CW00336436

The Cunninghams

The Cunninghams

David Ballantyne

Auckland
Oxford University Press
Melbourne Oxford

Oxford University Press
Oxford New York Toronto
Delhi Bombay Calcutta Madras Karachi
Petaling Jaya Singapore Hong Kong Tokyo
Nairobi Dar es Salaam Cape Town
Melbourne Auckland
and associated companies in
Beirut Berlin Ibadan Nicosia

Oxford is a trade mark of Oxford University Press

First published in 1948
Reprinted as a New Zealand Classic 1986
©David Ballantyne 1948

This edition ©the estate of David Ballantyne 1986

This book is copyright. Apart from any fair dealing for the purpose of private study, research, criticism or review, as permitted under the Copyright Act, no part may be reproduced by any process without prior permission of the Oxford University Press

ISBN 0 19 558158 X

Cover photograph by Kim Christensen
Cover designed by John McNulty
Published by Oxford University Press
5 Ramsgate Street, Auckland 5, New Zealand

CONTENTS

BOOK ONE

PART I

Chapter		Page
1	Waiting	11
2	A Letter to Mum	15
3	Visitors	20
4	Eels	23
5	The Most Popular Boy in Standard Four	26
6	The Baptist Minister	33
7	Evidence	37
8	There's Always Something	42

PART II

9	Gert and the Dummy	48
10	Grant Me Thy Grace	56
11	Escape	59
12	Many a Heart Then Is Broken	61
13	Christmas Letter	64
14	Night of December 24	66
15	A Sentimental Time	70
16	Reaction	72
17	Destiny Waltz	75

Chapter *Page*

18 MacPherson's Bush 80
19 Reflection 86
20 The Paper Run 90
21 The Quarrel 92
22 One Rainy Night 97

PART III

23 After the Storm 99
24 Kath Smith 103
25 In the Barber's Chair 107
26 An Attempt at Escape 110
27 Comeback 114
28 Links in a Chain 117
29 We're Only Human (R.K.O. Radio) 120
30 The Opportunist 123
31 The Disturbing Influence 126
32 Good News 129

BOOK TWO

1 Twelve Is Quite Old Enough 133
2 Ordeal 137
3 His Majesty's Earnest Hope 141
4 Scent Can Choke You 143
5 Over the Sink 148
6 No Place for Dreamers 152
7 The Radio Man 156
8 The Lost Sheep 160
9 A Crazy Thing To Do 163
10 Wishful Thinking 169

Chapter *Page*

11 The Big Game 172
12 Husband and Wife 177
13 Twosomes 182
14 A 1937 Christmas 187
15 Teddy the Butcher 191
16 Murder in Lovers' Lane 196
17 To Hell with Worrying 199
18 The Smoker 203
19 Night Journey 208
20 On the Peninsula 211
21 Street-Corner Radical 219
22 Sleepyhead 222
23 Maytime 224
24 A Link Is Severed 228
25 Ceremony at the Family Home 232

BOOK ONE

PART I

Chapter One

Waiting

I

GIL CUNNINGHAM worked out how much of the sun would be under the green veranda blind in an hour, in two hours. He figured it would be all over the veranda by noon. His bed was still in the shade, and this extended as far as the cabbage tree on the lawn a couple of yards in front of the gate. Good to have the sun again after weeks on end of cold winds and rain flapping the blind.

Drawing his sheet under his chin, he pushed the bed-end with his feet, pressed his head back on the pillows. Though his eyes were closed he saw the hills across the flats, the grey-white snow on the green and blue hills. In all his life in the bay he'd been up in those hills only once, he told himself. Always seemed to head north, to sheep stations where squatters got him to build sleeping porches and outhouses, and the Gladston agents of overseas meat interests like Vestey's had him first repair freezing works then pull them down, and he certainly spent a lot of time up the coast; but looking back he could remember just once going into the hills around Gladston. When he was sixteen he went deerstalking with some other young fellows, and it came on to rain pretty heavily, and everybody was soaked and got bad colds. He was in bed six weeks with bronchial-pneumonia, he nearly died. That was when he was going with Kath Smith, and she told him to see what came of his preferring other people's company to hers. 'Course they were only kids, it was all a long time ago.

He heard his wife come out onto the veranda, through half-opened eyes saw her watching him with hands behind her back. "Postman been yet, dear?" she asked. He pretended he was dozing and sleepily said Eh? and she said, "I was just thinking we should hear from the pension people any day now, shouldn't we?"

"We might," he said.

"Surely they can't keep us waiting much longer," she said. "I've been expecting it every day and every day old Huxley rides by and says no mail. How do they expect us to live, Gil?"

"They take their time all right," he said. He didn't know how bloody often he'd said that.

"Oh, well, thank goodness it's sunny," she said. "Won't be so chilly out here for you. It's been an awful winter." She went inside.

The hold-up in the pension must be pretty worrying for her, he thought, fingering his thighs. They certainly needed money badly wherever it came from; times were hard. By Christ she was getting stout, he thought. Her hair was fuzzy, she needed another perm. She'd been wearing one of her thin silk dresses and didn't appear to have corsets on, or maybe she had the old ones on, and they were nearly as bad, she used to say, as having no corsets.

—"Joy you get out of that bed, golly, don't know where you kids think you are—in the Grand Hotel? Lying in bed this time of day!"

They should be out of bed by now, should be helping their mother tidy up, nine o'clock was no time to be lying in bed. He felt like shouting to them, only he couldn't think what to say, and he wasn't sure he'd be heard if he did say something.

—"If you kids don't get out of bed I'll come in and drag you out, what do you think I'm here for, what's going to happen to the breakfast I cooked you, I get up and cook you things then you won't get out of bed. When you going to the butcher's, Gilbert, how much meat you think he'll have this time of day? And there's the bread to be got."

He laid his hands on the starch-white quilt, the sallow skin and prominent veins making them seem like a pattern on a cushion cover. There'd been times when these hands were lean and tough, they were tanned, and he'd been proud of them; and sometimes they'd been tired, tired from work. All his life he had worked hard, even in the depression when other good men were unemployed. The hands were still lean, but the toughness had long since gone from them.

II

He took a detective magazine from the locker.

He had a system for using up the day so's time didn't drag too much; the same idea as jokers at work, breaking the day into periods. From early morning to morning smoko, to lunch, to afternoon smoko, then to knockoff. Only with him there was no knockoff, and there was an evening stretch. Where reading was concerned a good detective yarn was best. In the locker he had a bonzer collection of *True Detectives* and *Master Detectives*, with stories in them like "The Roadhouse, the Moll, and the Man With a Limp" and "The Gory Secret of Locomotive 1122."

Though he listened to the radio occasionally he wasn't extra keen on it. One new tune in particular he didn't like—"Smoke Gets in Your Eyes." Might have something to do with the quack telling him to cut down on the tobacco. And he didn't go for Larry Adler, that mouth-organ virtuoso.

He glanced over the magazine, saw Marjorie Young standing on the top step. Sometimes he felt tender towards the girl. Other times he was amused because she was pregnant and so melancholy looking. Just now he was in a sympathetic mood; he guessed being up the duff to a young quarter-caste who was out of town was no joke even if she *had* been a fast number.

She said, "One thing about the veranda, Mr. Cunningham, you get the sun, don't you?"

He nodded. "How's everything?" he asked.

"All right, thanks," she said.

Still, she didn't look too good, he reckoned. He remembered her as a real frisky piece, gallivanting around all over the place. But the quarter-caste had stopped her. Well developed for nineteen, she was not painted and varnished as she once had been; her straight fair hair was neatly combed and held in place by a blue ribbon, and she wore a mauve shawl over her smock. You could tell by her legs she'd been brought up in the country; not exactly thick, they were strong looking.

"Think I'll wait for the postman, thought I heard his whistle," she said.

He watched her walk heavily down the three stone steps from the veranda. Watching her, he remembered Helen and her pregnancy times. If Joy, his eldest, was born in 1923 she was thirteen now, and Helen would be about the same age as Marjorie when she had her first kid. He remembered the times before each of his kids was born—Joy, Gilbert, Frank, Sydney, and little Helen.

He reached for his tobacco, rolled himself a smoke.

III

Marjorie rested against one of the squat pillars at the bottom of the steps. Then she scuffled along the path.

Young Frank had scooped spadefuls of metal from the roadside last time the borough council trucks were around, and he'd brought the metal inside and spread it over the paths. That kid liked messing about; once he trimmed the lawn back six inches, and it would have been all right if he'd made a good job of it, but the lawn edge ended up crooked as a dog's hind leg. The young devil, Gil thought.

He looked at the curling cigarette smoke.

There was the sound of cars and trucks from Massey Avenue about a hundred yards from the house. Saturday mornings Gladston was generally pretty busy with people from out on the flats coming in to do their weekly shopping and Maoris from the coast gathering on the river banks to talk and laugh and drink beer and eat fish and chips.

One of the kids ran along beside the house. It was Gilbert, tall and thin with a big head, big nose, big ears, and freckled face, and wearing his usual silly grin. You'd like to be closer to your eldest son, but the kid was so awkward; he was eleven, entering the gawky period. Watching him walk up to Marjorie, you felt scornful.

"Good afternoon, Gilbert," said Marjorie. "So you did get up?"

"It's Saturday morning."

"Oh, of course you studied *so* hard during the week."

Gilbert blushed.

Gil stubbed his cigarette irritably.

Helen came out and yelled to Gilbert to hurry to the butcher's before everybody else bought the best meat, he was probably too late as it was. The kid ran off.

"Postman not been yet, Marj?" called Helen.

"Not yet," Marjorie said. "Thought I heard his whistle, but I must have been mistaken."

Helen looked at Gil. She said she supposed Mr. Simmons would probably be turning up soon.

"Something to look forward to," Gil said.

He couldn't decide whether there was any jealousy in his attitude towards George Simmons, but he did know he was narked that the night watchman at Gladston freezing works should cut his hair, not that it would matter if Simmons were a garbage collector, but he was such a bloody loudmouth. So was his old woman. A beaut pair of gossips.

"I suppose it's decent of Mr. Simmons to think of sick people," Helen said.

"The money he gets for it probably makes it easier," he said.

"Didn't think of that," she said.

He could imagine George Simmons doing anything for anybody for nothing!

When she had gone inside he lit another cigarette and flipped the pages of the detective magazine. He looked over the veranda rail, saw old Huxley draw up before Marjorie, and leaned back out of sight. Huxley was always telling him he should have stayed in the post office with him, he was an old fool.

"Something for you, Mr. Cunningham," said Marjorie, handing him a long envelope. "On His Majesty's Service."

"Time that came," he said. "Nothing for you?"

She looked blue. There was never anything for her.

He opened the envelope.

Chapter Two

A Letter to Mum

I

WHEN HELEN had written

Dear Mums,

I received your ever welcome letter this morning. I was glad to hear from you. You are really too good to me. Always sending me things but I don't want to be robbing you. Cheer up we may be together soon. One thing if anything happens to Gil I would leave Gladston as soon as possible I am sick of it.

she put the pen-end in her mouth and had a bit of a think.

She didn't want her mother thinking she was dumpy; but everything was so unhappy these days. She'd love to tell Mum about Fred Burgess, but she was scared. People reckoned Fred was a shrewdie because he did some bookmaking outside his warehouse business, but she knew he wasn't, and he was very good to her. She'd been dying to tell Mum about him ever since they had been introduced to each other by Marjorie's mother. Flo Young was another good friend, but of course she was up the coast.

Marjorie came into the dining-room and sat in the sedan chair by the radio; she put her hand into the sun dust that streamed through the window and wiggled her fingers. She pulled her smock back from her knees. The radio was playing "Steamboat Bill."

Helen asked, "Any mail, Marj?"

"Just one On His Majesty's Service for Mr. Cunningham," the girl said.

Golly, the pension may have come at last, Helen thought. How much easier things would be if it did come! She put the pen on the table.

Out on the veranda Gil was looking at a paper; he passed it to her without speaking.

She read aloud: "War Pension, Dear Sir, the War Pensions Board will sit in the Gladston Borough Council Chambers next Wednesday and desires to see you in connection with your disability."

It was as if all her worries had gone and then returned; things were the same as ever. "That's not much better than before, is it?"

"Doesn't look like it," he said.

She couldn't tell what he was thinking.

II

Angry at the pension people, wanting to tell her mother about them, she sat at the table in the dining-room. She couldn't think what to say.

She looked at Marjorie sunning herself. Seeing Flo was such a great friend of yours you didn't mind her daughter boarding with you, but the girl was terribly lazy, she lay in bed waiting for breakfast to be taken in, as if you didn't have enough to do looking after Gil and the kids, and she didn't do a hand's turn. And fancy getting stuck on a Maori.

"Funny you haven't heard anything from Joe yet, Marjorie."

"He'll be writing any day now, I expect."

"Do you think something might have happened to him?"

"He's working, that's all. Last time he wrote he said it's been awful with Californian thistle up there this year."

Helen nodded understandingly. She returned to the letter. Goodness, what can I tell Mum? This pension business was terrible. Took her all her time to buy food let alone the clothing the kids needed. Mum was a great help sending clothes the way she did. It was good to have someone like her to write to. And being with Fred, sitting in his car or dancing, was like the old days up the coast again. But it wouldn't do to tell Mum that.

Oh well, better get the house tidied, she told herself; no use moping around like a wet blanket all the time. She could finish the letter later.

"Hope old mother Simmons doesn't come today," she said, getting a dusting rag from the sideboard drawer. "That tart gets my goat."

"Don't think I met her," said Marjorie, who was listening to "The Continental" being played over the radio.

"You know, that skinny old biddy with the bunhair, she talks and talks."

"Sounds good."

"She's a talkative old thing and a half, she gets my goat," said Helen, rubbing the little ornaments on the mantelpiece. She'd been lucky to get these souvenirs of her uncle's visit to England with the Rugby League team before the depression; the ornament Fred gave her, the bulldog frowning out from a kennel, fitted in well with the others.

She glanced at Marjorie, thought how enormous she was. She hoped none of the boys came in and saw her sitting like that with legs all bare. Wonder how she felt inside and was the baby giving much bother, she thought.

Joy nosed in. "Tea made, Mum?"

"Fine time you decide to get up for breakfast."

"I was tired," Joy said.

"Well, you just get your own breakfast now, you wouldn't get up when I called you. And take these rugs outside."

Joy took the rugs away to be shaken.

Her eldest kid's looks were improving, Helen thought. The past couple of years Joy had been awfully gawky—a real tomboy, wrestling with her brothers, playing cricket—but now she was getting quite nice to look at. She was highly strung though, and inclined to be lazy; and sometimes the questions she asked were embarrassing.

Marjorie stood up yawning and said she was going to have a lie-down.

Getting ahead with the cleaning, Helen replaced the rugs in front of the sewing machine, the fireplace, and the doorway. She pulled the blinds down to within a few inches of the window sill; it was always nice to have one tidy room in the house, and the half-darkness made the place look ready for any visitors who might turn up.

She sat at the table once more.

We have a girl staying with us, she is Mrs. Young's daughter, you know Mrs. Young she was such a friend of mine up the coast and I miss her terribly down here. Marjorie is all right but not like her mother—she is you know to a Mạori. I thought couldn't she do better than that but you know what these young things are.

Better say something about the pension. Oh, how sick she was of cadging from the Citizens' Defence Fund! How she hated standing before the board members every time she drew the money! She never did like the idea of charity.

And Mums darling, we still haven't got that pension, I'm sick of waiting I wish I could get away from Gladston I hate everybody here, I've got no friends at all except—

No, she'd not tell Mum about Fred yet.

Wonder what that Marjorie's doing, I bet, I bet. . . .

She walked up the passage. Sure enough, Marjorie was sprawled over the bed in the front room, on the pink eiderdown, too. She lay with her eyes closed and one hand stroking the eiderdown, and the sight made you wild. You'd think she'd have more consideration for other people's things.

She returned to the dining-room where the radio was playing the first religious record of the morning devotional service. Golly, why couldn't they play something cheerful, something by the Comedy Harmonists or a march, something anyway that would cheer you up?

III

She frowned at Joy, who sat in the kitchen drinking tea and reading a *True Romance,* then peeped into the kids' room where the little ones were playing with Plasticine.

She loved her kids, she thought as she watched them. Bubs

was like a hothouse flower and it was a shame her eyes were so weak she had to wear dark glasses outside. Frank was a slow sort of kid, only a class ahead of Sydney at school though he was a couple of years older. Sydney was a casual kid, and he'd be a lady-killer when he grew up. He hadn't spoken a word till he was nearly five, and she'd fretted thinking she'd brought a dumb child into the world.

What did she want, Sydney asked, surprising her because she didn't think he'd seen her there.

"Gilbert not back from the butcher's yet?"

"No Mummy, he's not, he's not," cried Bubs, running to her.

She kissed her baby, and she would always think of Bubs as the baby though she was in Primer Two at school now. Ruffling the kid's thin hair, she remembered how some dirty tike had rubbed its head against Bubs when she first went to school, and how Bubs came home lousy and had to have all her hair cut off. "Play with the boys, lovie. Mummy wants to tidy the house."

She ordered Joy away from the kitchen table and, grumbling, Joy went onto the back veranda, still reading the *True Romance*. She came back in a hurry and said old Simmons was getting off his bike out there.

Then the man himself appeared in the doorway, said "Good morning" brightly. He carried his box of hairdressing gear.

"Oh, hello, Mr. Simmons." She pretended she was surprised and glad to see him. She certainly wasn't, though, she thought as she looked at his fat belly and fat fingers. And she hated his look that seemed to say he shared a secret with her.

"Gil's been expecting you," she said.

He looked pleased. "I just came from the hospital, thought Gil was due for a haircut. Reckon it makes a difference to a sick person when his hair's cut."

She went up the passage with him, saw him walk towards Gil, then returned to the dining-room to write some more of the letter.

Chapter Three

Visitors

I

"BE A hot summer this year, Gil," said Simmons, working the clippers. "Fellows up the hospital will be glad of a change, you know."

Watching him, Gil remembered when he'd been no mean hand with the clippers himself; no trips to the barber shop for the kids those days. "Weather's been pretty bad, all right," he said.

"Yes, I just came from the hospital," Simmons said. He walked to the front door and yoohooed for a chair.

Helen passed one out, and Gil lifted himself from the bed and, feeling weak, let Simmons arrange a towel around his neck. Then, snipping the air a couple of times with the scissors, Simmons got to work. He stood off every so often to see how he was doing, and he breathed hard.

Gil waited for him to start yarning.

—God, all the different kinds of visitors you had when you were lying in bed! Most of them had good intentions, you guessed, but a lot were damned nuisances. You didn't mind the fellows from the freezing works, only they made you tired always telling you you'd been loony to go into the freezing chambers, reminding you you'd been sent home from the war with pleurisy and ought to have known better and should have stayed on boxing; and when you told them the screw was better in the chambers they wanted to know what was money when you didn't have your health, as though you hadn't thought of that. Other visitors who were bearable were the blokes who'd been your cobbers in camp, and these were around the forty mark and looked like they were headed for the grave, but it was good remembering 1917, the front line, billets in France, Marie-Rose, the years of trenches and mud and lice. You weren't too keen on old Ma Jacobsen, who handed you holy messages over the rail then scooted round the back before she caught your disease, or on the wife's friend Bella Simpson, who visited you one winter day and kept telling you how unhappy she was, how winter weather gave her the blue spiders. Then there was John Weaver, your old schoolmate, a tall broad-shouldered chap with straw-yellow hair, who told you of a town where you picked up gold from the streets and reckoned you ought to visit this town and get rich; everywhere John went he was followed by a bodyguard, and people reckoned the bodyguard was as crazy as John; they took John back to the wow because one night at tea he grabbed a knife and reckoned he was going to chop the head off the first one to look up from his plate. . . . Yes, these were your visitors, and they had their good points. But this homey Simmons was a loudmouth with a big opinion of himself. God only knew what women saw in him. . . .

He was saying he was putting up a shed at the works for the men's bikes. The boss had asked him to, knowing he was handy with tools, he said.

You were wild at Simmons' fancying himself a carpenter. The long years you'd spent learning to be a carpenter! And you'd be well off today for the trouble, too, but for the depression.

II

"Reminds me of the time down south when I was watchman at a brewery," Simmons said.

Gil shut his eyes while the other clipped a fringe.

He listened to a pointless yarn about how Simmons saw an orange glow one night on his rounds and it turned out to be a fire and he smashed one of the windows and got in and put the blaze out and he cut his hand pretty bad and you could still see the scar and the manager was so bucked up about the save he got a door built in a wall of the brewery and told Simmons he could walk in any old time and help himself. And there was a tenner for Simmons, too. He'd never forget it, he said.

Best to change the subject, Gil thought. "Heard from the pension crowd this morning," he said.

"Good news?" Simmons asked.

"No better than before," Gil said. "Got to try to get down to the council chambers next Wednesday. Could be half-dead, and they'd still want me to hike down there."

"Pretty tough, all right," Simmons said.

"Thought the Labour Party would make a difference when they got in," Gil said.

All politicians were the same, Simmons said.

"Still, I suppose it'll be okay once Mickey Savage and his crowd get things running," Gil said.

Simmons said it might. "How long you been in bed now, Gil?"

"About three years," Gil said. "Blame some of it on the quack, you know. Think he thought I was swinging the lead, trying to get a pension for nothing."

"You don't say?"

"Make a difference when we do get that pension," Gil said. "Times are hard, as you know. 'Specially if you have a wife and family to consider."

Simmons stood off to see what he'd done. "She's going to be a scorcher, all right," he said. "Know what the highest temperature was down the beach this week? Eighty-two degrees. Give the cockies something more to moan about. First wool of the season was over at the works on Wednesday. Only in the store an hour before they had it on the boat."

Gil felt a little chilly. He didn't like the damp touch of Simmon's fingers, and he hoped he finished before starting one of his yarns that would take all morning to tell. He kept telling the same stories too, like the one about the former Mayor of Gladston who was kicked out of his church for interfering with a youngster in a Sunday School class, and the one about the manager of the Majestic Theatre who had been seen embracing the girl from the *Age* office in a milk bar in town, and the one about the headmaster of Gladston Central School who beat his pupils on the backsides with a golf stick, and . . . oh the ones about the sheilas who took on any old jokers.

But he was wiping your neck with a towel, so it was over. You stood up shakily, got Simmons a shilling from the locker, then sat on the edge of the bed, and you felt better for the haircut.

Simmons collected his gear, pushed his hat back, and wiped his forehead.

"Like a cup of tea now that's done?" asked Helen in the doorway.

"By Jove, I'd love a cup, Helen," Simmons said, smiling at her.

Gil was wild at the way Simmons talked to his wife, sort of intimately, as though what he said was for her alone. It was always the same.

She was inside a few minutes and returned with the morning tea on a tray. She was sorry there was no cake, she said. Then she got the shovel and broom, swept up the hair, and returned inside.

When he'd finished his cup of tea Simmons lit his pipe and had some more chinwag. He probably saw you were bored, though, and presently said he'd be going, Myrtle would be expecting him. You were glad to see him ride out the gate.

You felt the sunshine that was beginning to cover the veranda, just as you'd figured. Really you hadn't minded Simmons' visit, it relieved the monotony. But you didn't like the idea of that joker hanging around your wife.

III

Bubs came out onto the veranda. " 'Lo, Daddy."

" Hello, Bubs," he said. " What you been doing this morning?"

" I been playing Plast-cine, Daddy."

With her dark glasses the poor little tike looked awfully fragile. " What that smell, Daddy?" she asked, snuggling against him.

" Only Daddy's medicine."

He noticed Sydney standing by the cabbage tree looking towards the veranda, and, since it was the first time he'd seen the boy this morning, he called a greeting.

" How you feeling today, Dad?" Sydney called back.

" Not bad at all, son," he said.

And just now, not thinking of the pension or any other worry, and with his baby beside him and young Sydney on the lawn, and the sun shining, he did feel all right, he thought.

Chapter Four

Eels

The Dodge was parked on the edge of the bush. Waiting for Fred to return from spearing eels, Helen couldn't hear a sound, and all she saw when she looked through the car window were the shapes of trees and shrubs. She imagined him floundering through the night, splashing into the creek, jabbing at the eels. He'd catch his death of cold if he didn't take care of himself.

She didn't hear him coming from the bush until he opened the back door of the car and laid a couple of eels on a sheet of newspaper on the seat.

" Bit on the small side tonight," he said. " Must have taken all the big ones from that creek."

She didn't know how he could handle the greasy things, she

said. She couldn't stand eels and didn't know how he could go for them like he did.

He switched on the roof light. Twisting round, she watched him carefully covering the eels with newspaper.

You could tell he'd been an athletic man in his youth, she reckoned, even though he was getting rather stout now, and his dark hair was turning grey. She supposed his playing Rugby for so long meant that he'd live to a good age; he'd kept so fit. And she bet not many men over forty played cricket every day in summer like Fred. Oh, he was wonderful, and she didn't believe what they said about his being a bookmaker and that sort of scandal. He made life bearable, and she was never dumpy with him like she was at home.

"Feeling cold, love?" she asked.

"A little," he said.

"You ought to take care of yourself, Fred. Don't want to get sick for the sake of a few silly eels."

He shut the back door, slipped into the driver's seat beside her. She rested her head on his shoulder.

"Well, what's the news?" he asked after a bit.

"Nothing much," she said.

"How's the hubbie?"

"Seems to be doing all right," she told him.

"Have any trouble getting out?" he asked.

"I said I was going to visit Bella. Poor old Bella. Always the same, always moaning about something. She annoys Gil. He says she's not the right sort to visit the sick. He says she makes him feel worse."

"You certainly don't want that sort around you too much."

"Oh, Fred, I had a letter from Flo Young today."

"Anything new?"

"Got it here somewhere," she said, searching her purse. "Here, I'll read it. 'Well we are still deciding or trying to decide about Christmas,' she says, 'and it's pretty close now but at present I'm a cripple and am wondering if I will be able to get around without a stick by Christmas time. I was putting up curtains in my room the beginning of the week and had two boxes one on top of the other. I was trying to get down and overbalanced the boxes and came down with a crash and put my knee out. I think it went back again but my heavens if it didn't give me agony for a while. It is still swelled and very painful if I do much hobbling around on it and I have been making use of my mop handle to help me, so I'm hoping I won't be still lame at Christmas and have to take the mop handle with me. I was glad to hear particulars about Marjorie in your letter, she's an awful correspondent. We get about a letter a month from her and nothing in them, just scribbled in a desperate hurry. Well, old dear, I'll close now as news is scarce, pleased to hear Gil is so well, I hope the summer won't be too hot for him. Cheerio, best of love to the kids. My kindest regards to Gil and love to you from your pal, Flo '."

Helen looked dreamily at the letter. "Hope her accident's not serious, hope she gets down for Christmas," she said. "Flo's so much of a bright spark about the place."

"Doesn't hear much from the girl, I see."

"No; isn't Marjorie a corker, Fred? Think she'd write and let her mother know how she's getting on, wouldn't you?"

"She heard anything from her boy friend yet?"

"Not yet. If he doesn't hurry she'll be dropping her bundle at our place."

"Is it that close?"

"Well, just about. I got nothing against the Maoris, Fred, and I always say my Maori blood is the best blood in me, but there's a difference in the way they look at things. Especially these coast Maoris. They're very casual, and of course Marjorie's white, and the older Maoris are funny that way, they sort of look down on girls like Marjorie marrying the young Maoris. Mum's mother was a half-caste, you know, Fred, so there's quite a bit of Maori blood in me. Anyway, Marjorie knew what she was doing."

"Suppose so. Heard any more about the pension, love?"

"Gil had to go to the council chambers the other day to get examined, but nothing's changed. They won't tell him anything. They don't seem to believe he's seriously ill. I think myself he should try a specialist in the city. They make me boil that pension crowd, don't know how they think we're supposed to live. Seem to want us to go on forever living on charity."

They were a queer bunch, Fred said.

"Gil always used to talk about what the Labour Party would do, but he doesn't say so much now," she said.

"Don't know whether the Government's to blame," he said. "You know some of the tricks these quacks can get up to."

She thought how good it was talking things over with him.

"Things will straighten out in the end," he said.

"I suppose so," she said. "Feeling cold, Fred?"

"Am a bit. I could go a good feed of eels just now."

"Oh, those awful things," she said.

"I like them," he said.

"We better turn back then," she said. "Your brother at the hotel might let you cook them there."

He started the car. " A feed of eels would be nice and warming all right," he said. " As good as a dance."

" I get the shivers every time I think of them," she said.

" That's because you fancy they look like snakes," he said. " You ought to try some, love."

" Gosh, no thanks," she said.

Chapter Five

The Most Popular Boy in Standard Four

I

THE SUN was going down, and the late afternoon was chilly. Some Central School kids came from the schoolground, started running when they heard a kid on the corner of Saint Matthew's Street and Stout Road yell, " Fight! Fight!"

Schoolbag over his shoulder, Barry Andrews wondered whether to follow the others or to go home and do his homework so's he would have time later to add a new packet of stamps to his album. He decided he'd better see what was going on, and walked slowly towards the crowd gathering outside a house up the street.

He bet the masters would be angry to see how the big jokers were shoving the small kids from the fence. Old Shimmering would have something to say on dignity and discipline if he saw his pupils now.

Reaching the group outside the unpainted cottage that stood in the shadow of big timber sheds, he looked up at the shed walls, at the sign GLADSTON TIMBER CO. LTD., then down at the cottage. He couldn't make out what was happening. The big kids stood on tiptoe, looking over the heads of those squinting through the grey fence slats. A couple of girls giggled.

Glad he was tall, he stood on tiptoe himself. Now he could see everything. The cottage veranda gapped in places; the bottom halves of the two front windows were blocked with sacking; between the veranda and the fence were a small yard, a broken concrete path, grass clumps, tobacco tin lids. A large woman holding a broom stood shouting in the open doorway. There was a heck of a lot of noise going on, he couldn't understand—then things began to straighten out. The woman shouted, the kids talked and giggled, and a baby howled in a cot on the veranda left of the door. The woman started to use the broom on a Central School kid who stood there letting her hit him. He couldn't make out who the kid was, and, tiring of standing on tiptoe, he stepped back to the footpath's edge and listened to the comments.

"Shucks, I bet that hurt."

"Look at her getting red in the face."

"Boy, that was a beaut stroke, Russ."

"See that wrist action?"

"How'd you like her on your side, Russ?"

"Quite a style, eh? And what a figure!"

Making out they thought the boys shocking, the girls talked about the boy.

"Oh, I think he's a silly goof, why doesn't he shift?"

"Mm, you'd think he'd move away, wouldn't you, Judy?"

"Funny, isn't it?"

"The poor thing."

"Isn't he red in the face?"

"Listen to the poor baby bawling its lungs out."

"Wonder what he was doing."

"Who is he?"

"That's the dopey Cunningham kid."

"He's brainy, isn't he?"

"He's dopey."

It was certainly a surprise to discover the kid was Gilbert Cunningham. He didn't know what Gilbert was doing on somebody's front veranda getting hit with a broom. And Gilbert was not dopey, it was just what those kids would think. His friend didn't say much at school because he was shy, and he knew this because he felt the same way himself sometimes, when he forgot to think about anything but what he was reading or saying. That was why he was friendly with Gilbert.

On tiptoe again, he had another look. Behind him on the roadway two little girls sang, "Jesus loves me, that I know, 'cause the Bible tells me so." Gilbert's forehead was cut, blood trickled down his cheek. The woman had stopped using the broom, the baby was now whimpering, and the kids were watching in silence. Why did he do it? the woman kept asking, and got no reply. She was big as anything, she had a big bum. At last she took the baby from the cot and walked inside, down a gloomy, uncarpeted passage.

Gilbert walked across the yard to the street. Several kids asked him what was wrong, but he wouldn't tell them anything. He dabbed with a hankie at the blood on his face.

The kids left the fence and drifted along Saint Matthew's Street. The little girls singing " Jesus loves me, that I know, 'cause the Bible tells me so " were holding hands and skipping up the street.

Barry walked on slowly, waiting for Gilbert to catch him up. He wasn't like those other stickybeak kids, he reckoned; all the same, he thought, he was dying to know what the fuss was about.

II

" Gosh, you take a lot of books home, don't you?" said Gilbert.

" Like having everything with me when I do my homework," Barry said.

" What course you taking when you go to High, Barry?"

" Don't know yet. You going there?"

" Might," Gilbert said. " Two more years yet."

" We don't have to worry about passing, anyway."

" No, we're all right," Gilbert said. He'd been top of the class every term in Standard Three and the second term in Standard Four. The only one he and Barry had to worry about was Ashley Harper, who suffered badly with asthma and was off school a lot. He got top whenever Harper was away.

He wondered what Barry was thinking. You never could tell. Barry was like you only he hardly ever blushed.

" Hear old Baldy this afternoon?" he asked. " Start practising for the breakup ball end of this week. Remember all the practising we had last year?"

" I might not go," Barry said.

" Think I will," Gilbert said. But he wasn't going in school uniform this year, he thought. He'd have a fancy costume like most of the kids. And, boy, he'd try and get a dance with Carole Plowman.

" Going to wash that blood off your face?" Barry asked.

He felt crook again, remembered the old tart hitting him with a broom, the kids watching. He'd seen the baby in a big cream-coloured pram outside Mrs. Morpeth's dairy a few days before, and it was such a lovable sort of tike he wanted to see it again, watch it smile the way it smiled outside the dairy. He used to see the mother wheeling her baby along the streets of the town; she lived in the cottage with her husband, a small joker with a black moustache, who worked on the nightcart. Passing the cottage this afternoon, he couldn't resist the desire to look in the cot on the veranda, and he unbound the wire securing the front gate, walked to the cot, and gazed at the baby that lay there pink-faced and contented. And he stroked it under the chin, and it awakened, studied him drowsily for a moment, then got into a sleepy bad temper and bawled like mad. Once it stopped bawling when he made a funny face but not for long. Then the mother appeared with the broom.

" I was only looking at the kid," he said.

" That all she hit you for," asked Barry.

" It woke up," he said.

" Oh," said Barry.

They walked across the school playground, and Gilbert washed his face under the tap next to the woodwork room. He asked Barry if there was much of a cut on his head, and Barry said Not much. He thought of the crowd outside the cottage and remembered seeing Moira Thornton, and he hated her because once he borrowed a silver pencil case from her and forgot to return it and she looked in his schoolbag and reckoned he'd stolen the case and called him a thief, and he'd hated her ever since.

Back across the playground they met Mike Park who had some cricket gear resting on the crossbar of his grid. Gilbert didn't like the sound of Mike's voice when he said Hiya and though he couldn't have heard about the old tart yet there was something in his voice that scared you.

They parted at the school gate. One of these days he'd go home with Barry, thought Gilbert. Barry was his best friend. He didn't have many good friends. Earlier in the year there had been a popularity contest, and he was voted the most popular boy in Standard Four, but he guessed this was because he was top of the class and didn't take sides with other kids in their scraps; he didn't sling off at anybody, either. Russ Willis said his win was a fluke, and he bet he didn't win when the whole school voted on the most popular of the most popular boys. And he didn't win, didn't expect to; he knew the kids would vote for the Form II joker, and they did sure enough. He didn't want to win anyway, he felt foolish standing in front of the school while the kids voted.

III

Standing on the corner by Mrs. Morpeth's dairy he watched the workers riding home on their bikes; nearly everybody in Gladston owned a bike, the country was so flat; maybe next year he'd get a bike himself. He couldn't make up his mind about going home. The public library was at the other end of town but no use going there again; he'd read the latest *Daily Mirror* overseas edition and the other magazines in the subscribers' room.

He entered the dairy. Inside was a smell that was not in any other shop in town. Mrs. Morpeth sold milk, cream, ice cream, bread, scones, all sorts of sweets—chocolate, fudge, toffees, cinnamon bars, changing balls—and blocks of cake and tins of biscuits; but you couldn't tell where the smell came from.

He bought a penny sante bar, then stood outside pondering over the smell the way he always did when he visited the dairy. It was like other mysteries coming into your life; you thought about them but never understood.

He'd walk along the block to Mr. Herbett's, see if there was a new *Champion* or *Triumph* he could add to his collection in the bottom drawer at home.

Down opposite the front gates of the Central School he strolled past Mr. Herbett's shop, waiting for somebody else to enter ahead of him.

Generally he sold bottles to get the threepence for the *Champion*, sometimes his mother gave him the money straight out; once he pinched her change, and she found half a dozen pennies where he'd hidden them in the gutter under the bridge—but he didn't think about that time too much.

Two small kids came along with comics in their hands and went into the shop. He followed. The kids pretended to study the papers on the shelves; he knew that as soon as nobody was looking they'd slip one comic inside another and hand Mr. Herbett two of their own comics as swap for the double one; they were going to rook the old boy out of a comic, he'd done it himself. Out of the corner of his eye he saw Mr. Herbett watching, and he skimmed through the magazines quickly so's it wouldn't look as though he were reading anything.

The kids got away safely, and he asked Mr. Herbett if the latest *Champion* was in. No, said Mr. Herbett, his popeyes suspicious, his thin fingers tapping the showcase monotonously. He coloured and, feeling old Herbett's eyes following him, left the shop. He was lonely.

IV

All along the streets of the town the workers were going home in the dusk. Gilbert followed some fellows up Stout Road, listening to their loud talk, thinking they were funny when they laughed, and it wasn't what they said, it was the way they said it.

A long walk in the cold night. Gosh, there was lots to think about. The girls cycling past made him think of Carole Plowman, but that was so uncomfortable he forced his mind onto something else, and he got hot thinking of the broom and the watching kids. Oh, if only something could happen to him before tomorrow! Say he could be knocked over gently by a car and have to stay in bed for a few days. He always thought like this when something was coming off at school. Anything to get out of standing before the class with the kids looking on. It was not good to think of such things, and he was glad when he reached Livingstone Road.

Marjorie Young stood at the front gate, apparently watching the yellow street lights plopping on to glow smudgily.

He asked her if she was getting some air, and she didn't reply for a while, then said, "Eh?"

He asked if she was waiting for somebody, and she told him she wasn't.

—Never would he forget what had happened between him and Marjorie one day up the coast when he was a kid. He met Marjorie and another girl down by the swamp when he was about to cross to the other side by the plank bridge. They were yarning about fellows they'd met at a dance, and he glanced at them curiously, and Marjorie noticed him and then this thing happened. "Look, Gilbert, have a look," she said and she unbuttoned the housedress she wore and showed him her breasts, and they were clean as anything, and she kept telling him to look. "Go on, Gilbert, good, eh? Want to touch?" And she made him touch her breasts, and they were nice and soft, and they moved beneath his fingers. But she scared him the way she looked at him. Fixing her clothes, she said to her girl friend, "That was all right." The other girl laughed. He never forgot what had happened that day.

"Heard anything from Joe yet, Marj?"

"No."

"That what you're waiting for?"

"Eh?"

"You waiting to hear from Joe?"

"Is it worrying you?" she wanted to know.

She needn't be so snaky, he told himself as he walked in the gate. He saw his father's head shadowed above the veranda railing and, thinking he could see his eyes, said Hello, but there was no reply, and he felt foolish. You'd think a man would say Hello when his son greeted him. He pictured his father sitting in bed hugging his legs with his long arms, face resting on his knees. Dad was good-looking—light brown hair, narrow face, thin lips, wrinkled forehead; he was sort of like the returned soldiers who visited him. But fathers were stern, and you preferred Mum to Dad even though Mum reckoned God wanted you to love both your parents the same.

V

Away across the paddock beside the house he could see lights in the brewery tower. The silence of the paddock was disturbed by strange night scurryings.

Inside, the family was starting tea. He was hungry.

"Where you been all this time?" his mother asked.

"Down the library," he said.

"We thought you were run over or something."

"I was reading a good book," he told her.

"You ought to let us know when you're going to that place."

"I bet he's been tarting," Joy said.

He blushed. "Aw, shut up."

"Don't say 'Shut up'; it's not nice," his mother told him.

"She must have hit you," Joy said. "How'd you get that cut on your forehead?"

"I fell over; it's nothing," he said.

His tea was placed before him, and he ate soft juicy cabbage, clean white potatoes, roast beef slices and sauce, and it all tasted pretty good. He felt better eating. Mum was a great cook.

"How about making us some costumes for the breakup ball at the end of the term, Mum?" he asked.

"Golly, what next? You kids seem to think money grows on trees."

"Me and the other girls and boys having practice now for the big dance, Mummy," Bubs said.

"Are you, love?"

"We all going to this dance?" Frank wanted to know.

"You're looking ahead," his mother said. "Who knows what'll happen between now and then?"

"I want to be cowboy," Frank said.

"I didn't say you could go, did I? I didn't say you could have costumes, either."

"I don't want to go if we can't have costumes," Gilbert said.

"Is Sydney going to the dance?" Frank asked.

Sydney ate his tea, not taking much notice of what was happening. He said, "I want to go as a cowboy, too."

"I'll see what I can do," their mother said. "Don't expect

too much, though. Frank, run and tell Marjorie her tea's waiting; don't know what that girl does out there in the cold. And go round the side so's you don't disturb your father."

Gilbert slowly ate a piece of bread and butter. He saw himself dancing with Carole Plowman, laughing with her, talking to her. He wished the breakup ball were not so far away. He wished it were next week. But it wasn't, it was right at the end of the year.

Chapter Six

The Baptist Minister

I

THE REV. BERTRAM KENT, Gladston Baptist minister, had parked his small Ford just outside the gate, and Gil could see the kids examining it, shoving it forward a little then back again. Sitting on the bed in his dressing-gown, he wondered what the devil Hilda meant by sending the minister to see him. Mr. Kent, who was tall and fair-headed and had a holy air that maybe you imagined, didn't seem a bad sort; but you liked to say what was on your mind in plain language, and you couldn't do that with sky pilots.

"Yes, feel livelier these days, don't want to lie in bed so much as I used to. Still shaky on the pins, though. But I can make the gate now. Feel a lot better."

"My, that *is* a good sign," said Mr. Kent, posing carefully on his chair so's not to crease the trousers of his navy-blue suit. "It's good insofar as the family is concerned, too. It does make a profound difference to children if they have their father's guiding hand. How *are* the little ones, by the way?"

"All right," Gil told him. "Gilbert's the brainy one, but just between you and me I think young Sydney will put the others in the shade."

"Your sister wasn't sure whether or not the boys were going to Sunday School at the present time," said Mr. Kent.

"Matter of fact they're not," Gil said.

"Are you against the idea of Sunday School as a matter of principle, Mr. Cunningham?"

"Certainly not," Gil said. "Reckon kids these days need to know a lot more about—about God."

"Quite so. The boys were going to our Sunday School regularly a few months ago, but lately they seem to have dropped away altogether. Do you think we could get them back?"

"Young blighters!" Gil said. "You know what growing boys are."

"I'd even go so far as to say—I believe I'm right—that Sunday School can play as important a role in the life of the growing boy as ordinary day school."

"That's what I reckon," Gil said. "You know, I won a first prize myself at the Baptist Sunday School."

"Did you really? That's most interesting."

"I'll show it to you," Gil said. He walked inside, thinking what an effort it had been to do this a few weeks ago. He had been very weak when he first got up, but now he was getting on fine. The weather, of course. It had stayed warm and without rain right through October to November, and in the mornings there was frost on the grass, and the sun shone all day long. He used to watch people passing the gate on their way to the beach at the end of Livingstone Road, and there were young fellows and their girl friends in bathing costumes with towels across their shoulders and, in particular, there was a nice-looking blonde who passed the gate every afternoon, and he would wait for her to pass and feel somehow better when she did. These days he felt like talking to people. His cobbers suggested he'd soon be back at the freezing works, and they had some good laughs together. Most of all, though, he was pleased to be so interested in his kids. All his kids were good, they didn't give much trouble. If he did catch any of them going the wild way, smashing windows or pinching things, he'd make them feel it, he'd tan their backsides for them.

He pulled things out of drawers in the tallboy in the spare room next to the veranda until he found the Sunday School prize under his canvas bag of carpenter's tools.

"Here it is," he told Mr. Kent. "*Martin Rattler*. A great book for boys. See what I wrote in the cover when I got it?"

Mr. Kent read: "'Gilbert Cunningham received this book as a token from his teacher on condition that he must keep it clean and read it every year and keep looking at the Scriptures'."

"Held on to it all this time," Gil said.

"I should think your sons would want to follow in their father's footsteps," Mr. Kent said.

"I'll talk to them," Gil said. "A bit of church does nobody any harm."

"Very true," Mr. Kent said. "You see, there is so much we offer young people besides the teaching of the Lord's wisdom. We have reading clubs, discussion groups, tramping parties, and of course our church is not against young people conducting their own musical evenings so long as these functions are properly controlled. There's really a lot of healthy fun in going to Sunday School."

"I'll have a word with them," Gil said.

Mr. Kent stood and patted his trouser legs. "That's excellent. I'll leave this card for the boys. It's something of an invitation. By the way, did you read the Scriptures as you promised you would?"

"Not always," Gil said.

"Ha ha," Mr. Kent laughed. "Bye-bye, Mr. Cunningham."

"Hooray," Gil said.

II

He sat on the steps in the sun. "Hey, Gilbert!" he called.

Gilbert walked across the lawn. "Yes, Dad?"

"Come here, I want to talk to you about something. Why haven't you been going to Sunday School lately, son?"

Gilbert said nothing.

"You got to have some religion," Gil said. "You don't want to be called an atheist, do you?"

Gilbert said No, he didn't.

"Well, you better go to Sunday School and take a few Bible lessons," Gil said. "Don't want people saying I let you become an atheist. Had to go to Sunday School myself, most kids did in my day. Can see what'll happen to you kids if I don't do something about it. You'll be a pack of bloody heathens."

Gilbert said All right.

"You see you go tomorrow, then," Gil said. "No shinnanicking now, you get dressed tomorrow and go. Tell Frank I want to see him."

Gil felt good telling his son what to do; he wasn't letting the boy become a heathen if he could help it. He had to put his foot down.

"What you want, Dad?" asked Frank.

"Here, read this card Mr. Kent left for you," Gil told him.

The card showed four small boys, pink-cheeked, round-faced,

each wearing a white collar and tie, peering from a church window as though looking for somebody. Under the small boys was

WHERE WERE YOU SUNDAY?

The boys in our class are here on the jot,
But there's something that's missing alack!
'Tis your own jolly self that we're needing a lot.
Won't you hurry and come right back?

COME SURE NEXT SUNDAY

"See, Frankie," Gil said, "it says they want you to go to Sunday School, they miss you."

"I know it says that," Frank said.

"You going?"

"I don't want to go."

"Why not? You believe in God, don't you?"

"'Course I do, Dad," said Frank. "But I don't like the kids at that Sunday School."

Gil told him it wasn't the kids at Sunday School that mattered, it was what they learned there. "You get dressed tomorrow and go with Gilbert," he said.

"All right, Dad," said Frank. He went out the front and yelled to some kids and they played in the gutter.

III

Gill wondered what the kids these days were coming to. Sunday School was just what the young devils needed. He felt they were giving him cheek, not wanting to do as he said. He was only thinking of their welfare, it was for their own good.

Helen came out and wanted to know what Mr. Kent had to say.

"We had a good talk about the boys and Sunday School," he said. "Reckon those kids need a bit of religion, they're just at the age when they might go wrong if they don't learn the proper things."

"There's nothing wrong with our children," she said.

"Sunday School certainly wouldn't do them any harm," he said.

"Oh, I suppose that Hilda sent old Kent here."

He supposed she had, Gil said. Helen was always saying Hilda poked her nose in their affairs and it'd be different if it was money she gave instead of so much advice, not that she'd accept charity from any of his sisters. Well, Hilda had certainly done all right marrying Bill Coulter, the freezing works engineer, he thought, but her intentions were good.

"They can go, I suppose," Helen said.

"Do them no harm," he said.

She mumbled something, then went inside.

A man didn't know why he should worry about his wife. Maybe it was because there were so many other matters you thought you weren't worrying about but were. Maybe you didn't really think she was carrying on with some other joker; maybe it was the other worries mounting up so that when you thought about her you were actually thinking about everything, everything—hell!

He got restless, couldn't settle down to a detective yarn. He walked to the locker and got the black tin box that contained his war papers, letters, photographs, blueprints, bills—things from the past. He sat on the steps remembering the old days.

Chapter Seven

Evidence

I

HE REMEMBERED back to when he was nineteen.

His old lady, wearing one of those billowing black dresses, looking sorrowfully proud of him, gave him this prayer as she said good-bye:

Our Father in Heaven
Give me, I pray, clean hands, clean words
    and clean thoughts;
Help me to stand for the hard right
    against the easy wrong;
Save me from habits that harm;
Teach me to work as hard and play as fair
    in Thy sight alone as if all the world saw;

Forgive me when I am unkind, and help me to
forgive those who are unkind to me;
Keep me ready to help others at some cost to myself;
Send me chances to do a little good every day,
and so grow more like Christ Thy Son,
for His sake.
Amen.

II

He remembered his cobbers in camp—Tup Haines, Tom Burkett, Perc Bates, Jim Lewis. There was a photo of the reinforcements the day they were mobilised at Gladston Race-course. Some wore uniforms; those in civvies certainly looked funny now, trousers narrowing at the bottoms, hats all shapes, sober-looking jokers in black suits, hayseeds, a queer-looking bunch now. They had a good time in camp, swearing, talking about girls, acting tough, soldiers of the King. And five officers, one holding the collar on a black and white retriever; four sergeants, each with a handlebar moustache, the dead spit of Lord Kitchener. The year 1916.

III

His brother Raymond was twenty-two when he died, and eleven weeks married. Smiling into the camera, Raymond was a handsome boy, hair dark and long, shoulders a little hunched; he stood with some older fellows, outside a tent, a dixie on the ground, the boy trying to look like the others because he was in camp with them, hoping to get a lash at the Huns.

" My dear Gil, this is a pc of some of Ray's mates in camp, can you pick Ray? Jim Bishop and Phil Sanders in the back and John Hickman and some others in the front. You will know by now that Ray has been turned out of camp on account of his age. Phil is up on final, he has been here all day, he does not know what to do with himself. Love, your sis, Denise."

IV

It was a dingy Gladston in August, 1916. In the foreground the river, anchored coastal boats and scows, narrow wharves, waterfront pubs, Gladston Hotel white and important at the back, smoking chimneys of the freezing works, the shaded hills, all in a basin and the river flowing across the flats. The same firms as now, many of the same buildings.

"Dear Gil and Jim, I received your welcome card and was very pleased to hear from you and that you are well as it leaves me at present A.1. So you only had a week in Egypt, well did not see much there but what you did see was quite enough for you. I bet you thought it was a dirty place and you would not be far wrong as it is one of the dirtiest places on earth and you will see the difference in France. Do not make love to the girls over there as you might be bringing one back with you and I might cut you out for her so beware. Well you met a lot of the old boys there. I am glad and I hope they are all well. Well Gil you say to let you know how the old town is. Well it is still in the same place and I will be glad when all the boys come back as the town is very dull and slow. Well Gil, this is all this time. So Aur Revoir, Perc."

"Dear Son, I have been going to write you a few lines for some time but somehow or other something or other has always come in the way. I have got twenty pounds from Blake. I told Blake that was the amount he was indebted to you but if there was any more you could settle with him when you returned. I have got fifty-five belonging to you in the post office. Jim has thirty-two pounds in the post office. I had a very poor potato crop this year; the blight took at least half but I put in marrows and pumpkin and have any amount of them. I will try and get as much of your section in crop this year as ever I can but it requires a lot of labour to get it fit for anything and I don't feel quite so willing as I used to be, though I have had the best of health since you left. My birthday will be next week. Only seventy and still going strong. We had the borough elections the other week. Mills stood against Delaney for Mayor but lost by 160 votes. Now, Gil, I wish you would hurry and get the war over. I want a hand to cut up the big pine tree we cut down before you left—I have got all the branches cut up but the trunk is too much for me and Ray is very little good. It takes about five minutes until his hands are covered with blisters. May God be with you and Jim until we meet again. Your affectionate father."

V

Lewis mg instruction 71 weeks soldiering.
On fatigues in supports and front line heavily shelled . . . fine day on railway fatigue paid 35 frs . . . wet day on railway fatigue boots repaired . . . on sick parade no work very ill stomach trouble . . . on fatigue near trenches very tiring day Wet day left Pradilles

9.15 a.m. arrived Wallon-Cappell 12.15 p.m. eight kilometres 74 weeks soldiering . . . wet day left Wallon-Cappell 9.15 a.m. arrived Tatingham 4 p.m. 21½ kilos . . . rifle drill etc. received letters from home . . . leave to St. Omir—good day's outing had photo taken . . . fine day wrote Marie-Rose and home firing at range average 53 of 75
Arrived billet near Nippe 1 p.m. marched past General Godley and General Russell . . . camp heavily shelled all night letter from Marie-Rose . . . on sick parade LD slight cold . . . arrived reinforcement camp . . . fine day on carpentering work letters from home Denise Hilda Kath Smith . . . in Bulford Camp inspection by General Godley and staff . . . three balloons burnt and one enemy aircraft brought down
Hun airplanes dropped numerous bombs at night French church shelled and several women wounded and killed ghastly sight . . . left Bulford Camp for Aldershot Camp . . . arrived Catacombs marvellous piece of underground work holds 5,000 men
Fine day reported ill with heart excused duties . . . sent to hospital milk diet . . . from hospital to rest station and immediately to clearing station . . . left station per hospital train travelling slowly all day . . . arrived Rouen 11 a.m. to U.S.A. hospital plenty to eat well treated . . . operated on and had considerable amount of fluid removed from side complaint—pleurisy . . . marked Blighty in very high spirits
Sailing tonight
Foggy day in channel arrived Southampton 12.30 p.m. arrived Brockenhurst 6.45 p.m. recommended for board for N.Z. weight 9 stone 6 pounds . . . went for drive New Forest temp high sent to bed bad fever 103.8 sister fears relapse bad night . . . little better . . . quite recovered . . . visited Brockenhurst Church got stem of yew tree at church
Seven days leave in London went to theatre visited Westminster Abbey Trafalgar Square Leicester Square etc.
Arrived Glasgow 7 a.m. my 21st birthday spent in Wishaw
Arrived Motherwell 9 a.m. owing to raid met by Jean went to Glasgow with Jean theatre late train applied for extension until 16th glorious time . . . left Motherwell 10 p.m. parting hard numerous presents
Arrived back Torquay . . . left Torquay for embarkation Tainui
Left Plymouth rough weather strong escort of destroyers eight boats sailed in convoy. . . .

VI

—He received a certificate stating his conduct had been good,

had been issued with no medal on date of discharge, was on service 2 years 104 days.
—Raymond, who died of peritonitis, was a musician, and people reckoned he could make a violin talk. When he was dead, his eldest sister, Hilda, kept the violin on top of the sleeping porch cupboard. Anne, Ray's wife, married again ten years after his death. (The feelings about your return were mixed up with the feelings about Ray's death.)
—He became engaged to Kath Smith. Then he met Helen. He was on holiday spending the money his Dad had saved for him. Helen, smiling, white teeth, dark hair, beautiful, worked in a country hotel. He a returned soldier, Helen seventeen.
—Marriage. Foreman of his job in the city, children coming along, shift to the country, freezing works, woolsheds, the depression. Selling his section in Gladston for a hundred, the money disappearing God only knew where. (Remembering the bad times, don't forget the happy times.) Helen—Marie Antoinette—winning first prize in a costume ball, white wig, gorgeous dress. Not so bad up the coast, though the river was flooded a lot in winter so's you couldn't get to the store. Plenty of bills.

Dear Sir, Many thanks for your remittance of £3 2s. od. which has been correctly credited to your Morris Chairs Account, and from the attached receipt you will observe that while you are evidently of the opinion that £3. 2s. od. is sufficient to complete the purchase, there is still £1. 2s. 6d. outstanding. We think that the enclosed statement will be sufficient proof that our estimate is quite correct.

VII

"Dear Daddy, We are living in a house with a copper and tubs inside. This house has got one small room and one big room. There is an old truck here and Bubs gets in it and plays cars. Joy doesn't want to go to school. She said she doesn't want to go. I have just written a letter and picture and Frank tore it. We can't turn the taps off properly here. I have just had my breakfast. They still run a little bit. It will soon be Sydney's birthday. Ten more days. To Daddy, From Gilbert."

Chapter Eight

There's Always Something

I

HELEN TURNED into Massey Avenue. A gust of wind blew dirt clouds from the places where the borough council had planted native trees, swept her skirt about her legs; but it didn't matter these days if a breeze ruffled your dress, it was not like in your giggling young days. No pretty dresses these days, only the shiny costume the old biddies told you had been good to you, meaning it was shabby, and it was about time you got another.

Outside the bakery Mr. Moore, who was watching the traffic, said Hello, and she said Hello back, thinking he'd get his money all right, she'd pay him what she owed.

All this worry was getting her down, she thought, it wasn't good for her. Oh, if only she could get away from Gladston—mustn't forget to post the letter to Mum, she didn't know how she'd get along without her mother's letters and parcels. Good old Mum might be able to help with the machine, the cheek of those Singer people taking away the machine when so much of it was paid off, it was more hers than theirs. It made her frightened as anything getting the summons. Then she was wild as anything. Was there no end to her worries? Nearly drove her mad trying to make both ends meet on the money she got. Why didn't that pension come? They kept putting you off. Asking Gil for his unemployment levy coupon-book for inspection, if you please.

She was very dumpy, wished she could cheer herself up. She would call and see Fred, but first there was the shopping to do. She'd have to buy something for tea. Mince didn't take much preparing, and Marjorie might have the spuds done, and you could get a cabbage or cauliflower; then you must try and get some material for the kids' fancy dress costumes, the poor kidlets were entitled to their good times even if the creditors had to wait a bit longer. You knew how you yourself liked dressing up when you were a kid. Bubs must have something nice—she could be a pixie or a fairy. Both the younger boys wanted to be cowboys like Buck Jones, Tim McCoy, Ken Maynard, and all the other cowboys in the pictures. Gilbert could go as one of those pierrots that entertained people on beaches, the costume would suit him. Well, she would do what she could for the kids, but she certainly wasn't going to help at the tables on the big night, not like last year. Let the Gladston Central School Parents' Committee get somebody else this year, let them do their dirty work themselves, give them a change from bossing others around.

Mrs. Logan and Mrs. Webb were having a great yap a few yards in front of her, and she walked slowly so's not to catch them up. When they turned into Mercer Street, probably going to an afternoon's gossip at a bridge party, she hurried on down the avenue.

In the grocery Mr. Fields looked her over as though he thought she'd give him a big surprise and pay her bill. But she certainly wouldn't give him that sort of surprise. She asked for some tobacco, some butter, and a pound of tea. He asked "Will that be the lot, Mrs. Cunningham?" She noticed how he always asked "Will that be the lot?" with her but with others it was "Will that be all?" He needn't worry, he always got paid—sooner or later. She hated it when people thought they were doing her a favour; they always got paid.

Mr. Fields asked, "You placing your monthly order, Mrs. Cunningham?"

She was surprised that he asked for the order. Must think the pension had come. "Oh, yes, I suppose I could now." She gave the order, and he said he'd have it delivered. She took the bag of sweets he always gave with the order and said she'd share them out evenly among the kiddies when she got home.

He asked, "Heard any more about the pension, Mrs. Cunningham?"

"No," she told him. "Expecting word any day now."

He said, "Oh." Poor joker probably wished he hadn't asked for the order. He smiled Good-bye though, quite civilly.

II

There were such a lot of women in town today, hurrying, dawdling, yapping to one another. She was glad she didn't know many of them to talk to, it didn't do to get too friendly with other women.

Waiting her turn in the rest room in the Electric Power Board building, she listened to two women yarning about their jobs and felt dumpy again, thought some women could work and she couldn't and it would help a lot if there were some extra money coming in. But she wouldn't make much and the Civil Defence

Board would withdraw its allowance if she got a job, and there was a family to keep fed, clothes to be washed—a hundred and one things at home nobody else could do. Sometimes you wondered how it was all going to end.

III

Down by the river she studied the front of Fred's warehouse; the brown paint was faded, there were no boxes on the loading platform. Two old jokers, one of them Porkie St. John the remittance man, sat in the sun on the warehouse steps, not noticing each other, the one who wasn't Porkie nursing a beer bottle.

She looked down at the river, at the Maoris gathering pippis on the mud flat, two Maori women bending over and half a dozen kids putting the pippis in flax kits. Behind her the two old jokers began slinging off at each other, then Porkie St. John mooched away into a section back of the shops.

She walked up the steps to the warehouse, past the other old chap. It was half dark inside, a couple of lights glowed dimly from the rafters. The liquor smell was pretty strong. There was nobody in the small office on the right of the large room, but she could hear a tap running in the bottle-cleaning room at the back. She walked around the groups of empty bottles, looked at the faded newspaper clippings on the walls, the jokes cut from *London Opinion* and *The Bulletin,* the coloured whisky advertisements, the drawings of old-time bathing belles.

A fair-headed young fellow came from the bottle-cleaning room and told her to please take a seat in the office. She sat down and the young fellow returned to the bottle-cleaning room. She got restless. It was nearly three o'clock, the kids would be home from school by four, she really ought to be there to stop them messing in the cupboard, cutting bread, covering everything with jam. She hoped Fred wouldn't be long.

When he came in they kissed, she thinking how glad she was to see him and letting him keep his arms round her. Fred was the only person in Gladston to whom she could turn for help and comfort; she hadn't realised how lonely she'd been till now. She wanted him to hold her like this all the time, not let her go. He called her love and darling, apologised for keeping her waiting. Then he let her go, went to the cabinet for a bottle of stout, and filled two glasses.

He said, " So you couldn't make it on Saturday?"

" I simply couldn't get away," she said. " Gil's brother-in-law, Bill Coulter, called, and of course I couldn't think of leaving while he was there. Make me sick that crowd. Know what Hilda had the cheek to do last week? Sent the Baptist minister to our place about the kids! Wish she'd mind her own business, that woman."

"Ever give you any financial assistance?"

"Not a penny piece. All Gil's sisters are the same. Denise did send some clothes a couple of years back, but nothing else since. Still, I don't care. Don't want their charity, thank you."

"How's hubbie?"

"All right," she said. "Better than he's been for years, Fred. Even talks of getting a job. But you know what this T.B. is. I don't think they can ever be properly cured. Still, it's nice to see him walking around again. He's not so helpless these days. Makes it easier for me in some respects."

She drank the stout quickly, and Fred poured another glassful. Mustn't drink too much, she thought, didn't want her breath smelling when she got home. Stout was good, though, pepped you up. Oh, it was nice talking to Fred, he was lovely company.

"How's the girl?"

"Another three or four weeks yet."

"Joe not down?"

"No sign of *him.*"

"Another spot?"

"Just a little, love."

"Think you'll be able to get out next Saturday afternoon? Thought we might have a bit of a drive up the coast."

"Wish I could, love, but I don't know. Just like Hilda or Mrs. Simmons to come when they're not wanted. Might get away for a few minutes on Sunday afternoon now the kids are going to Sunday School, but then Gil might fancy a walk to the beach or somewhere."

Golly, she thought, the stout made you feel you'd been sparked up with electricity or something. She was sorry she couldn't go with him, sorry for his sake as well as her own. It was simply awful the way his people treated him, throwing insults every time he went home, treating their visitors better than they treated him. And now that he wasn't living with them any more she bet they wished they hadn't made his life such a misery.

"You comfortable in your lodgings, Fred?"

"Quite comfortable, thanks, love," he said. "'Least I don't feel like an intruder."

"The business doing all right?"

"God, I've been rushed off my feet all week."

"You don't want to overwork, dear."

"I'm looking after myself."

They looked at each other for a bit.

"I'll have to be going now," she said. "Must do some shopping for the kids. Poor tikes want me to make them costumes for the fancy dress ball."

"Want any money? Here, take this."

He gave her a couple of quid. She tried to tell him No, but he wouldn't listen. He kissed her good-bye, and she felt the dumps coming back now she was leaving him. He said he'd see her next Thursday night, and she thought he was a good man, and she loved him.

"Good-bye, love," he said.

"Good-bye, dear," she said.

"God bless you, love." He stood on the warehouse steps watching until she turned the corner.

IV

The bus was crowded, and she was lucky to get a seat. Through the window the shops went past, then the telegraph poles, then the trees in Massey Avenue. Just think. Christmas again. She supposed she'd have to think about presents for the kids, there was always something. Yes, Christmas, and her still in Gladston. Fat chance she had of getting away!

The bus stopped at Livingstone Road. She saw Mr. Moore watching from the bakery but made out she didn't notice him. Trixie Sutherland, the imbecile girl, called Hello and watched her walking home. The dusk was cool.

Bubs, Sydney, and Frank came running along the footpath, the two boys letting Bubs reach her first. "'Lo Mummy," said Bubs, holding out her arms.

"Hello, darling, missed your old mother, eh?" You cursed the kids sometimes, but it was nice when they met you like this. She frowned at Frank; he'd just touched Sydney to start a scrap, but Sydney wouldn't bite.

Marjorie was waiting for them at the gate, and they walked to the veranda together. Gil sat on the bed in his dressing-gown.

She pursed her lips at the top step to let him know she'd had a tiring afternoon. "Any visitors?"

"Not a soul," he said.

"You look worn-out, Gil," she said. "Why don't you get into bed and I'll bring your tea out?"

"I'll be all right," he said. "Bit hot this afternoon. Made me tired."

"Golly, it was suffocating in town," she said. "Such a lot of people doing their Christmas shopping already. And me looking in shop windows thinking what I'd buy if I had the money."

She went into her room to change. She could hear Gil laughing with the boys.

In the kitchen Gilbert wanted to know if he could get a bike for Christmas so's he could have a paper run, and she asked him how he thought she could afford to buy a bike these times. He said it wouldn't cost her much, all she had to do was pay the ten shillings deposit, he'd pay the rest off himself every week when he got the run.

"I'll see about it," she said, "but those things cost money."

He said he didn't want anything else for Christmas if she paid the deposit on the bike, and she wished she hadn't said she'd see about it, he'd expect the bike now, would be disappointed if he didn't get it. She knew who would have to pay the instalments if he lost the run, just supposing he got one.

"I had the devil's own job getting something for the kids' costumes," she told Marjorie, who was scraping spuds under the tap in the pantry sink. "Hunted all over town then only got enough for a costume for Gilbert. He can go as a pierrot."

"That's a sort of a clown, isn't it, Mum?" Gilbert asked.

"Can't imagine you acting like a clown, biglugs," Marjorie told him.

He frowned and bent over the exercise book on the table before him.

—Golly, but Marjorie was big. She waddled like a muscovy duck. Wouldn't be surprised if she had twins.

Frank hobbled into the kitchen bawling that Sydney had kicked him. "Oh, you kids," she said. Then he wanted to know if she'd got his cowboy costume, and when she said No he asked Why not? Because they were always tormenting her with their scrapping, she told him. He said she'd promised. She said she didn't recall promising anything of the sort. Frank told Sydney they weren't going to the dance after all, and Sydney said he didn't care.

"For goodness' sake, shut up," she told them. She got the bag of sweets from the bedroom and gave the kids three each, telling them not to worry her any more. She mentioned to Marjorie how Fields fell in thinking she was going to pay him and how he asked for the order.

"Young devils," she said, when Frank and Sydney had run up the passage with a sweet for their father.

Telling Gilbert to set the table, she went out to the veranda. She heard Gilbert asking why Joy didn't come and set the table but took no notice of him. He better watch himself if he wanted that bike, she thought.

"The boys just told me a Mae West yarn," Gil said.

"They didn't!"

" It was a clean one," Sydney said.

" It was clean, all right," Gil said. " Tell your mother, Syd."

Sydney told how Mae West walked into a hotel one day and asked for a bath then went upstairs and had the bath and that was all there was to the story and it was a clean one, wasn't it? She laughed at him.

Gil said he'd made up his mind, he'd have his tea in the kitchen tonight. So they all walked down the passage. Joy came in, explaining that she'd had some work to do after school, and they told her she'd spent a long time about it. That kid would have to be watched. But she wasn't bad, all your kids weren't bad. And it was nice having the whole family sitting at the table like this eating their tea. Just like in the days when Gil worked over at the freezing works. Made you feel comfortable. Life wasn't really so bad after all. Then you remembered Fred, and remembering him you were sort of worried underneath.

PART II

Chapter Nine

Gert and the Dummy

I

GILBERT WALKED with his brothers and kid sister down Massey Avenue to school. There'd been a frost, and he and rosy-faced Frank and Sydney had their grey shirtsleeves down. Bubs wore her woolly green jumper. Though the sun was pretty warm, you could see the backs of your hands red and blue with cold.

Looking up from the school journal he was reading, he asked Bubs, " Want to hear a poem about a little girl called Janet who wanted everything she saw in shop windows and ended up being a window dummy herself?"

Bubs nodded, and he said : " Listen to this—' Janet when she went out shopping had a tiresome trick of stopping every yard to point and say " Mother, buy me that I pray " '." He looked up. Bubs was watching Frank and Sydney scuffing their shoes in the gutter. The borough council jokers had been working along the avenue, and there were piles of weed and dirt beside the scooped-out gutter. " What you doing in there?" he asked.

" Just walking along," said Frank.

" Well, get out and use the footpath," he told them. " You'll get your shoes all dirty for school, and they won't let you practise dancing for the fancy dress ball."

Taking their time about getting out of the gutter, Frank and Sydney started singing " No more spelling, no more sums, no more teachers to whack our bums."

He got thinking of all the good things happening in the next fortnight. First the breakup when they'd learn where they came in the class (Ashley Harper had come to school pretty regularly this year, so you didn't think you'd be top; and you weren't sure about Barry Andrews, either), then the fancy dress ball (you hoped not too many kids went as pierrots but you hoped a few did so's you wouldn't stand out; you were glad the practising was nearly over; if only you could be smart and ask Carole Plowman for a dance), then Christmas Eve (you'd wear your cream longs and maybe you'd see Carole down the street and you'd talk to her).

Frank asked if there would be many cowboys at the ball, and he thought the kid must have been thinking the same way as himself. There might not be many, he said, but he knew there would be because most boys went as cowboys or Mexicans and most girls as fairies or gypsies. Sydney shouldn't have wanted to go as a cowboy, too, eh? said Frank. He said it wouldn't make much difference if they both went the same. They were only kids, he thought.

II

Some Form I and II kids were playing cricket on the concrete pitch, and Phil Chalmers' big brother Syd, who knew all the strokes and played them beautifully, was swiping the ball everywhere.

Gilbert reckoned he wouldn't mind playing cricket if he could play like Syd Chalmers. Might start playing next year, there was more chance to learn in the higher classes. He walked over to Barry Andrews near the woodwork room. They watched the game.

" Well," he said, " getting my bike tonight."

" New one?" Barry asked. " Not second-hand?"

" Brand-new B.S.A.," he said.

" Might get one at High," Barry said.

"Mine's a Christmas present," he said.

"Be all right for the holidays," Barry said.

Syd lashed out with the bat; the ball flew over the swimming baths into somebody's back yard. The kids told Syd what a corker sixer it had been. Syd leaned on the bat. Gilbert looked at Barry, and Barry raised his eyebrows.

Laurie Bowden came up rubbing his finger across the dark fluff under his nose. Barry told him Gilbert was getting a new B.S.A. for Christmas. Yes, they were the best, Laurie said. He might get a paper run, might be able to sub for Syd Chalmers, Gilbert said. Syd would be a good joker to sub for, all right, Laurie said.

Then Barry said poor old Phil would be about the only one in Standard Four to fail. Laurie laughed a bit and said he didn't know about himself yet. They told him he'd pass for certain, but he made out he was worried.

The only fight he'd had so far at school was with Phil Chalmers, Gilbert remembered. Phil had some dirty tricks and didn't play games like his brother, though they were both pretty tough and lived in the part of Gladston where the houses were mostly unpainted with rusted roofs. The fight had started as a boxing match, but he got wild and slung Phil to the ground and punched him, and Phil was scared and wouldn't look up. So all the kids reckoned he won the fight.

Somebody bowled Syd with a tricky ball that broke in sharply and made Syd look silly.

He'd play next year all right, Gilbert thought. He liked watching other kids playing, so he might not be so bad himself.

Laurie said, "That wasn't a bad drawing of Mickey Mouse you had in the kids' page last Saturday, Gilbert."

"Just a little sketch," Gilbert said, feeling warm. You got bucked up when anybody spoke about your items in the children's supplement. It was good.

III

The teachers frowned at the yapping girls, and the Be Quiet whisper ran along the class groups. Baldy Shimmering stood on the first-floor balcony. He led the singing of "God Save the King," then stamped from the balcony and strode up and down the aisle. They'd reached the end of another school year, he told them, and though he had some complaints he was quite satisfied on the whole with the progress they'd made. He wanted them to enjoy their six weeks' vacation and come back fresh for the new year. He said there were just two things, he didn't want anybody using the school baths over the holidays and he didn't want any of them breaking the traffic laws; Mr. Nolan, the traffic inspector, would tell him of any pupils caught riding on the footpath or without a lamp at night or violating the regulations in any way and the individuals reported would be whacked hard. They should remember everyone knew they were Central School pupils by their uniforms, he said, and he didn't want those uniforms disgraced. He walked inside. A Form II boy beat on the drum, and they marched into class.

By gosh, it was certainly a long morning. There was nothing to do except clean up the classroom, sandpaper and scrub the desks, throw out old papers, talk. Down in the teachers' study Mr. Martin prepared the reports and thought out whose scrapbook was best. You bet Dennis Shaw won the scrapbook prize, he had a shiny-papered scrapbook with typewritten headings and articles, and seeing he was the only son of an important businessman his scrapbook should be better than your own which was of brown wrapping paper with the Majestic Theatre's monthly programme as a cover.

Bill Murray, a real sheik, talked with the girls, he and Des Curtis asking them what they were doing in the holidays, making them shriek with laughter at things that didn't sound a bit funny.

You wished, as you sorted your textbooks, that you could talk to Carole Plowman the way Murray talked to girls. You were sort of excited thinking about Carole and, telling Barry you were going downstairs for a few minutes, you walked along the passage to Form II room, and the kids there were busy cleaning up, too. Old Miss Drake looked at you when you nosed in the doorway, so you hurried back to Standard Four room. But you'd seen Carole, she was looking through some books on her desk, her fingers up to her golden-coloured hair. You remembered once again the time you saw her crying under the stairs at the front of the school and telling another girl that Mr. Shimmering had said something to her that made her scared. Gosh, if you weren't so bashful you could dance with her at the ball. Maybe Mum would put some make-up on your face so you could feel brave and not worry about asking Carole for a dance. . . .

IV

Mr. Martin wrote the names of the first ten kids on the blackboard.

1 Ashley Harper
2 Gilbert Cunningham

3 Moira Thornton
4 Barry Andrews
5 Dennis Shaw
6 Erica Morgan
7 M. Park
8 W. Murray
9 Edna Robinson
10 L. Bowden

It was a surprise to see Laurie's name on the board, but you had an idea he was trying to make out he was worse than he really was. Well, now the reports were handed out there was no need to worry any more.

Mr. Martin said they'd be interested to learn that the first fifteen in the class would be known as Form I A next year and would study with Form II under Miss Drake; the remainder would study under Major Howard as Form I B. You were pleased and looked at Barry. He was pleased, too.

Mr. Martin passed round the essays and scrapbooks. He said your name and said what you had written was a good effort and would you mind reading it to the rest of the class. It would pass the time away, he said.

You didn't have time to feel embarrassed, but you wished it was another essay because this wasn't your best. Then you noticed Baldy Shimmering standing in the doorway, and you concentrated on reading the essay:

> The Phoenicians, who were the neighbours of the Jews, were a Semitic tribe who lived along the edge of the Mediterranean Sea. Their land was made up of rich fertile soil, and on this they built two well-fortified towns, Tyre and Sidon. In the course of time they earned the monopoly of trade on the Western Seas. Their ships went to Greece, Italy, and Spain, and they even ventured beyond the Straits of Gibraltar to the Scilly Islands, where they obtained tin. Wherever they ventured they built small trading stations which they called colonies. . . .

Baldy walked up the aisle and patted you on the head, saying it was an excellent essay and could he have a look at it. Then he said, "Hello, Gert," and the kids laughed, and he told you that you had put "G. Cunningham" at the top of the essay, and who knew what the G. stood for? Better watch it, he said. Then he wished everybody a Merry Christmas and a Happy New Year, and everybody wished him the same.

When Baldy had gone Mr. Martin called to you, and thinking maybe you were going to be congratulated on the way you'd read the essay, you walked to the front of the class. But Mr. Martin only wanted to whisper that your fly was undone, and you did it up back at the seat. You didn't mind Mr. Martin telling you about your fly because just now you were certainly pleased with yourself. Gosh, you bet when you told Dad how you'd read your essay on the Phoenicians to the class with Mr. Shimmering listening he wouldn't think you were so stupid after all.

V

Waiting for his mother, the schoolbag over his shoulder full of books, he watched the kids entering Mr. Herbert's shop. One of them came out reading a *Champion,* and he recognised Fireworks Flynn on the cover. They always put Fireworks on the cover, they never put Colwyn Dane on.

Some girls crossed the road from school, and he made out he was interested in *A Mystery of the Broads* by Percy F. Westerman that he'd won for his scrapbook (Presented to Gilbert Cunningham 1st Prize Scrapbook S4 Boys 1936).

"You're wanted on the phone, sir!" announced Patrol Leader Jack Manly of the Otters of the Nth. Putney Sea-scouts. Mr. Forbes, Scoutmaster of the Troop, received the information without enthusiasm. Being merely human and not a superman, he muttered "Bother!" under his breath and hurried toward the telephone. . . .

The girls walked past.

—Gee, I was pretty sure Dennis Shaw would win that scrapbook prize.

He bet his mother would be surprised; she was always going crook at him for cutting up paper on the kitchen table, making a mess with the flour-and-water paste. And now he'd won a prize for all the mess he made. He hoped she didn't forget to meet him. She *must* pay the deposit on the bike tonight; when he got the paper run he'd pay the instalments out of the money he made. Boy, he was going to have some beaut times in the holidays, riding to the beach and out in the country.

He watched the people passing the corner. There was only a week left to Christmas, and everybody was rushing to buy presents—brightly tinted wooden horses, trains and trucks in loose paper wrapping, wooden shovels and tin buckets, kids holding Christmas stockings, kids blowing squealers . . . his only present would be the bike, and that's all he wanted.

Joy and some other High School girls went past yapping like a bunch of old women. She better come home early for a change tonight, he thought, she ought to do more in the house instead of leaving everything for him to do.

He saw his mother coming toward him. She was better looking than most mothers, didn't have grey hair, though one or two silvery hairs were starting to show above her forehead.

"We'll have to hurry," she said.

"Can I have threepence for the latest *Champ,* Mum?"

"Oh, later; I'm in a hurry."

They walked down Stout Road. He told her he'd seen Joy, and she said Joy ought to be home getting the tea for her father, she left everything to her mother. He showed her *A Mystery of the Broads,* said that's what came of paper and paste. Then he told her he'd come second in the class, and she said he'd done all right this year, he should tell his father when he got home because he'd be pleased. She always knew he was going to be clever, she said; even when he was a baby he pointed to pictures on the wall and chuckled in a knowing way, and she'd leave him on his own in the dark and go back later and there he'd be with his eyes wide open and not a murmur from him.

He sure hoped his father would be pleased about his winning the prize and not look at him as though he thought him silly and only a kid; he didn't like his father when he looked that way at him. Dad got wild easily lately; must be rotten to be sick and not able to work. Different from the old days when he was tall and brown, and you were up the coast, and Mum came down to Gladston to have Bubs and you stayed behind with Dad, and he gave the house a coat of paint and the both of you drank all the ginger beer Mum made before she left for Gladston. He said, "Another thing, Mum, I'll be in Form I A next year."

"That's good, love," she said with a proud glance at him.

The schoolbag got heavier and heavier, his legs ached. Then they were at the bike-shop and looking at the window display of head lamps, handlebars, bells, tins of paint, and two glistening bikes. They looked terribly expensive, she said. They were the dearest sort, she didn't have to buy one of those, he said. She said she didn't intend to and, seeming nervous about going inside, told him she didn't know why he couldn't have waited another year. "I'll get a paper run, you don't have to worry, Mum," he said. "You only have to pay the deposit." She grimaced.

The girl behind the counter had a nice smile and made the arrangement seem easy as one thing. She took the deposit, wrote out a receipt, entered all particulars on a card, then explained everything about the bike. She opened the bag hanging from the seat of the bike, displayed the tools, told how the Boesch light worked and how to oil the chain and hub and how tight to keep the tyres. The way she talked and smiled made him feel good.

VI

Outside on the footpath, the sun on the bike made the handlebars, rims, spokes, and mudguards shine. He would look after his bike, it would never become as dirty as some of those going past.

His mother hung her shopping bags on the handlebars, told him to be careful riding home. He said he'd be all right, he could ride. Soon as he was home, he thought, he'd turn the handlebars so's they faced away from him instead of towards him.

Riding off, he glanced quickly over his shoulder and saw his mother waiting by the bike-shop corner for the bus. He was soon moving along pretty fast. He passed an old joker in working clothes and told himself he'd passed the first person on the new bike. He pushed harder on the pedals when he thought he heard somebody puffing behind him.

Up at the beginning of Massey Avenue, he saw his cousin, Ralph Coulter, standing astride a flash red and blue racing bike, talking to one of his tarts. Ralph was always talking to girls; he had a good time, Uncle Bill gave him plenty of money. Ralph was so handsome he made you feel foolish about your long legs and close-cut hair. You were glad he didn't see you with Mum's shopping on the handlebars of the bike because he'd crack one of his jokes for sure.

He rode in a neat curve from Massey Avenue into Livingstone Road, one eye on Mr. Nolan who stood in the centre of the crossing directing the traffic. He remembered what Baldy Shimmering had said about anybody being caught breaking the traffic regulations and thought he'd have to watch out for Mr. Nolan.

He slowed to turn in the front gate, and a fellow sped past on a bike, but he figured that didn't count as somebody having passed him on the new B.S.A. because he was slowing down on purpose.

"Want to have a look at my new bike, Dad?" he asked, stopping before the veranda. His father told him to bring the bike onto the veranda so he lifted it up the steps, took the shopping bags from the handlebars, and wheeled it along to where his father sat. Closely he watched the inspection of the machine—opening the oil caps, trying the pump, thumbing the tyres. "How much did it cost?" "About twelve pounds, Dad." "They don't make bikes like they did when I was a boy. Well, you won't have any excuse for not going to Sunday School now, will you?" "No, I won't, either."

Suddenly: "Where's your mother?"

"Waiting for the bus," he said, wheeling the bike back along the veranda. "She won't be long, Dad."

"You take good care of that thing; it cost enough."

"Yes, Dad," he said. He'd intended telling his father how he'd got on at school, but somehow he didn't feel like it just now.

Chapter Ten

Grant Me Thy Grace

"MUMMY!"

She put her hand on Bubs' head. "Sh sh," she whispered. In the night she could love her kids free of the thought of the dog's life they gave her with their squabbling, could tell herself they weren't bad kids. "Keep still, love," she whispered, listening for the noise again. It was the third night she'd heard it.

Moonlight shone through the window. Into the awful silence, like a scream in a Prince Edward melodrama, came the sound of a car on Massey Avenue. Then there was that other noise once more. She sat up in bed, tucked the blankets under Bubs, and lifted her legs—the lino was cold.

She knew it couldn't be mice or a cat. And what would any burglar want in this house? You had to be careful though; think of those murders in Gil's detective magazines when a burglar lost his head. But she knew very well it was no burglar who was responsible for the noise.

She got back into bed. Marjorie slept soundly on the other side of Bubs.

—Near-asleep, she saw a mixed-up Gil at different times of life . . . lovemaking, crying, vomiting, smoking, sitting on the veranda bed in his dressing-gown, poor tired-looking Gil. Herself . . . dragged to this small town, sickness, kids, charity, parted from old friends. She remembered her mother and the prayers one said when in trouble and with nobody to comfort one. What a lot of worry there must be in the world, you'd think God would do something. No, you had to think things out for yourself, and it was certainly hard sometimes. Prayers of comfort? Jesus, the only thought of Thee with sweetness fills my breast but sweeter far it is to see and on Thy beauty feast . . . She was scared old biddies like Mrs. Simmons would find out about her and Fred (Fanny and Peter; their little joke) . . . She should never have left the city when she was a girl, she'd be a lot happier there, and the kids would grow up to get good jobs. When she was small Mum gave her half a crown and sent her on a message and she spent the change on lollies and told Mum the things cost more than they did and Mum went crook at the old woman in the shop for overcharging and when the old woman said the change had been spent on lollies didn't Mum get wild— "You wicked girl! You'll never come to any good!" Golly, that was a long time ago; now you were married and with five kids of your own. And it was another Christmas, and you were getting older and older. Merry Christmas and Happy New Year, they said. Ha ha, you said. My sweetest Jesus, be not to me a Judge but a Saviour.

She heard footsteps in the kitchen. Bubs groaned, and she patted her head. Marjorie was breathing heavily. Heavens, what a size that girl was!

—O Almighty God, I wish from the bottom of my heart that I had never sinned against Thee (what were her sins?), but since I've been so unhappy grant me Thy grace that I may never offend Thee more (all she wanted was to be a little bit happy and to have her affairs straightened out).

"Mummy."

She whispered consolation to Bubs. She had such lovely children, people reckoned, they'd be a big help one of these days. She could scream at Hilda or Denise when they said that; they didn't realise the worry there was in rearing kids.

The noise was in the dining-room now. A chair moved. Everything was so quiet outside. Must be after midnight. People would still be dancing in country halls. There'd been some great times in tumble-down halls and woolsheds up the coast. She and Flo Young had fun. In the meantime in between time ain't we got fun . . . there's nothing surer the rich get rich and the poor get poorer. . . .

—God was on her mind. He'd take care of things if she prayed and believed. Those kids would have to go to Sunday School as Gil wanted them to. She didn't like the Baptists though, had had a derry on that crowd ever since Hilda took her to an evening service and she saw them being dipped in water, coming out like drowned sheep, and Hilda telling her it was the most sacred thing in their church. No, her kids would be confirmed in the Catholic faith, she'd see a priest about it . . . God knew everything. All marriages should be in the church, Marjorie should have waited. The Catholic faith was the true faith, all others came from it . . . Dressed as Marie Antoinette she won a fancy dress prize at a ball up the coast. She sent to the Country Trading Company in the city for the costume and everybody said she looked lovely and the judge, the big station owner, wanted to kiss her more than once but she wouldn't let him because Gil would be narked . . . And she was still young, too damned young to be buried alive in Gladston.

What was he doing in the dining-room? The summer was so hot, it was worrying waiting for the pension, the kids troubled him with their noise, and he was fretting.

—She was going to lie awake all night thinking, she'd never get to sleep like Bubs and Marjorie. That girl was a poor thing, waiting for her Maori joker to turn up. Poor Marjorie, poor Gil, poor everybody—especially herself. God, the only thought of Thee. Fred pouring black stout into glasses, she dancing round the warehouse as Marie Antoinette, a French song. A grocer named Mr. French belonged to her childhood and one day she asked him if he was a Frenchman and her father said "Hear that, Charlie, she wants to know if you're a Frog" and he got a big kick out of it. "No more stout thanks, love."

She'd been near sleep. Better get out and see what he was up to.

She put her slippers on and tiptoed into the passage. Through the house came the dripping of the tap in the pantry sink. She saw a glow in the dining-room and peeped round the door. He stood by the mantelpiece holding a match, looking at the ornaments. The match burned out, and he lit another one.

She tiptoed back up the passage. In bed she cuddled Bubs to get warm.

Chapter Eleven

Escape

THE SUN shone in a cloudless sky, there was no wind, like it had been for weeks now. Gil sat on the bed browsing through a *True Detective,* thinking about the characters in the magazine and the horrible things they did, thinking about crooks.

Some people sympathised with crooks because they were the underdogs. Think, though: if all returned soldiers got the idea everybody was against them where in hell would the country end up? You couldn't go around shooting your fellow men . . . you had to keep a hold on your feelings.

Funny how detective yarns were generally illustrated by a picture of a small town and small towns seemed to be the same the world over though America was a big place all right and you got many sorts of people there—murderers along with great singers like Paul Robeson. And the photographs of molls and police officers. You could see the girls used more make-up than was decent, or maybe it was the way the photos were taken; and the cops looked more like crooks than the crooks did. Ah, the familiar faces, the familiar old yarns.

> HARMONICA NELL—*The Gun Girl Who Came Back*
>
> San Franciscans wondered what had become of Nell Hood, the harmonica-playing newsgirl, when she vanished suddenly from the waterfront. But their questions were answered when Nell returned—a gun moll who was to stage a series of the most sensational prison escapes in California's crime history.

Hhh, you didn't get that sort of tart in Gladston. All right reading about them, though. "Thrice she made good her boast, flaunting iron bars and scaling wire barriers to win freedom. What was her ultimate fate?"

Escape—that's what all crooks, locked up or otherwise, wanted. And not only crooks, either.

He shut his eyes. He got droopy a lot these days. Like the paper said, Gladston seemed to be getting the tail-end of everybody's weather, and it was simply one hot day after another, and he became very tired. Might be better if he went to the city, as Denise wanted him to.

Reaching for the tobacco on the locker, he touched the book Gilbert had won for his scrapbook. He was glad his son was so clever at school; he hoped he got cleverer and made a name for himself. It would show Denise and Hilda and Elaine that you didn't have to be in the money to make a success of your life. He sort of wished he were closer to Gilbert, but the kid irritated him.

—Wonder what Helen's doing now?

He knew something was going on where his wife was concerned. He was wild at himself for roaming through the house at night, looking at writing pads and poking in drawers, for being jealous of her, but hell she was his wife, and she had no right running around with another joker. She went out far too often, and he didn't believe the tale that she was visiting Bella Simpson because he didn't know how anybody could seek Bella's company, while he knew that Helen had never cottoned on to Jim's wife, Rose, who was also supposed to be on the visiting list.

Christ, he might be going crazy . . . like poor old John Weaver. Surely he hadn't reached that stage, though.

Yes, he needed a change of atmosphere. That was it. When Denise came up in January he'd go back with her, have a month's holiday, away from such worries as the pension, scrapping kids, Helen, moping Marjorie. Didn't his cobbers from the works reckon a change would do him good? The whole trouble, they said, was he'd never had enough holidays. He needed a damned good spell from Gladston, they said.

Still, Gladston was where he'd been born and brought up; his old people had settled here long years ago. You got attached to your home town. But you'd be weak not to want to say goodbye to tarts like Mrs. Jacobsen, or Bella Simpson, or Mrs. Simmons, or any of them. The only one he knew who had the right idea about invalids was Flo Young, and he saw nothing of her these days. Bright and breezy, Flo loved an argument; she argued for the sake of arguing, and that was all right because it showed she had a mind of her own and knew he had one, too, wasn't feeble-minded because he was crook. Be all right if Flo came down over Christmas like she'd told Helen she might.

Maybe he'd feel better by Christmas. He'd cut the kids' hair; nothing depressed a man so much as kids walking around with hair down over their ears like Rudolph Valentino, that film star bird everybody went mad about a few years ago . . . back in the depression when they were up the coast and he and Jim were getting along all right with their building. Didn't see much of Jim these days, must be busy. He still worked even though he'd gone to the war, too, and got shot in the right thigh.

Oh, the days were hot and long and he was tired and he'd die if he didn't get away. That's how he felt. It was a feeling that had come slowly up from inside him, was now certain and urgent. He'd go with Denise and Elaine, get an eyeful of the city they were always talking about. He'd walk through their lovely homes, meet their charming friends. That's where money got you—money and plenty of luck. Well, a man might be up to hobnobbing with the nobs for a month. They were no better than he was.

Well, that was a problem disposed of. He could have another go at the *True Detective*. He settled back on the pillow for a read, flipped over the pages of the magazine until he came to

SEATTLE'S LOVE BANDIT
AND HIS 75 GIRL VICTIMS

> Rising hysteria gripped Seattle as a phantom attacker, preying upon scores of helpless women, continued his mad career. No woman was safe from the fiendish prowler, yet police were unable to trap him until a series of letters furnished a clue which was to end the lone bandit's infamous forays.

Chapter Twelve

Many a Heart Then Is Broken

FROM THE hall doorway, Gilbert, grinning and trying to look casual, watched the dancing. It was after ten o'clock, and the fancy dress ball was still going strong. The kids whirled past, some in gay costumes, others in queer-looking hoboes' and bakers' rigouts; all dancing, shouting, having a great time.

On his face the charcoal beauty spot had smudged; his eyebrows were thick black bands, the charcoal streaking across his forehead. He shouldn't feel foolish about his pierrot's costume seeing other kids wore fancy dress, too, but he did, and he wished the ball were over. Behind him Baldy Shimmering was talking to the lady who'd taken the money at the door, and he knew there'd be a fuss if any kid was seen going outside on his own.

The ball had certainly been different from what he'd expected. At least, that's what he tried to tell himself. But he might have known it would end up this way. Right from the start he'd been as nervous as ever; he didn't enjoy himself at all. He'd felt silly walking along the street with Frank and Sydney even though there were lots of others in loudly coloured clothes and with make-up on. And he'd felt silly when he and his brothers had their photographs taken on the lawn at Aunty Hilda's place with their cousins, Ralph and Donald. Ralph was pretty impressive looking in his white Roman gladiator's costume; Donald, who was a pale, quiet kid, wore a page's uniform. Even Donald was having a good time tonight from the look of it.

He'd felt all right in the Grand March, parading round the hall with Edna Robinson, not minding the parents and teachers watching, and some of the simple dances like I See You were good, and he danced them with Edna, too, but then she danced with other boys, and he got tangled up doing the Military Two-step and The Skaters, even though he had no trouble practising them at school. He danced with boys who couldn't find girl partners, then edged to the wall to watch. A teacher wanted to know why he wasn't on the floor, and he said he was resting. Phil Chalmers, who was resting too, told him he'd hang on till the supper dance, then grab the best-looking tart on the floor and take her to supper. When suppertime came Phil got a girl—Moira Thornton, who certainly wasn't the best-looking one on the floor—and took her upstairs, but *he* couldn't get anybody. He tagged onto the boys standing in the small room at the side of the hall where they gave out orange and raspberry drinks, and drank a lot, then joined in a furtive chase around the hall to the big dark room under the stage. Through the cracks in the stage they could see the orchestra, and Phil Chalmers reckoned he could see right up the dress of the lady playing the piano. At first the others didn't believe him, but they had a look, too. Then they got a couple of primer kids under the stage and scared them with spooky noises. Before the dancing started again a Form II girl sang "Cherry Ripe," and Mr. Shimmering made a speech. He watched on once more, and Aunty Hilda came up and said she hadn't noticed him for a long time and why wasn't he dancing, and, to please her, he had a dance, but he couldn't stop thinking of the people watching and probably saying he was stupid looking, and he was embarrassed, and that was the last dance he had.

So now he was standing in the hall doorway waiting for a chance to sneak away home . . . Carole Plowman danced past with a Form II joker; she looked as beautiful as anything in a long white evening dress that showed her skin down to where her breasts began. She was the most beautiful girl in the hall, and you felt lonely looking at her. Oh, her eyes were sad, but when she laughed she was better looking than any of the actresses you saw at the Majestic Theatre. He was jealous when he saw her dancing with Ralph and wished he were as handsome as his cousin. And he thought about Carole the whole time, but he couldn't ask her for a dance. He had figured he might wait until after the ball and walk home with a girl; it would be the first time he had ever done this, and it would be wonderful. But now he wanted only to get home as fast as he could, he didn't care if he never got a girl. He was glad Joy had been unable to come, otherwise he'd never hear the end of it. And he was glad, too, that his mother had not come.

"How's things?" Phil Chalmers wanted to know.

He grinned. "All right."

"Had many dances?"

"A few."

"This is all kid stuff," Phil said. "Not like the big dances. You get sheilas you can do something with at big dances. No mommas watching them, boy."

"A few good-looking girls here," he said.

"About three," Phil said. "That Plowman tart's sizzly."

"She's all right," he said.

They watched the dancing.

Phil said he'd shove in and get a dance with the Plowman. He said he liked her looks. But he didn't get a dance with her because she sat down and when Phil spoke to her shook her head. Then she walked around the hall and went into the dressing-room.

He watched the dressing-room door and the dancing at the same time. Aunty Hilda spoke to him again and said wasn't it a marvellous dance and everybody was having such a lovely time. She asked if he'd seen Ralph, and he said he hadn't though he recalled seeing Ralph going outside with a girl. Gosh, it would be corker if he could go outside with Carole Plowman—or even Edna Robinson. Fat show!

Suddenly he noticed Barry Andrews sitting with his mother, and he realised that he hadn't seen Barry dancing, and he was pleased because Barry was a lot like him. Funny how he felt like talking when he was with Barry but not when he was with anybody else. He felt braver now, and he would ask Carole for a dance as soon as she came from the dressing-room.

But when she did come out she wore a blue cardigan over her dress and she walked outside. Upset, he waited a minute or two, then went outside too. He couldn't see her.

A cold wind cut through the thin material of the pierrot costume; he shivered as he walked towards home.

Chapter Thirteen

Christmas Letter

IT MADE no difference that it was only a few days to Christmas, the housework still had to be done, Helen told Marjorie as she turned the wringer handle. There was a lot of washing where there was a family, she said, and Marjorie would find that out soon enough.

Marjorie was just the sort to have a large family, too, she thought; thank goodness the arrangements had been made for her to go into the Salvation Army home when the time came. It was a pity Flo couldn't come down for Christmas, a girl's mother should be near for the first baby. Not that there was anything dangerous about it. Golly, she'd had five kids, and Mum was not always standing by, though you'd been grateful when she was.

She must drop her mother a line, she thought. She'd be worrying whether anything had happened, and she was so kind with the parcels and cheering words she sent. Still, you'd been very busy these past couple of weeks, you really hadn't had time to write letters. Gil's things had to be got ready for his trip; Denise and Elaine would have no excuse for saying their brother was not looked after properly. Nobody could say Gil had been neglected. That was half the trouble; if you'd been like some women you wouldn't have worried so much about him, you'd have had a good time, never mind what was said.

She sighed as she put the clothes through the wringer. "Oh, well, the change of air might do Gil the world of good."

"It should," said Marjorie, who was sitting on a box by a heap of clothes behind the door. "It's so awfully hot here in summer, worse than up the coast. We had nice summers up there."

"Yes, I didn't mind living up the coast," Helen said. "Of course Gil was well then, no sickness. It would be different now."

Marjorie nodded.

Helen thought the girl looked paler than usual. "Why don't you go inside and have a lie-down, dear?"

"Think I will," Marjorie said. She left the wash-house.

She'd finish wringing the clothes, then she'd peg them out and duck inside and scribble a few lines to Mum, just to let her know she was still alive, Helen thought. She'd mention that Gil was going to the city for a month or so and she'd have a welcome holiday though it would hardly be a holiday seeing the kids wouldn't be going to school and she knew from experience what that meant. She could mention, too, what a good friend Fred was to her, hint that she and Fred hoped to enjoy themselves while Gil was away; but it wouldn't do to say too much to Mum.

"Lovely day, isn't it, Helen?"

She was so busy with the wringing that she didn't notice Simmons until he spoke. She was annoyed at him for sneaking up like that, felt like telling him it was a rotten day. But she said very politely it was a lovely day, all right. She was sick of the sight of him, he always looked at her in that knowing way, making her feel awkward. She hoped he didn't come round when Gil was away, you couldn't trust a man like Simmons.

He said, "Quite a lot of washing today."

"Never seem to get to the end of it," she said wearily.

"Can I help with the wringing?" he asked.

"I'm just about finished," she said. "Thanks all the same, Mr. Simmons."

He stood watching until she had wrung the last of the clothes; then, when she stooped to pick up the basket, he asked if he could carry it down the yard for her. She said she'd manage, but he took the basket and followed her to the clothes-lines.

He watched her pegging out the clothes. "Hear Gil's taking a holiday," he said.

"Yes," she said. "Going to his sister's place."

"Do him good, eh?"

"He's quite excited about it," she said. "Might make all the difference."

"You need a good holiday now and then," he said.

She moved farther down the yard, and he called that he was going in to have a yarn with Gil. She thought good riddance and went on pegging out the clothes.

After she had filled two lines she walked inside, feeling very tired. The kids had gone to the beach, and the house was peaceful. She sat at the dining-room table thinking out the letter to her mother.

> I hoped you'd be able to come down Christmas time but I know what Christmas is. Not much money and heaps of things to get and don't trust strangers to your house Mum you are too good at heart and you have been had before by heaps. I would love to see you but I would hate anything to upset your place just through my wanting to see you. Do write to me often I just long for your letters they are all I have to look forward to. We are still in as much a bother as ever with no pension yet and the kids wanting things and all my creditors worrying me. But Gil is going away for a few weeks to his sister's place and I'll have a little rest. I hope it does him good poor Gil the weather has been very trying for him—

Chapter Fourteen

Night of December 24

I

"SEASON'S GREETINGS," said Mr. Moore from the bakery.

"Same to you, Mr. Moore," Gilbert said.

In the dusk people streamed down Massey Avenue towards town: buses and cars sped past, and lizzies and truckloads of Maoris, the older Maoris bundled beside one another in shawls, the younger ones singing and blowing on mouth-organs. Christmas Eve was always a busy and exciting time.

He'd played cricket in the brewery paddock this afternoon and rubbed his sand-shoes on some cow muck, marking them, and, as he said to Marjorie before he left, the dirty shoes sort of spoiled the effect of his cream longs and too-short navy suit coat. He wished it would hurry up and get dark. Maybe he should have waited for the others and walked down-town with them, he thought. Only he'd been in such a hurry after thinking about Christmas Eve so long that he couldn't wait, and he might meet some of his schoolmates, too, if he got down early enough. He should have arranged to meet Barry; then they could have had some fun together. But if he did meet Barry he'd miss the chance to speak to Carole Plowman, and that was no good because he still thought he might talk to her even though he'd had no luck at the fancy dress ball and, anyway, he would have spoken to her there if she hadn't gone home so soon.

Down the road a bit old Porkie St. John stood on the footpath telling the people who passed that they were mad, they sneering at him for being drunk, and some saying that it was awful how a man with connections in the Old Country could go to the pack like this. And one or two grown-ups smiled at the old man while kids imitated him by swaying sideways and talking thickly.

He wished he had more to spend so's he could buy some throwdowns. All along Stout Road kids were exploding throwdowns on the footpaths, making women and girls squeak. Once he bought a couple of ice creams and a soft drink there wouldn't be much left of his two bob. Not much use hoping Mum would give him something to spend, she was always saying how short of money she was.

Yes, he hoped it got dark pretty soon. Some nights he had frightening thoughts of the murderers he read about in *True Detectives,* but generally the darkness was good. For one thing, in the dark people didn't say how tall he was.

A gang of Maoris ran past, laughing in their own way, different from the way Dad and the men from the works laughed. It would be good to laugh with somebody the way the Maoris laughed.

II

He bought an ice cream from Mr. Herbett and waited on the corner. He saw Phil Chalmers and some other Standard Four jokers skiting like one thing on the opposite side of Stout Road. Phil yelled to him, but the others merely had a look, then walked on. Anyhow he didn't fancy going with them. They'd have a wild time and end up on the river-bank smoking cigarettes. He wondered what it was like to smoke a cigarette. One of these days he'd have a try.

His mother came along with the kids. Sydney was looking in shop windows, and Frank was looking wherever Sydney looked. Bubs saw him eating the icecream and asked for one too, kept on asking until Mum told him he had no right letting Bubs see it, and he said she shouldn't want everything she saw. For the sake of peace Mum bought them an ice cream each. Then she spotted a friend and yapped with her about husbands and kids as though they'd never stop. Near by a drunkie fell over and hit his head but got up painfully and wobbled on. People in coloured costumes were singing and dancing near the clock tower.

Aunty Hilda gave him a big smile as she walked by with Donald; Mum was too busy to notice her.

He asked Frank and Sydney if they wanted to go down the busy part of Stout Road with him; he might see Carole there, he thought. They walked away and Bubs started whimpering and they told their mother they weren't going far so she said Bubs couldn't go where the boys were going.

They wandered among the happy people, watched the giggling girls holding one another's arms, laughed at the kids with the throwdowns. Streamers wound about everybody. There was music from the Salvation Army band and from young jokers with ukeleles, and every few minutes a trumpet rose above everything. You could hardly move in the shops, especially in Woolworth's.

He told his brothers to hold onto his shirt so they wouldn't get lost, mentioned the little girl who was lost at the A. & P. show one year and was found dead in a swamp; she'd been kidnapped by a bad man and murdered. They better stick close to him if they didn't want that to happen to them, he said.

They had two drinks and an ice cream each at the Orange Fountain; Sydney and Frank bought squealers, and Gilbert a Sexton Blake comic with an exciting cover. Soon their money was gone, and they felt lonely and poor. Gilbert met Des Curtis, who showed him a pound he had to spend, then disappeared into a music shop to buy a mouth organ.

Strolling into a sidestreet where lots of cars and trucks were parked, they saw a man standing against a fence with his hands down in front of him; they saw a young fellow and a girl going into an empty section and listened until there was quick talking and noises from the girl; they saw a woman going from car to car placing pieces of paper inside, and when they were close they saw she was old Mrs. Jacobsen. They walked round the block.

III

When Gilbert looked round Frank had disappeared. Sydney said he'd gone into Woolworth's. They waited uneasily, but he showed up after some minutes with a large toy engine. He said he saw it lying on the floor in Woolworth's so he picked it up. He said there were more in there, and Sydney could go and see if he wanted to. They told Gilbert they wouldn't be long and went into Woolworth's. When they returned Frank held a large coloured ball and Sydney a mouth organ. It seemed funny to him, Gilbert said. They'd found them all right, they said.

Up near the clock tower, they stared at half a dozen girls wobbling like drunks, swinging their bodies, one of them all the time hitching up her undies through her dress.

Their mother wasn't where they'd left her, so they walked back to the Spot Cash Stores. Frank and Sydney ran ahead, and when Gilbert caught up with them they were standing by the confectionery counter behind a crowd of men and women. He saw Frank reach through to the counter and grab a bar of chocolate, then saw Sydney do the same thing. Shocked, he looked to see if anybody had noticed his brothers, but nobody seemed to have. Frank and Sydney told him to look at what they'd found. Go on? he said, thinking he wouldn't mind a bar of chocolate himself, he was hungry. So he asked Frank if he could find one for him, too, and Frank said of course he could, but as soon as he asked he felt scared, and he walked out of the store. They wanted to know why he didn't wait for them, and he told them it was pretty dangerous finding things like that, they could easy get the police on their trail.

The clock struck half-past nine as they walked up Stout Road towards home. He'd had a good time downtown tonight even though he hadn't seen Carole Plowman. He remembered the strange things he'd seen, like the men and women in the side-streets, old mother Jacobsen, the music and the streamers, the throwdowns, the Maoris, and the Salvation Army band.

Then they met Ralph Coulter and a couple of girls, and Ralph started showing off by poking fun at Gilbert's longs and coat and kept it up until the girls told him to stop. Ralph thought it was a great joke.

Gilbert tried to think of something to make himself feel better. Well, he was having some good rides on the bike; only he wished he had a paper run. And, gosh, it was Christmas Day tomorrow, and there'd be Christmas cake and fancy things on the table, presents, and the special radio session. Christmas Day was about the best day in the whole year, and it seemed funny that it was tomorrow.

"We had a good time tonight, eh, Gilbert?" said Frank.

"Not bad," he said.

"I did, anyway," Frank said. "Didn't you, Sydney?"

"'Course I did," said Sydney.

Frank started singing "The Daring Young Man on the Flying Trapeze." The kid was certainly happy.

Chapter Fifteen

A Sentimental Time

GIL RECKONED he was the soberest one on the veranda; all the same he felt pretty good. Decent of Bill Coulter to bring along some booze, he thought; gave Christmas Eve the necessary kick. Decent, too, of Bob Davidson and Harry Braxton to call.

"How about a song, Bill?" he said.

"Yeah, shoot the works, Bill," said Harry, who was usually very quiet but got rather talkative in drink.

Bill put them off. "Have another spot?"

Gil said, "Only one; too much of this stuff isn't good for an invalid, you know."

"Just the thing," Bill said. "How about you, Harry—Bob?" They held out their glasses.

"Can't beat spirits," Bill said. "Reckon I ought to shoot home and get some?"

"This'll do, Bill," Gil said. Beer was strong enough for him.

"Wonder how the wife's getting on, Gil," said Bob. "She should have finished that bottle by now."

"I'll take another one in," Bill said. He rolled a bit as he crossed the veranda.

His brother-in-law was getting fat, Gil thought. Had high blood pressure, according to Hilda. She said he didn't eat much, she surely didn't know why he should have such a tummy. There were not many people who didn't like Bill. Though he'd got himself a position in life he'd never developed a swelled head like Hilda; you'd think she made the money.

"Glad to hear you're doing so well, Gil," Harry said.

"Yes, I feel all right, considering," Gil said.

"Still waiting for the pension?"

Gil nodded.

Bill returned to say the girls were fine; they were getting the kids' Christmas presents ready. "I told Marjorie she wants to take it easy," he said. "Jove, Gil, Helen's looking sparkling; must give you a thrill to have such a nice-looking woman waiting on you."

"Oh, yes, it does," Gil said. He guessed he hadn't done so badly. At times, when he was in that damned jealous mood, he acted crazily, but he couldn't really complain. She had stuck to him through the years, and what was he? An invalid, no good to himself or to anybody.

"Worrying about the trip?" Bill asked. "You'll be all right, fellowmelad."

"When you going, Gil?" asked Bob.

Gil said to ask Bill.

"January," Bill told Bob.

"How long you reckon on staying?"

"Few weeks," Bill said.

"Be great, Gil," said Bob.

"Mmm," said Gil. He wouldn't let on that, after thinking twice about the trip, he wasn't so keen to go. He reckoned he might as well take what was coming to him and not worry about growing strong and healthy.

"Cheer up, Gil," Bill said. "Mightn't be true, old chap."

Gil laughed. "How about a song?"

"Yes, come on, Bill," said Bob.

Bill coughed, stood in the right attitude, then started on "Wagon Wheels." He did little more than shout a song, though he was supposed to have been pretty good in his younger days. But it was Christmas Eve, and anything with a sob in it went over well, *Wagon wheels wagon wheels keep on a-turning . . . wagon wheels . . . carrymehome . . .*

Very good, they told him when he finished.

Christmas was a sentimental time, Bill said.

Everything seemed great at Christmas, Bob said. You'd think there was nothing in the world to trouble you.

"Always been the same," Gil said. "Remember how they stopped scrapping one Christmas during the war to swap greetings and puddings with the Huns."

"Shows you who wants wars," Bob said. "It's not the ordinary joker, it's the bastards on top."

"Too bad it isn't Christmas all through the year," Harry said. Harry was the diplomatic type; he didn't go for arguments, and once you got arguing about wars you never knew where you'd finish up.

Gil thought back to the trenches.

"Yes, we ought to have a good time down in the city, Gil," said Bill, who hadn't gone to the war.

"Be a change," Gil said.

"Wonder how the girls are getting on," Bill said. He went in with another bottle.

"Bill's a good sport," Gil told his cobbers.

"A decent joker," they said.

Gilbert, Frank, and Sydney walked up the steps. "Hello, Dad," said Sydney.

"Hello, son," said Gil. "Have a good time?" Proud of the boys, he told them to say Hello to Mr. Davidson and Mr. Braxton.

Bob said they were the dead ring of Gil, especially Gilbert. The kids looked embarrassed.

Bill came out, and the boys said "Hello, Uncle Bill," and he gave them a couple of bob each for Christmas. They hurried inside, the men calling Good night after them.

Yes, Bill was a decent joker all right, Gil thought. The way he went on you'd never think he was one of the most important men in Gladston.

Chapter Sixteen

Reaction

GILBERT NOSED in his mother's room. Marjorie lay on the bed, a glass in her hand, her hair mussed up. He felt like he felt down the street when he saw the drunken girls. Sydney and Frank wanted a look, too, but he told them to hurry to bed because it would be Christmas when they woke up and they'd get their presents.

They walked down the passage and squizzed in the dining-room where their mother was preparing the presents on the table. She hurried to the door and kept them from seeing. Gilbert guessed from the smell of her breath that she'd been drinking beer. Everyone seemed to drink beer on Christmas Eve, he thought.

She said, "You'll have to keep out of here, darlings."

"Look what I got, Mum," Sydney said.

"Where'd you get that, love?"

"I found it."

Frank held out the fire engine and coloured ball, said he'd found them, too. And they'd also found some chocolate, he said.

Worriedly, Gilbert told them to shut up. They said they were going to show their finds to Dad and went up the passage. He followed and stood in the doorway.

The men were saying good-bye to Dad. "So long, old boy," Uncle Bill said. "Keep your pecker up, want you in good shape for the trip." The other fellows said, "Don't go worrying about anything."

"Thanks for calling," Dad said. He looked pleased but not drunk like the others, who sang as they went down the steps and kept singing until they got to Uncle Bill's car.

"Hey, Dad, I found a corker ball and an engine," said Frank.

"Found them?" said Dad, gazing at the empty bottles on the veranda.

"In Woolworth's," said Frank.

"How could you find expensive toys like that?"

"They were just lying there."

"Where?"

"Not on the counter. Dad, they weren't on the counter."

Gilbert moved back. His father yelled at him to stop, asked him what the devil had happened. He didn't know where they got the toys, they told him they found them, he said.

"My own sons turning out thieves!"

"We found them," Frank said. "Didn't we, Syd?"

"Aw, shut up, you," Sydney told him.

"You damned young devils," their father said. "What'd people say if they knew? You're old enough to know what's wrong and what's right. Hell, don't we always give you what you want without you having to steal? You're thieves, that's what you are."

Frank and Sydney didn't say anything. They looked ashamed. It was a long time since their father had been so wild. He certainly looked very angry, as though he'd jump out of bed any second and wallop them. Gilbert wished he could go inside so's he wouldn't have to stand there wondering what was coming next.

"As for you, you clumsy-looking big—you oaf, you can't tell me you didn't know what was going on."

"I didn't, Dad."

"Oh, God 'struth! Get out of me sight. And you're the one that didn't want to go to Sunday School!"

Gilbert went inside. He felt his father hated him, and he was unhappy because he couldn't decide whether he'd known his brothers were stealing or not.

He got into bed with Frank and Sydney and lay in the dark listening. Presently his brothers were breathing deeply in sleep; but he couldn't go to sleep himself. He heard people going past outside on their way home from town, but there was no sound in the house. All of a sudden he felt sad as anything, he wanted to cry. Something inside came up in his throat, a tear rolled down his face, and he touched it with his finger. Gosh, he felt queer. A lot of things went through his mind, like Carole Plowman and Ralph Coulter, and all those people in the main street, and Marjorie, and school, and his bike, and Dad, and Mum. . . .

He must have gone to sleep because next thing he knew it was light outside. He remembered instantly what day it was. But there were no presents by the bed. He was puzzled.

He hopped out of bed, went to the dining-room. His mother sat sprawled across the table—asleep. About her head were the presents—comics, stockings, soft drinks, fruit. Sleepdopey, he walked to the veranda, awakened his father, and told him Mum was asleep and they wouldn't get the Christmas presents at the right time. He was ordered back to bed. It was still early morning, his father said.

So he lay in bed waiting. He hoped his mother didn't stay asleep too long. Gosh, she just had to wake up.

Chapter Seventeen

Destiny Waltz

I

FRED'S DODGE sped along Massey Avenue out of town. People on bikes blinked into the headlights, then were gone. White stones in the cemetery shone as the Dodge swept round the bend from Massey Avenue into the North Road.

Fred brought the car down to thirty, the engine droned evenly. They passed country pubs and stores and saleyards until they drove along beside the sea, Helen nestling against Fred, her head on his shoulder. He was a good driver, seemed to have perfect control over the car, you felt safe sitting beside him. It was nice driving along a lonely country road with no worries, no howling kids, the smell of the sea through the open window, a cool breeze rushing past. Everything was peaceful.

She looked at him. He glanced a smile. She said, "I like this, love, don't you?"

"Not a bad night for a drive," he said.

"It's lovely being out in the fresh air away from that prison," she said. "It's great having a car."

"Wouldn't be without one," he said. "Must bring the kids for a ride one of these days. Think they'd like it?"

"They'd love it," she said. "Poor kids don't get much pleasure, all said and done. I just can't afford to do all I'd like to do for them."

"How are they?"

"All right," she said. "But you know what kids are, they wear you down."

"Miss the hubbie?"

"In some ways," she said. "But it takes a lot of worry off my hands him being away."

She thought about Gil. When Bill Coulter called and drove him away she felt as though she was chasing him from home. It was a silly way to feel; she supposed it was because she really had been looking forward to his going. Golly, it was a change to go out at night without having to worry about anybody knowing. A change from visiting Bella Simpson and Rose Cunningham. Women were always slandering somebody; she'd like to know what they called her behind her back. That Rose was a jealous thing, too, she crawled to Hilda, and she'd be darned if *she'd* crawl to Hilda, she didn't care what Rose said about Hilda having a corking home and she was going to buy this and that simply because she'd seen Hilda with it. Jim was a decent fellow, but Rose was inclined to be common. Jim, who was supposed to be fond of his bottle these days, got more like Gil as the years passed. Once you wouldn't think they were brothers, Jim was the carefree sort while Gil was quieter; but apparently poor old Jim was beginning to feel the effects of the war and hard work. You didn't blame him for drinking because you knew how much a drop of stout helped when you were dumpy; you'd have to watch you didn't get too much into the drinking habit, though.

She said, "Bring any stout, love?"

Fred said, "What, already?"

"Not just yet," she said. "I only wanted to know, dear."

"Some in the back seat," he said, watching the road.

She said she hoped the kids were all right. He wanted to know if she was worrying about them, and she said you couldn't be certain what they got up to when you left them on their own. Couldn't Marjorie look after them? he asked. Marjorie needed looking after herself, she said, she was going into hospital next week. He asked if there'd been any news from Flo. No, she said, her accident must have been pretty bad.

II

She could hear the breakers rolling in on the beach. He turned the Dodge into a sand hollow, then up the other side, and stopped. They were overlooking the sea. It was beautiful, the noise of the breakers close, the moon shining on the white tops of the waves. A little chilly, though. She rested her head against Fred, and he put his arm round her shoulder. He was a good man, so understanding. He was getting on for fifty, she was thirty-three. Older men were more understanding. Not all older men, though. A person like Simmons was a lot different from one like Fred. Simmons was a bad man, she hated to think what would happen if he and his old biddie got spreading tales about her.

"We might as well get what fun we can out of life, eh, love?"

"Of course," he said.

She knew from his tone that he was brooding over something; probably about his unhappy home life. And he was having financial worry about the warehouse, too. She'd have to cheer him up. " What's wrong, Peter? They say it's no use worrying."

He touched her on the chin. " Who's worrying, Fanny?" he said. " Just thinking about getting old, everybody going."

" Who's going, love?"

" All my old cobbers," he said sadly. " Jokers I used to play football with."

" We've all got to go sometime, I suppose," she said. " But when you hear of anyone's death and you know them it always brings back sad memories of those who have gone. Perhaps some day we'll all meet again."

Perhaps they would, he said.

" Wish I knew where you could rent a nice quiet room, Fred." She sighed, opened the dashboard compartment, and brought out a couple of glasses, rubbed them, and reached over to the back seat for a bottle of stout. She poured a drink each. " Here's luck," she said.

He held up his glass. They drank the stout.

" Anyway I'm glad Gil isn't snooping round the house," she said. " He used to terrify me, Fred, I couldn't sleep till all hours. He looked at the writing pad, trying to read the impression of the pen, and I even caught him looking at the ornaments on the mantelpiece and the one you gave me, Fred. Things like that worry you."

" Well, you've got a few weeks' break from that now," he said. " You want to make the best of it."

" I'm going to do that, all right," she said.

III

They were going to forget their worries dancing, they'd waltz and fox-trot, they'd be in each other's arms. It would be like up the coast where there were dances every Saturday night and she danced with Gil and there was no thought of sickness. Fred brought back the good old days, days of laughter and song. Be nice if she could get an evening dress; she'd like a dark dress, black suited her better than colours. But it was only a country dance, there would be plenty of ordinary frocks.

Fred drew up the Dodge behind some cars parked outside a country hall. There was a lighted porch, and through the door came the sound of " Destiny Waltz." It was a lovely waltz, melancholy, something from the happy coast times. . . . Outside the hall, in the dark, somebody sang " Frankie and Johnny," and there was a strangeness about the little hall and the two songs. She listened thoughtfully until "Destiny" was finished and the dancers clapped.

They got out of the car, walked to the porch.

The hall was fairly crowded, and people sat close together on the benches. Coloured streamers and decorations left over from Christmas hung from rafters and down the walls.

The band played "Three O'Clock in the Morning," and they joined the dancers on the floor. She wondered if there was anyone in the hall who knew her; there was no telling who might see you, put your pot on. Next they shuffled around in a fox-trot, then there was a Monte Carlo, but she didn't win it and she didn't expect to; she had never won a prize for anything yet. She was enjoying herself, she thought. Only thing, she was getting rather tired, must be out of practice, she'd have to sit down for a few minutes. She sat with Fred and watched the dancers go past.

Suddenly she got a great shock.

She saw Emily, the plain-faced girl with straight black hair who was Hilda's maid. She wore a long frock with a spray of blue flowers; oh, she was sure to tell Hilda she'd seen Mrs. Cunningham dancing with a strange man, she was one of those sticky-beaked tarts who knew all the gossip going. She was only making out she hadn't seen you so's you wouldn't get the breeze up. Well, they were wrong if they thought they'd separate you from Fred.

She looked at him.

"Tired?" he asked.

"Am a bit," she said. "I think we'll go now, dear."

"Righto," he said.

They walked outside.

It was terrible having your evening spoiled like that. You would worry about what Emily might say to Hilda, what Hilda would do. Golly, though, you weren't an old woman, you were entitled to your pleasure. Damn what they said.

"Have a drink, Helen?"

"That's just what I feel like," she said.

IV

They sat in the Dodge drinking another bottle.

"Have a good time?" Fred said.

"Very nice, thank you, dear," she said. "Some of those girls have lovely evening dresses, don't they? I often wish I had one, too."

"I'll see what I can do," he said.

"Oh, I don't mean that," she said. "You've quite enough expense as it is, Fred."

"If you want an evening dress I'll try and get it for you. I'm not that broke, you know."

"You're a darling," she said, bending over and kissing him. "Makes you wild when you think how people like Gil's sisters get everything they want because they've got money and no kids. Denise has had so many permanent waves she's nearly bald."

Fred laughed.

"Makes me weary when I think of all the scratching and scraping I've got to do," she said. "The latest worry is paying for Gilbert's bike. He said he was getting a paper run, but he hasn't so far."

"He's a good kid; he'll get one I should say," he said.

She shivered. "Golly, it's cold."

"We'll move," he said. He warmed up the Dodge.

They sped along the highway at about fifty. It was good speeding through the night, as though you were leaving all cares behind. The Dodge was touching sixty now. With anybody else she would have been frightened.

"Good?" he asked.

"It's very fast," she said. "But it's just what I feel like doing. I want something exciting to happen."

You got into those moods, he said. "Hell!" he said.

They were passing a big mail lorry that was rumbling along the highway when suddenly the lorry swerved and the Dodge smacked the back of it. Helen screamed. The car slithered across the road, struck the earth bank, went over on its side.

She fell against Fred, but she wasn't hurt. She felt sick but not in pain.

Down the highway the lorry skidded and stopped, she could hear men running back. She called to Fred, asked if he was all right. The men from the lorry flashed a torch, and she saw Fred looking white as a ghost against the door. She knew something bad had happened to him.

"I think my leg's broken," he said.

Chapter Eighteen

MacPherson's Bush

I

GILBERT WAS oiling the chain of his B.S.A., and Joy was polishing the bike she'd borrowed from a girl friend who'd left Gladston for the holidays, when Mrs. Simmons came round the back, said Hello, and went inside. She was a funny-looking old tart, her bunhair made her look old-fashioned. And, boy, could she yap!

Gilbert said he was going for a ride, and Joy said she'd go with him. He told her to hurry up.

Then Ralph Coulter, wearing khaki shorts and shirt and his legs and face and arms brown, rode into the back yard on a blue and white racer. "Hiya, beautiful," he said to Joy.

Joy said, "Well, it's Romeo himself."

"Be seeing a lot of you this year," Ralph said.

"Something to look forward to," she said.

"You bet," he said. "How's the new bike, Gilbert?"

"All right."

"Looks as though it wants breaking in."

"I've had a good few rides on it," Gilbert said.

If he really wanted to break it in, Ralph said, he should go for a ride to MacPherson's Bush.

He wouldn't mind that, Gilbert said.

"How about you, honey?" Ralph asked Joy.

"I'm easy," Joy said.

"Needn't come if you're too proud," Ralph said.

"I'm not proud," she said.

"What about lunch?" Gilbert asked.

"Hop in and cut some sandwiches, Gilbert," Ralph said. "Cut some for your sister, too. I'll get something to drink from home."

Gilbert was wild at his cousin for ordering him about; he didn't know why Ralph always acted as though he were dumb, he wasn't really dumb or he wouldn't have come second in the class. But he did as he was told.

In the pantry he prepared the sandwiches. The house seemed empty since Dad and Marjorie had gone. You expected to see them on the veranda or in the kitchen, and it was certainly queer their being away. He could hear his mother and Mrs. Simmons gossiping in the dining-room, and they sounded like they'd be there all day.

He put the lunches in his schoolbag and went outside.

They pedalled up Livingstone Road to the brewery, then turned into the dusty road that led to town. Ralph showed off, riding no hands and skidding in the loose metal. They had a race to Aunty Hilda's, and Ralph gave them a head-start but he couldn't catch Gilbert. It made Gilbert feel good to think that he'd beaten Ralph.

He looked at the Coulters' home while Ralph went in for his lunch. This was the house where the Cunninghams had lived when they came to Gladston in the early days. It had been done over when Uncle Bill bought it, but it was still in the family, it was still a noble-looking place, sprawling and low-lying but sort of dignified. There were lemon trees and native shrubs in the front and patches of brown earth on the thin lawn. He had never known of bamboo rakes until he had seen Aunty Hilda raking leaves from this lawn with one. The Coulters had lots of unusual things. They had an electric stove, a latest model radio; they had a drawing-room besides a dining-room and a sleeping-porch and a guestroom; they even had a maid called Emily. It would be good to have enough money for all these things, he reckoned.

II

Ralph came out with a small case hanging from the handlebars of his bike and a BB-gun strapped to the crossbar. They could have a drink of lime juice inside if they wanted one, he said, but they refused.

They rode past the Central School, and Gilbert had a scary feeling inside when he thought what would happen when school started and Baldy heard from Mr. Nolan that he'd been riding on the footpath. The traffic cop had told him he was going to report him to Shimmering when the holidays were over, and now he could see Shimmering telling him off before everybody for breaking the traffic laws, and maybe he wouldn't go into Form I A after all, maybe he'd go into Major Howard's class. Except for this happening he'd been having a great time on his holidays.

Pretty soon they were out of town. When they were passing a

block of shops just across the bridge a sun-tanned woman in beach pyjamas rode in front of them, and she leaned over to get off her bike by the footpath and he saw her breasts clear as one thing. He looked around, and Ralph grinned and said "Not bad, eh?" and he grinned, too, but felt uncomfortable.

They turned off the main road, pedalled along the road that ran beside the river out to MacPherson's Bush. The B.S.A. moved very nicely, and Gilbert pretended he was in one of those streamlined De Sotos that some of the Gladston nobs owned. He was certainly glad he had the bike; only he wished he could get a paper run.

The road climbed, and they had to get off and push. It was good coasting down the other side, though. Pushing was hard work, Joy said. The exercise would do her good, and anyway they could have a swim out at the bush, Ralph said.

Down in a valley they saw some men harvesting. An old Ford was tearing out into a paddock, pushing loads back, chugging away while the driver dug the grab prongs into each load. Another joker giddaped a horse that hauled the loads into the air. The valley was noisy with the Ford's chuttering.

They parked by the fence and watched the men at work. The joker in the Ford came pretty close, and they yelled out, and he yelled back. He was red-faced, and it certainly must be hot making a stack on a summer day like this.

They rode on towards MacPherson's Bush, the river beside the dusty country road a stream now, with strips of shingle and large boulders in it, the hills about them mostly brown. At the gate to the bush they hid their bikes behind a hedge, climbed a gate, and walked along a track through the trees. They came out onto a hill slope that fell to the stream.

Ralph ran down the slope and sat on the bank of the stream loading his BB-gun.

Joy flopped tiredly a few yards from him. She said, "What you going to do with that? Shoot some poor harmless birds?"

"Maybe," Ralph said. "See that lid on the bank over there? What you bet I can't hit it from here?"

"No bet," Joy said.

Ralph fired the gun; they heard the BB's striking the tin lid on the opposite bank.

III

Gilbert went for a walk. Everything was quiet in among the trees. He saw cigarette packets and food tins left by picnic parties but it was so quiet at this moment that it was as if nobody had ever been to the place. He could imagine himself living in a tent up here in the hills, like in those dreams where he was a sort of Tarzan who came down from the bush for food in the middle of night. He'd be naked, he'd hide in the treetops when he heard anyone coming. No need to go to school. He'd be like Robin Hood only there would be no merry men—

He heard Ralph calling about lunch, so he walked back and ate his sandwiches. Ralph shared a bottle of lime juice with him and Joy.

"Well, what you think of your cousins?" asked Ralph.

"Tui and Virginia?" Gilbert said.

"Sure," Ralph said.

Gilbert thought back to the day before his father left when Aunty Hilda brought Aunty Elaine's two daughters, Tui and Virginia, to the house. His cousins talked like those English actresses in the pictures, and he guessed this was because they went to college. He stayed in the bathroom pretending to wash his feet while they were in the dining-room. He heard them talking about him, saying how clever he must be spending so much time compiling scrapbooks and writing magazines, and he was pleased when he heard Tui say she didn't know how he did it, but he was scared to go into the dining-room so he stayed in the bathroom; and when his mother came looking for him he told her he was busy washing his feet. And he didn't move till the visitors left. So he couldn't remember much about them except their voices. But he told Ralph they weren't bad.

"Stuck-up, if you ask me," Joy said.

"Puss puss," Ralph said.

"Shut up," she said.

"Tui plays the piano and dances," Ralph said.

"That what they teach her at college?"

"Funny how sheilas get jealous of one another, Gilbert," Ralph said.

"Yes, it is."

"Your mother's not bad on the dancing, is she?" Ralph said.

"How do *we* know?" Joy said.

"Thought you might," Ralph said.

Gilbert wondered why Ralph was asking about Mum, wondered if he knew something concerning her that he didn't. He was curious about the talking in the dining-room when he was in bed; when he asked his mother about it she said he imagined things.

One night recently this joker Fred was in the dining-room. Mum said he was Marjorie's uncle. But you didn't understand what was going on, and you were puzzled.

" Who do you like best, your mother or your father?" Ralph asked.

" Don't be stupid," Joy told him. " We like them both the same, of course."

" I like my father better than my mother," Ralph said.

" Because he gives you money, I suppose," Joy said.

" That's one good reason," Ralph said.

" You should love them both the same," Gilbert said.

" Why?" Ralph asked. " They're human beings, they do bad things the same as anybody else. Didn't you know that?"

" You're only talking for the sake of talking," Joy said.

" One day you'll grow up," Ralph said. " You'll find out things you don't know about now."

" You don't say, grandpop," Joy said.

IV

Ralph got out of his clothes in a hurry, dived into the stream where it was pretty deep. Gilbert undressed slowly, taking off his shirt, then his singlet, then his socks and shoes. He stood in his pants. He glanced at the dark hair on his cousin, thought how his own hair had just started to grow; it was strange when the first hair came, a long curly hair, and you kept looking to see if any more grew.

" Come on in," Ralph called.

Gilbert got out of his pants and jumped into the stream. The water was nice and cool, it was good dog-paddling around. He liked swimming with nothing on. Sometimes at the beach he slipped his togs down soon as he was out a bit, let the water slide between his legs; but he'd never really swum with nothing on before.

" How old's Joy?" Ralph asked.

" Nearly fourteen," Gilbert said.

" She looks more than that," Ralph said.

" She does, all right," Gilbert said.

" Got a nice pair of bubs," Ralph said, ducking under the water and swimming along, legs threshing the surface. He got up on the bank, looked into the trees. " Won't be long," he said. " Want to visit aunty."

Gilbert stood and looked after Ralph. He had a feeling he knew where Ralph was going. He got out of the water and followed his cousin through the trees. Ralph worked his way in a bit and then, further down, came back towards the stream. From behind a bush, he stared out. Keeping a good distance away, Gilbert looked where Ralph was looking.

Joy swam naked in the stream. Now and again she looked towards where she had left Ralph and Gilbert, then she stood, dived into the stream, and stood again.

Gilbert eyed Ralph, then studied Joy as she turned round and faced them, rubbing her hands over her body. Gosh she had changed since the days when she had her baths with him and Frank and Sydney. Except for the one thing her body then had been the same as theirs, and nobody took any notice. Now her body was no longer like a kid's, and her freckles were going and she was good-looking. He'd known she was growing different though because she had stopped having a bath with the others and she wanted a room of her own; he had felt the same way when he got older.

He could make out her breasts, small smooth-looking round lumps, the soft look of her body, the way her legs were thick above the knees. It was the first time he'd seen so much of a girl's body—a grown girl's body—and he felt himself getting warm all over. He put his hand down in front of him, then took it away, and gosh, it was a queer feeling, like you were doing something terrible but good all the same. He remembered how he felt that time up the coast when Marjorie made him touch her breasts; it was the same way he felt now.

Joy got back under the water. He hurried through the trees to his clothes, dressed, and sat waiting for Ralph.

V

After the swim there didn't seem much to do except sit on the bank while Joy dried her hair in the sun. Ralph fired at a bird, and when it dropped in the stream Joy told him he was cruel, but he only laughed and shot another bird. Then he handed the gun to Gilbert, told him to see what he could do about the lid on the opposite bank. Gilbert had a few shots but couldn't hit the lid.

Ralph told a dirty story and laughed loudly. Then he mentioned their mother once more. "You want to keep an eye on her," he said. "She's quite a number."

"You better watch what you say about her," Joy told him.

"Want to know something?" Ralph said.

"No, we don't," Joy said.

"Righto, then. Far be it from me to enlighten you."

Joy told him to go jump in the stream.

Bending over to lace his shoes, Gilbert felt a sudden pain in his behind, and the tears came to his eyes. Ralph laughed. "See him jump! Bee sting you, Gilbert?"

Gilbert grinned, but he was wild at Ralph for shooting the BB's at him, and he didn't feel like laughing.

"You're dangerous," Joy told Ralph.

"He can have a shot at me if he likes," Ralph said.

Gilbert refused the offer. He reckoned his behind wouldn't feel any better if he shot Ralph.

"I think it's time we went home," Joy said.

"There's a spouting geyser up the bush a bit," Ralph said. "Want to see it?"

"No thanks," Joy said. "We're going home."

"All right, if you want to be proud," Ralph said.

They walked to the bikes.

On the ride back to town Joy and Gilbert were silent. Ralph was grinning.

Chapter Nineteen

Reflection

I

Bob Davidson leaned against the veranda railing and rolled a smoke. "So you reckon the city wasn't so hot, Gil."

"I thought it was a bastard of a place," said Gil, who was sitting on the bed.

"Suppose it was the wind, eh? Blows a good bit down there. So they say, never been there myself."

"It's the place in general," Gil said. "I just didn't like the city or the people in it, that's all." It was true, he thought, he wasn't exaggerating. Gladston might be too hot in summer, too wet in winter, but it wasn't as miserable as that dump.

"See any quacks down there, Gil?"

"Had to visit the hospital as an out-patient," Gil said. "Did no good, though."

"Reckon we got as good quacks in Gladston as anywhere in the country," Bob said.

"They're okay as quacks go," Gil said. He guessed there was

a point where no quack living could do anything for a man.

"Don't suppose you had a chance to do anything about the old pension," Bob said.

"Hh, just live and hope where that's concerned," Gil said. God, he thought, he was getting to sound like Bella Simpson. Anybody would think he'd been to a bloody funeral instead of away for a holiday. Too bad if Bob Davidson told his cobbers Gil Cunningham was becoming a drip and there was no sense visiting him because he didn't appreciate visitors. He liked his old workmates calling on him and yarning, and he'd feel bad if they knocked off.

"Had a great time in the Businessmen's Club, Bob," he said. "Sister's husband took me along one morning. You never saw such a pack of fat contented idiots in all your life. They sat at posh tables taking it easy in sedan chairs. There were shining knives and forks and silver jugs and teapots; neat-looking waitresses brought plates of lettuce, cold luncheon sausage, and hot potatoes, and bread rolls and tiny pats of butter, and the boys yapped like a lot of old women while they ate their lunch. Then the chairman made remarks about certain members that were supposed to be funny, and he fined a few of them for something they'd done lately, like starting a new factory or something. Christ!"

"Bet they pulled the Labour Government to pieces," Bob said.

"You're right, there," Gil said. "They reckoned the National Party might go ahead with Adam Hamilton taking over from old Forbes. You never heard such a pack of old tarts. Here, take a look at this."

He handed Bob the card the club secretary had made out for him. On one side was

BUSINESSMEN'S CLUB

Honorary Member

Mr. . . . G. Cunningham
From . . . 3rd January to 3rd February
Introduced by . . . Mr. F. Searing

and on the other

IMPORTANT

Honorary members are not permitted to bring into the club premises or entertain therein any strangers without permission of the secretary. The attention of honorary members is drawn to the club by-laws posted in the club.

"Could see me getting into a club like that," Bob said, grinning.

"*I*'d never have got in but for having Searing for a brother-in-law," Gil said. "They're his people."

"They'd sling me out as soon as look at me," Bob said.

"Sooner Labour puts them out of business the better," Gil said. "Made me wild looking at those fools, they seemed so pleased with themselves, like they were on top and didn't give a damn for anybody else. Might be thousands feeling the pinch, but it wouldn't worry those bastards. The Labour crowd are only politicians like the rest, but you get your back up when you think what those business jokers would do to Labour if they got the chance."

"Yes, there's a big job ahead for Labour," Bob said.

"Certainly is," Gil said.

Bob thought a bit, then straightened up. "Well, I'll have to be running along, Gil. Thought I'd drop in on the way home from work, see how the holiday went. Glad you think old Gladston's the best place after all. You get fed up with it, but you appreciate it when you're away."

"You do, all right," Gil said.

"Looks like rain tonight," Bob said. "Some black clouds up there."

"It'll clear the air," Gil said. "Don't forget those *True Detectives,* Bob."

"Have a look right after tea and send the boy over," Bob said. "So long, Gil."

"Hooray," Gil said. He watched Bob hop on his bike and head for home. Bob was a good stick. A man made some real friends when he was working.

II

The dusk was humid with the summer storm that was in the air. The stillness was very oppressive.

—Seemed like you'd never been away, seemed like the last few weeks were not real. Good to be back near your bed so you could turn in whenever you felt that way instead of dressing up and being polite to people you didn't cotton on to. Funny how drowsy you'd been since you got back, as though you'd been drugged.

Helen came out. He was annoyed when she smiled at him. He

reckoned she ought to be ashamed to smile at him when she was running around with another bloke. 'Struth, he didn't mind her having a good time. But why didn't she say right off that she was fed up with looking after him and wanted a good time?

She said it was hot, wasn't it.

It was, all right, he said.

She asked, "You coming in for tea, dear?"

He said, "Don't think I fancy tea."

She said, "Oh, you must have something; would you like me to bring your tea out, Gil?"

He said, "Don't bother."

She looked at him as though wondering what was on his mind. But he wouldn't say anything until the right time, he thought. She asked about Bob, but it was only for the sake of saying something, he knew. She mentioned tea again, and he told her he didn't want anything.

Shaking her head, she went inside.

Fat lot she had to shake her head about! Wonder whether this man who'd taken her fancy was anybody he knew. You'd have thought she would have waited until he was dead. Elaine and Denise reckoned he'd never looked better; he wasn't going to kid himself thinking that. But he was not dead yet. Just another returned soldier waiting his time. He wouldn't kick when the time came.

Bubs skipped onto the veranda. Was he coming in for tea? she wanted to know.

"Tell your mother No," he said.

She was not disturbed. "When school start, Daddy?"

He told her to ask her big brother, he was the brainy one in the family.

Bubs left the veranda.

—Thinking back, you saw how you'd always looked forward to something better turning up, as when you were an ordinary carpenter and visualised yourself in the money with jokers working for you. You hadn't had much of an education, but your blueprints were praised by builders, and you always attended to the books when you and Jim were partners. But there was the depression and the damned sickness, and now you weren't much good for anything. You'd had some good times though, you'd been happy married to Helen. You could remember when you were younger how you lay awake nights thinking of Helen. And now she was still looking for something from life. Good luck to her. Only it hurt a man to wonder what sort of joker she preferred to you. It didn't seem right.

Then he thought that, seeing he had the energy to worry

about her, he might not be so crook after all. Maybe it was a good sign that he was worrying. Maybe it showed he had more kick in him than some people imagined.

Chapter Twenty

The Paper Run

GOSH, THIS job was worth more than seven and six a week, Gilbert thought, as the bag containing the papers got in his way when he turned a corner and nearly tipped him off the bike. He had learned the run from Basil Fisher in a week, now did it four nights weekly; Basil collected the full wage and gave him seven and six for being his sub. It was all right at first, and he liked riding down Massey Avenue with the paper-bag dangling from the handlebars, thinking maybe somebody who knew him was watching and noticing he had the run. But it was not so good having a *Star* run; the subscribers were scattered, and you had to ride a long way to finish the run. A couple of nights he had finished with two spare papers, and, seeing they counted them exactly at the office before you left, it meant two subscribers had missed getting their copies. He'd rather deliver *The Age,* the local paper, as his father had done on foot in the old days.

He leaned over the handlebars, watched the road slipping by. He saw some kids playing cricket in a section; a girl yelled to him, and he blushed but felt proud. The run was mostly down by the river where the houses were ramshackle looking. This was the part of town where Syd and Phil Chalmers lived and big families like the McDermotts, who were famous for their fighting.

The bike bumped onto the footpath. He had an excuse for riding on the footpath now. Might be able to work something out of that to tell old Baldy when school started next week. He had worried all through the holidays about the traffic cop catching him riding on the footpath, had tried to forget by telling himself it was a month before school started, then three weeks, then a fortnight; but now there were only four days to go. Gee, he might have an accident one night, might not have to go to school for a few weeks, and Baldy would have time to forget about Mr. Nolan.

A raindrop snicked his face. He'd have to put the papers in the letter boxes. 'Course it would rain soon as he had a job. It had been sunny all summer; once the rain started it might last for days and weeks. He had a good mind to tell Basil Fisher to stick his run. He'd met Fisher at Sunday School but didn't know he had a *Star* run until the first night. Some nights you were at the shop at five o'clock waiting for the mail truck to get in but it would be half-past six before it showed up and you wouldn't get home till after seven, and Mum, who had been going out a lot lately, went stinking. Now Dad was back she didn't go out nearly so much.

Since his holiday, Dad had been pretty bad tempered, he couldn't have enjoyed himself like you were supposed to on a holiday. His first question almost on his return was whether you were attending Sunday School regularly; you told him you were, and you were, too. But you didn't like the kids at Sunday School. You were in the Bible Class now, and some of the other kids were jealous, seemed to think you hadn't worked as hard as they had to pass from Sunday School to the Bible Class. Fisher especially kept asking questions about the Bible in front of the others to try and make you look foolish. Fisher was always trying to make you blush and look a dope. The other Sunday he talked about how he went to the beach often and got sun-tanned and healthy, and he looked at you as though telling the other kids to see how pale your skin was. Then he talked about how many baths he had, and you remembered you'd forgotten to clean your ears for some days and you supposed that was what Fisher was driving at. . . .

The run was taking a long time tonight. He was hungry, wished he was home. More spits of rain fell, and pretty soon it was raining gently. He pedalled harder.

He kept thinking he'd tell Fisher to do the run on his own. Be different if it was his run and he got the full pay. He might knock off Sunday School, too; lots of kids didn't go, like Ralph Coulter. He didn't see why he should have to go when his cousin never went.

It was getting cold and dark, the rain was thicker. Street lamps made the road shine. He bet not many kids had to work in the dark and the wet. His pants stuck uncomfortably to his thighs, the water splashed up over his socks; he worried about the effect of the rain on the chain and hubs of the B.S.A. Twenty more papers.

He neared the main part of town. People ran through the rain towards home and there was something good about them running along in the wet, the yellow street lamps, and the far-away sound of thunder. Passing the Presbyterian Church he saw Porkie St. John plodding along and he wondered if Porkie would shelter in the church, but when he looked back he could see the old man going on past the big building, and he could see a yellow light in the tower.

Sick of putting the papers in letter boxes, he tossed the last few onto verandas, then sped towards Stout Road. He rode by the house where the old tart had whacked him with a broom and then on to Mrs. Morpeth's dairy. He stood in the dairy doorway looking out at the rain.

Chapter Twenty-One

The Quarrel

I

GIL PUFFED on a cigarette. To hell with the quack, he thought.

He looked without enthusiasm at the covers of some magazines he'd brought from the city; you got magazines in the city you never saw in Gladston, like *Health and Beauty,* the one with naked tarts in it, some of them old and scrawny, the important parts touched up. No, he couldn't read; there was too much on his mind. He wished he hadn't told Helen he didn't fancy a cup of tea, he could certainly do with one just now.

He watched the end of the cigarette.

Helen poked her head around the door and asked was he sure he wanted nothing because she'd like to go for a walk later and if he wanted anything he better have it now.

Wild because she was going out and hadn't told him where she was going, he said once more that he wanted nothing. A hurt came and went inside him pretty suddenly, and it scared him a bit.

Sydney walked out the front door, hands behind his back, and stood at the top of the steps looking across the lawn. In the dusk Gil could just make out the serious look on the kid's face; he was rather old-fashioned, seemed older than his years, something like Raymond to look at except that Raymond had been dark. God, he wished he was healthy so's he could be a proper father to his sons and daughters.

"Hot today, Dad," Sydney said.

"Looks like rain, son," Gil said.

"Good job it kept off raining till the end of the holidays," Sydney said. "We had a good holiday, Dad."

"Keen on starting school again, son?"

"It's all right."

"You want to work hard and make the best of your school-days," Gil said. "You'll never regret any of your education. A man's no good in the world without an education."

"I might be a carpenter, Dad," Sydney said.

"You couldn't do better, Syd. Only you want to finish school first, so's you can get to be somebody in the trade."

"Might run my own firm," Sydney said. "Build houses and everything."

"Every man should have a trade," Gil said. "You don't want to go for these white-collar jobs if you can help it, Syd. Get out in the fresh air, keep fit, never do anything wrong. By gosh, I certainly don't regret I became a carpenter instead of staying in the post office. Fancy a man working like old Huxley every day of his life. Delivering the mail. A trade's the thing, my boy. Wasn't the trade that made your father sick, it was the war."

"I don't want to be a postman," Sydney said.

"You couldn't do better than be a carpenter, son."

"Reckon there'll be any more wars, Dad?"

"Who knows? They're awful damn things. I hope you don't have to fight in one."

"Know what a chap down the road reckoned the other night, Dad? He said the fighting in—in Spain, was going to spread all over the world. He said we'd be fighting, too. He was telling the people on the footpath this. Silly, eh? A policeman chased him."

"The world's always been fighting," Gil said. "Look at the Abyssinian business for instance."

Sydney sang:

"There's a war in Abyssinia
get your gun get your gun

Mussolini will be there
shooting peanuts through the air
there's a war in Abyssinia
won't you come, won't you come."

"Long as you kids only have to sing about wars you're all right," Gil said.

Bob Davidson's boy, a fat rosy-faced kid about the same age as Syd, walked up the steps. He handed Gil a *True Detective* Bob had found for him.

The two boys went out the front, and Gil browsed through the magazine. He couldn't find a yarn he fancied.

He looked up to see Frank watching him. "Where's your mother?" he asked.

"She's washing up, Dad."

"Joy inside?"

"She's ironing her dress for tomorrow night."

"She's always going out," Gil said. "Who does she go with?"

"I don't know, Dad."

"Miss me when I was away, son?"

"Yes, I did," Frank said.

"Have many visitors?"

"Not many."

"Who?"

"A few old women like Mrs. Jacobsen and Mrs. Simmons. Mum said she wished they didn't come. She said she was sick of them."

"What about Mr. Simmons?"

"He came once, I think. Mum doesn't like him either, she said."

"She washing the dishes, eh?"

"Yes, Dad." Frank waited, looking towards the gate, fidgety.

"You see you kids don't go far away," Gil said. "You'll be caught in the rain if you don't watch out. Anyway, it's getting dark, soon be time for bed."

Frank ran across the lawn.

II

Talking to your sons made you remember your own boyhood, the dreams you had, the way you thought the world was a great place and you were going to get a good job, marry, live happily ever after. Certainly didn't work out that way.

Kids had a marvellous time. You had good kids, they would grow into what the papers called worthwhile citizens, you could tell that by their ways now. If Marjorie's kid was as good as any of yours she'd be doing all right. Wonder if it would be a darkie like its old man. 'Course some white tarts had white babies to Maoris only the kids had funny skins, their faces looked like they should have been brown instead of white.

III

Suddenly rain whisked under the rolled-up veranda blind. He unrolled the blind and yelled to the kids to come inside. They tramped across the veranda. Sydney said " Abyssinia, Dad " and he said " Abyssinia " back to him. A good kid, that.

It rained steadily. He missed the noise the kids had made while playing; the rain-noise saddened him. He lay on the bed wondering what the hell to do; he didn't want to get under the bedclothes though he felt a little weak.

He walked along the veranda, looked out at the rain. A bike went past on the road, the rider hunched up, the lamp a jumpy glow. The rain got heavier. A wind gust chilled him.

He turned. Helen stood in the doorway all togged up in her best clothes—the costume, the dark coat with fur round the neck, the black hat that dipped over one eye.

" You're not going out in this rain?" he said.

" It's only a shower," she said. " I promised I'd drop in and see Bella tonight, Gil. I won't be more than a couple of hours."

" Surely she wouldn't expect you on a night like this," he said.

" Don't you want me to go?"

" Well, it's raining."

" Golly, I'm not a baby, Gil. I can catch the bus at the corner."

" Why couldn't you wait till tomorrow night?"

" Because I promised I'd call tonight. Bella's having a few visitors for a card evening. I should think you'd be glad I can get out at night after being stuck in this house all day long."

" Bet you weren't stuck in the house too much while I was away."

" What?"

" Nothing."

She looked wild. " What do you mean? Surely I'm entitled to leave the house. It hasn't reached the stage where I've got to be stuck here all the time, has it?"

" You can bloodywell do what you like," he said.

" You needn't swear at me," she said. " I won't go, then, if you don't want me to. I don't want to quarrel with you, Gil."

" You can bloodywell do what you like," he said.

"I'm not going to have you swear at me like that," she said. "What's the matter, Gil? Aren't you feeling well?"

"I'm all right," he said.

"You're not," she said. "You've never sworn at me like that before."

"You know damned well what's wrong," he said.

"I said I wouldn't go if you didn't want me to," she said.

"You can go to your bow-tie for all I care," he said.

She reddened.

He was angry, he didn't care what he said. But for a second he thought maybe he'd been mistaken; then he knew he hadn't, he just knew.

"What *do* you mean, Gil?" she said.

He could see she was trying not to shout. "You know damned well what I mean."

"You're a liar!" She always did have a temper. "You insult your wife and won't say what you mean. How do I know what you mean!"

He guessed he had more control over his feelings than she had over hers, seeing he wasn't shouting, too. "Keep calm," he said. "You'll have the kids coming out to see what's up."

"Who's this person I'm supposed to be running around with? What's his name? Go on, tell me!"

He said nothing. He wished he knew the name so he could say it.

"You're guessing," she said. "You're suspicious and jealous, and don't know what you're saying."

He smiled. He wanted her to say something she'd be sorry for.

She started howling. "All right, I *am* friends with another man. But he's a good man, he's been a marvellous friend to me. I'm sick of slaving my inside out every day. I'm not a frump, I want something more than this out of life. I don't—"

All of a sudden he hated her. It was different now that he didn't have to guess any more. And somehow it was worse than when he had been guessing. He stared at her, the hatred making him dizzy, and she stopped howling.

He stepped towards her, put out his hands. He was going to choke her.

She backed to the bed, brushed the hat from her head, took hold of his arms. He pressed her back, tried to force more strength into his body. She was stronger—God, he was too weak.

"Let me go! Gil, stop it!"

"I'll show you, I'll show—" His head felt full of something, he couldn't see her. He weakened suddenly, tottered. Could not see. Could not think. Words *what the hell what the hell* came, went. Tried to jolt back. Could not.

Your own fault, she said, *your own fault. Own fault own fault own fault. . . .*

Chapter Twenty-Two

One Rainy Night

GILBERT WAS pleased with himself, as though he had finished a hard day's work and was a workingman thinking of home. He wondered if any of these people sheltering under Mrs. Morpeth's veranda were thinking about his being a paper boy. He guessed he was a skite after all; he forgot his bashfulness when he thought somebody might be thinking of his being clever.

The rain was very heavy, and a cold wind blew up Stout Road. Now he was sheltering and the run was finished he didn't feel so bad, might not throw the run in after all. And it wasn't always rainy. Some nights it was nice and warm, and it was great delivering the papers. Another thing, he had some pocket money now he was subbing for Basil, didn't have to ask his mother for money for the *Champ* on Wednesdays and the Majestic on Saturdays. He could buy things like chaws and pies out of his own earnings. Gosh, he'd buy a pie now; he was cold, might be another hour before he was home.

He entered the dairy, thinking right away of the mysterious smell inside, a smell you couldn't describe or remember much about. He bought a pie from old Mrs. Morpeth, walked out the flydoor, stood against the bike watching the rain once more.

He loved the rain. It pelted on Stout Road, shimmered in the street lamps, spread to the gutters, filled them, flowed along. It was some storm, all right. He bet the brewery paddock was filling with pools; the stables over back of the brewery would be slushy, they'd stink. And the veranda blind at home would be down, the rain sliding over it, and Dad would be in bed maybe or in the dining-room beside the fire. Some of the things his father said made him feel foolish. Like last year when he waited outside for the paper, then went in and said it still hadn't come, and his father said it had come an hour before, and he was embarrassed and asked should he light the dining-room fire, and his father said he didn't know about the dining-room fire but somebody's face was certainly on fire. He could not forget that. Still, his father was sick, and you had to make allowances. He'd say Hello when he got home, ask how he was feeling.

He finished the pie. Over in the hills the thunder was rumbling. Better hold on, the rain might slacken off. Somehow it was good to think they'd be worrying about him at home.

There were lightning flashes; he was scared thinking he might be killed by one. Funny how frightened he got when he thought he might never see his mother again because she'd die or he'd die. He guessed he loved his mother, but not like in that article he read in the library the other day where a joker reckoned a boy, right from the time he was a baby, loved his mother because she was a female and boys naturally loved females. Gosh, the way he felt about Mum was different from the way he felt about Carole Plowman. He must be in love with Carole. It was queer being in love, especially when you didn't know the girl to speak to, you were in love through looking at her. Wasn't a bad feeling, but not too good, either. He would have to try and forget about Carole. She'd be going to High when school started, and he would still be at the Central. He'd thought about Carole all through the holidays. Every time he went for a ride he thought of meeting her, talking to her like Ralph talked to girls. A few times lately he had seen her with the little dark foreigner who played the violin in the string orchestra that had come from Vienna, so they said, especially to play at the Majestic for the holiday season. Carole would probably marry this foreigner, go to the city with him, then maybe overseas. And when he grew up he would meet her someplace in England or America and tell her he'd been in love with her when she was a girl in Gladston and maybe—

He came out of the dream. The rain had slackened. He jumped on the B.S.A., sped across Stout Road and up towards Massey Avenue, the dynamo whirring against the front tyre, the tyres making a ssss-noise on the wet road. He sped past Mr. Moore's bakery, skidded a bit when he turned into Livingstone Road, rode flat out along the footpath, and slowed to turn in the gate to home.

Somebody called to him from the veranda, where the blind

was down, the bed lamp shining behind it. He stopped the bike by the front steps. Joy, fingers to her lips, came down to him, said something terrible had happened.

He went up onto the veranda and saw his mother bending over the bed, and blood was pouring from his father's mouth into a bowl she held. She wore her best clothes, and they were covered with blood. He had never seen so much blood.

Suddenly his mother thrust the bowl into his hands, told him to run out to the kitchen and get another one. Feeling sick, he ran down the passage, past Joy who stood in the doorway to the kids' room with Bubs and Frank and Sydney trying to see from behind her. The blood spilled over the edge of the bowl onto the carpet.

In the pantry he got hold of the biggest bowl he could find and ran back up the passage to his mother.

PART III

Chapter Twenty-Three

After the Storm

I

IT WAS a frosty morning, it would be a lovely day afterwards. Helen thought her kids looked warm and tidy as they walked down the avenue to school. The boys were in the Central School uniform, and Bubs wore her new tartan skirt and red jersey, black stockings, and shiny shoes.

They turned and waved, and, standing on the corner, she waved once more, smiling at the way Bubs was walking backwards so she could keep looking at her mother. Thank goodness her baby didn't have to wear those awful shaded glasses any more, she thought. Golly, the kidlets were sprouting up. She'd be a grannie before she knew it. Who would be the first to make her a grannie? Probably Joy. Gilbert didn't seem likely to be the marrying type, though he was still too young for you to tell, and anyway he'd go to High School and get a decent education before he could think of marriage. Joy now was a girl, and girls thought about nothing else but getting married, they were much more trouble than boys. She bet Sydney would be a lady-killer, he was good-looking and very good-natured.

Gilbert rode up behind her, stopped by the tin fence round the place on the corner. Except for his long hair he looked smart. She gave him a shilling and told him to be sure he got a haircut tonight.

He looked at the handlebars, trying to see himself in them. She reminded him to look out for Bubs after school to see nothing happened to her.

He said Sydney and Frank could wait for Bubs; he had to get his hair cut, then do the paper run.

She didn't know what she'd do if anything happened to Bubs, she said. She could put up with the unhappiness Gil caused her, she thought, but not if anything happened to her kids.

Looking around to see if anybody was watching, Gilbert bent and kissed her good-bye. He was a funny kid, got into quiet moods; he was not yet twelve and shouldn't have worries. Perhaps he was annoyed because she told him he had to give up the paper run after this week. He was too young to be working, she reckoned, he should enjoy his youth while he had it. Time enough later in life to work. They might be short of money, but her son didn't have to tire himself out for a miserable seven and six. Besides, she didn't want his Aunty Hilda slinging off at her for sending him to work at such an early age.

She turned back down Livingstone Road.

Trixie Sutherland, the imbecile girl whose father had been somebody important at the freezing works until he had a stroke and went blind, walked up quietly behind her and said Hello suddenly.

"Oh, hello, Trixie." She looked at the girl's queer red-rimmed eyes, her turned-up nose you could see into, her blotchy skin. Trixie was a poor thing. But she was lucky in some ways; she didn't have the worries you had if you were sane, she would be looked after all her life, she wouldn't have to do her own thinking, and somebody would dress her in those dowdy-looking skirts and pullovers she wore, and she could walk in the sun thinking about nothing.

There was the other side to it, too. If you were like Trixie you wouldn't be able to have kids, and you didn't regret any of your kids. Yes, it would be awful to be like Trixie Sutherland. You should be grateful you had your health, you should stop worrying about things and be thankful you were alive and able to think for yourself.

II

She glanced at the bed where Gil had lain for so long before he had the haemorrhage and was taken to hospital. If he were home now the blind would be up because it was going to be such a beautiful day. She must remember to shift his things from the locker; they could have gone into the spare room if Joe and Marjorie hadn't moved in the day before yesterday.

She straightened the blue-and-yellow-flowered bedspread she'd put on the bed. It was a good idea to have the place looking as though she expected him home. The way Hilda looked at her the morning after he went up there you'd have thought he didn't need to go. She *did* want him to return home, anyway. But she wanted him to get better, too. And the hospital was the best place for him the way he was now. All very well for Hilda to think things, she hadn't had to live in the same house with him. You'd be a hypocrite if you said you weren't glad Gil was in the hospital seeing you were having such a good time with Fred, sitting in the car with him nearly every night, joking and having a cuddle every now and then, and telling him your troubles, and he telling you his and saying it would all be different one of these days. It was not for Hilda to know these things, though.

Golly, she had been worried when Fred said he might have to stay in hospital a long time after the accident; then the quacks found his leg wasn't so badly hurt as they thought, and now he was out and about again even though he limped and said he had some awful pains at times. Being able to chat with Fred lifted a great load off her shoulders; the drinks she had with him helped, too. But she'd have to go easy on the stout. She was drinking too much. She didn't want to take it like a drug.

III

Jack Daley was singing "When Irish Eyes Are Smiling" on the radio, and that was the only noise in the house. Not a sound came from the front room, even the baby was quiet. Joe and Marjorie must still be asleep. She had been able to lie in herself lately until the kids started school and she had to get them their breakfasts and see them off.

She went into the dining-room, pulled up the blinds, moved the rug from in front of the fireplace, and sat in the sedan chair by the radio. She lit a cigarette and looked at the grey-brown ashes in the fireplace. It had been cold and showery yesterday, and Marjorie had wanted a fire. The trouble with fires, though, was the mess you had to clean up afterwards.

She was fidgety. She hadn't yet told her mother about Gil's sudden turn, but she couldn't seem to settle down to letter-writing, and she got the fidgets when she put off doing something she really ought to do. She must get the housework over before ten o'clock. There was shopping to do, and tonight was visiting night at the hospital, and Mr. Braxton would be calling in his car. It was good of Mr. Braxton to call for her every visiting night, it certainly saved bus fares. He was a quiet chap, and the only thing wrong with him was that he was friendly with the Coulters, and she always felt she mustn't say a word out of place else he'd mention it to Bill, and Bill would pass it on to Hilda. Every Tuesday night when he called he brought the kids a bag of lollies, mostly licorice pipes and those orange-coated lollies with chocolate centres, and the kids thought there was nobody like Mr. Braxton. There were only a few people like him in Gladston. Most were like—like the Oldhams, for instance.

She looked out the window across the section and watched old Mrs. Oldham placing a paper package in the rubbish tin at the side of her wash-house, holding up her head as though she were a duchess. The Oldhams thought they were great because they owned the oldest boot shop in Gladston. None of them ever spoke to the Cunninghams—but who worried about that! She was so fed up with Gladston she didn't care if she never spoke to anybody in the place.

She finished the smoke. Better get some work done, she told herself, going out to the kitchen. She cleared the dishes from the table, then, looking through the pantry window down the yard, took her time washing them in the sink. It was a good job fine weather had come again. Better at night, too, when she and Fred were in the Dodge talking and having an occasional spot. She wouldn't mind a spot just now. Have to finish the sink first, though. Yes, it was a lovely day, the sort of day she'd like to spend on a beach somewhere with Fred, sitting in the sand, paddling in the sea, collecting beachwood, fishing, perhaps.

Golly, she must write to Flo, too. She just bet Marjorie hadn't written to her mother yet other than to send the telegram saying the baby was a boy. She'd been a queer girl these past few weeks; but now she'd had the kid and Joe was keeping her warm she might buck up. She certainly envied Marjorie in some ways, starting out in life with a young joker, plenty of what any normal person needed in life for the asking.

Oh, she was getting a headache, she'd just have to take a nip. She closed the pantry door and poured herself a glass. There was no sound in the house, and suddenly she felt very lonely, and she kept pouring more stout and drinking it down fast until presently she didn't feel lonely at all, only a little sad.

Chapter Twenty-Four

Kath Smith

I

SOON AS the haze cleared, and the white uniform that filled everything shifted, Gil took in the yellow-brown hair under the white cap, the slightly turned-up nose, the red lips, white teeth, freckled forehead. Not a bad piece, Nurse Evans; always had a bright word for a man, certainly cheered up the damned hospital veranda. But, wild momentarily at her disturbing him, he grunted when she said it was a nice morning wasn't it. And she made a ttt-noise so he said it was a nice morning, all right, and it wasn't bad, either, he thought. The sun was shining, and the rain seemed to belong to a long time ago.

It was comfortable watching the nurse fiddle around with the tray of glasses of liquid, small saucers, and tablets. She did everything very smartly.

He said, "You married, Miss Evans?"

"Why?" she said.

"You'd make a good wife," he said. "A man could take it easy and let you do everything for him."

"I get paid for this, Mr. Cunningham," she said.

"Well, you're very good at it," he told her.

She cleared the things from the locker top, wiped with a rag. "Thank you."

In the next bed Baker groaned and turned over. An old joker, white-haired and with some of his nose bitten away, hurried past towards the bathroom, dressing-gown tight around him.

Gil asked, "When will morning tea be round, Nurse?"

"What, hungry already? You only had your breakfast a while ago, Mr. Cunningham."

"Yes, but I had no tea. You people think we can hold out hours for a drink. Rather have a cup of tea than anything to eat."

"Oh, yes. Now, what about a basin of water and a clean pyjama coat, eh? Then it will be just about time for morning tea."

She got some water from the bathroom, watched him sponging his face as though wanting to do it herself as she had for the past week. She helped him change his pyjama coat, then he sat on a chair, feeling weak as hell, while she made the bed. He was glad to get under the clothes again.

Three patients came round and played quoits in the sun before his bed. Baker was groaning a lot; he was another digger. The joker with the crook nose said Hello to Gil, then watched the three playing quoits.

II

He had a pretty good possy on the veranda, Gil reckoned. He could see right across the flats to the sea, and down from the hospital to the paddocks were pines, and you heard birds making a row all times of the day. Looking on the flats was sort of like looking back over your life. You remembered when you were a kid and you and the other kids used to ask one another how long you reckoned on living, and some kids said they would live to a hundred but you couldn't think how old you'd live to be because you couldn't imagine any time when you wouldn't be living. And there was one kid who said he would be like Lord Byron, the chap that wrote poems, and die at an early age, reckoned he felt a lot older than the other kids already, and he'd be grey and stiff-jointed by the time he was thirty. That kid died of some sickness he caught in a military camp. Lot of other kids died at the war; those who returned were snuffing off like flies now. 'Struth, you remembered things from your childhood clear as one thing. The times you had with Kath Smith when you were around thirteen, for instance; you used to go tramping on your own, and the others would sling off at you and write GILBERT CUNNINGHAM LOVES KATH SMITH: KATH LOVES GILBERT in chalk on the footpath; but you didn't care. And one day when you were fifteen you and Kath went in swimming naked, and afterwards you sat next to each other by the pool, and presently you timidly compared your bodies and Kath let you feel her little breasts and she went red when she saw how this affected you and she seemed to want to giggle but she became very serious and said No, and repeated it several times, and you both became scared and hurried into your clothes, and you sat there in the trees out of town and told each other you were in love and life was funny and you wished you'd hurry up and get older so's you could marry. But you never did marry her, though you kept going with her till you went to the war and for a while when you returned. You went on holiday, met Helen, and the way you felt about her was different from the way you ever felt about Kath Smith. When you told Kath you were marrying someone else she burst out howling and told you you couldn't do it after all the times you'd had together, but soon as you married she wasn't long finding another joker, and she shifted south with him, and you never heard from her any more. Marriage was all right, and you worked hard, but when the depression came things seemed to go wrong, and now you were sick and waiting for a pension. What did a man live for? Was it to marry a girl, put her up the duff, slave until the pains came, and then wait for death? And when you died they'd say you were a jolly decent joker. And your wife would be able to give all her time to the fellow she'd picked up with. You wondered if the bastard went to the war. Good luck to him if he'd dodged. It was nothing to wish on anybody, even your worst enemy.

III

Nurse Evans bent over him, whispered "Mr. Cunningham?" He opened his eyes. Morning tea was ready.

The patients stopped the game of quoits and stood around the tea wagon, drinking tea from thick hospital cups and eating thinly buttered bread. Mrs. Simpson, said one, was a bitch to make the Duke of Windsor give up the throne. Somebody else said good luck to them both. That's the way he felt, Gil thought; Teddy was smart to do what he wanted to with his life, and he'd put the old girl in her place, though she was supposed to have been teaching the Duke of York all along for the job.

Then a fellow started on the Labour Government, said the country would forge ahead now the Tory crowd was out, and Mickey Savage was the best Prime Minister going. New Zealand would be the greatest spot on God's earth.

Somebody noticed Mr. Kent, the Baptist minister, coming down the path, and most of them wandered round the corner of the veranda.

The minister came beaming up the steps, drew up a chair

beside Gil's bed, and handed over a bundle of *Weekly News* and *Free Lances.* Gil reckoned Kent was better than most of the Bible-bangers who visited the hospital; he generally talked of everyday things and he didn't force the Bible down your throat. Mrs. Coulter, he said, had told him to say she'd be up tonight. Huh, showed he wasn't missing those outside, Gil thought; he'd forgotten it was visiting night.

"How is your wife, Mr. Cunningham? I haven't had the opportunity of calling upon her in recent weeks."

"Quite well, thanks. Those kids going to Sunday School?"

"I must say the young ones have been coming regularly," Mr. Kent said. "But Gilbert didn't attend Bible Class last Sunday or the Sunday before."

"Waits till I come to hospital, then jibs on it," Gil said.

"Boys tend to think they're above religion when they get older," Mr. Kent said. "If he came to Bible Class regularly he could quite easily win the same sort of book you won for your Sunday School attendance, Mr. Cunningham."

"I suppose so," Gil said.

He didn't much care what Gilbert did, he thought. He was tired, had had enough of Kent already. He tired easy these days. He couldn't be bothered with tales about kids, their mother was the one to go to now.

He listened to Kent's gossip and smiled faintly every now and again.

IV

Soon as Kent was gone he had a feeling of nausea, and he lay back and tried to get rid of it.

Hours seemed to pass before he was right again.

He wondered if he should go to the sanitorium like Hilda and the doc had advised. They always spoke as though they thought he'd get over this sickness. He didn't think so; one trip away from Gladston had satisfied him he'd never leave the town before he died.

He got to thinking some more of the times when he was a kid. He saw Kath Smith very clearly as if it were the other day he'd gone with her to the A. & P. Show, and he saw Raymond, too, and his brother wore a dark suit and one of those high-collared white shirts, and he bowed like an English gentleman when he met you with Kath. Kath wore a white frock and carried a blue pullover, and you rode on the merry-go-round together, fired coconuts at funny-faced dolls, and paid to see the fat lady and the leopard man and the tart with no head, and you sat under the gums beside the showground and had lunch, and later you walked through the paddocks, and on some hay you talked and kissed and you put your hand inside her dress. The longing you felt for Kath now was like the longing you had felt in camp and going over in the boat. . . .

It was like coming out of a dream to hear the others talking once more while they watched an airplane pass over the hospital, talking of Jean Batten and her great flight from England last October. That was years ago, so long ago it was hard to remember what it had been like on the veranda in Livingstone Road.

He hoped the visitors would not stay too long tonight. And when they left he hoped he had a good sleep, hoped he didn't kick the blankets off himself. He had a shrewd suspicion he'd been kicking the bedclothes around these past few nights so that the nurses, including Nurse Evans, saw everything he had.

Chapter Twenty-Five

In the Barber's Chair

I

GILBERT PARKED the B.S.A. outside the barber's saloon. Inside, the barber was cutting the hair of a man in working clothes so he sat on the couch, skimming through a paper, wondering if the man in the chair was looking at him and thinking what a big head he had and how long his hair was. When he looked up, though, the man was facing the end wall of the saloon where a poster showed a girl in a red bathing costume smoking a Craven A.

He studied the paintings that stood on a ledge around the saloon; some were copied from cigarette placards, others were of the Gladston countryside. Some of the noses and ears on the faces didn't look right, and the landscapes were blurry.

The man lifted himself from the chair, and he sat and waited while the barber got the customer his change. He looked at his hair in the mirror. Mum reckoned he had a worried look when his hair was long, and on Saturday, when he had gone to the hospital, his father had wanted to know if he was waiting until the price of wool went up. He didn't like getting his hair cut.

He watched the barber, an ugly little bloke with stumpy legs, thick body, shiny-bald head, and knobby nose, pour cold tea into a cup and drink it with a gulp. It was a small saloon, and there was only one chair, and the barber wasn't as smart as the barbers in Clyde Davies' saloon near the clock tower. But Davies' saloon was always busy, and the fellows would make fun of you if you went there.

Nice day, wasn't it, said the barber.

It was very nice weather, all right, Gilbert said, feeling his face get hot as it mostly did when he was spoken to. He felt the barber's warm-soft hands on his head, the towel being fixed between his shirt collar and skin, and he thought his face must be red as a beetroot but when he looked in the mirror it wasn't, and he wondered if when some of the times he was sure his face was red it really was not; but he knew he did go red because he looked in the mirror at home a few times right after something happened and, gosh, he was red all right.

Every time he looked at the paintings they got worse, he could think of plenty of prettier girls the barber could have painted; he could think of two, anyway. Gosh, Marjorie certainly looked better now she'd had the baby and Joe had turned up, she was nearly as beautiful as Carole. He felt funny when she kept talking to him about the baby, saying what it was going to be when it was older, and sometimes he thought she was making fun of him, but he liked her, and she let him hold the baby, and that made him feel a bit funny, too. 'Course he still reckoned Carole was the most beautiful girl in Gladston, but it was no use thinking about *her* seeing she went round with this foreign musician. He'd forgotten for a time that Carole was not at the Central School any more, he had been so pleased at Baldy saying he'd had good reports from Mr. Nolan who had no complaints to make. He bet Carole was having a marvellous time at High and the seniors would make eyes at her and she would kid them and go to dances. He wished he could stop thinking of her. When he was older he was sure to fall in love with a girl as nice as her and marry her and be like Marjorie and Joe and have kids. Must be great to be married. He heard Marjorie and Joe in the mornings and during the day giggling in their room, and they were always teasing each other no matter who heard.

II

He felt good when the barber asked if he'd been playing cricket, and said he had. The barber said he'd been interested in the game in the Old Country, and what was the rep team like in this town? Gilbert said the Gladston eleven had won the coast shield. The barber didn't seem impressed. Nothing in Gladston was up to much from what he could make out, he said.

Gilbert asked, "Don't you like Gladston?"

"It's the dirtiest town I've ever had the misfortune to be in," the barber said. "Look at the street outside, count the pieces of paper, the orange peelings, the horse droppings. It's up to the borough council to keep the town tidy, and if it doesn't the people should make a fuss. Seems to be no self-pride in the place, never seen so little civic consciousness."

Well, why did he come to Gladston if he hated it so much? Gilbert thought. Queer how people left England or some other place and when they came to Gladston did nothing but complain and if it wasn't Gladston that got their goat it was New Zealand. Just like Mr. Bridgen reckoned about those Communists; if they thought so much about Russia, he said, why didn't they go and live there, nobody asked them to live in this country.

After a silence, he asked the barber if he liked painting.

It passed the time away, said the barber. Did he do any?

A little, Gilbert said.

He could bring some of his drawings to the saloon if he cared to and he'd criticise them for him, said the barber. He didn't mind helping young people improve themselves.

Gilbert remembered his drawing of Mickey Savage that Marjorie's uncle, Mr. Burgess, had posted to the local Member of Parliament. The Member said he considered the drawing very praiseworthy especially in view of the artist's age and he'd sent it on to the Prime Minister. It was good of Mr. Burgess to send the drawing away, Gilbert reckoned. He used to lie awake at night listening to the mumbling in the dining-room and wondering what they were talking about. One night while they were talking somebody knocked on the back door, but they didn't hear the knocking because the dining-room door was shut, so he jumped out of bed and went to the back door and it was old Simmons, and he said Mum was out and Simmons looked at him in a funny way and asked whose car was that parked out the front, and he said he didn't know, perhaps somebody's from up the road. Then Simmons left and he told Mum about the visit and she said he was a good boy, and after that he sat up some nights with her and Mr. Burgess, playing cards. He liked those nights, felt that at last he was nearly a grown-up and, by gee, he'd be glad when he *was* grown-up. Because then he wouldn't be so puzzled about things; he'd understand Mum and Dad, and why he should have to go to Sunday School, and why he loved

Carole Plowman, and why he wasn't smart like Ralph Coulter, and why Dad wasn't a working-man who came home every night and took off his boots and washed his face and hands and sat down to tea, and why he was embarrassed when he saw girls together, and why he hated reciting poetry in front of the class. And lots of other things. Gosh, he wondered whether many other kids were like him. Barry Andrews might be. He was going to Barry's birthday party next week, and he'd have a good time—he hoped.

III

He jumped a little when he felt the hair being wiped from his neck. Looking in the mirror, he saw the barber staring at the back of his head, saw his hands come up, and then he felt thumbs pressed in his ears, the hands settling on his cheeks.

Then a man walked into the saloon and sat on the couch.

"There we are, son," said the barber.

Riding home for the paper-bag, he thought it just as well his mother had told him he could knock off working; he'd be able to play cricket after school when he didn't have the run. He wondered if he should go to the hospital tonight, seeing Dad hadn't been so pleased last Saturday. No, he would stay home and do his school work. And when Mr. Braxton came for Mum he'd get the lollies off him and share them out among the other kids and maybe there'd be a lucky-packet or licorice pipe over that he could have besides his proper share.

Chapter Twenty-Six

An Attempt at Escape

I

"You SURE you don't want anything, dear?" asked Helen.

Gil shook his head. The bedside lamp shining on the starch-white pillows made his face look like a crayon drawing on white paper. His skin was yellow and shrunken, his eyes were way back in his head. He looked awful.

She had wished that Hilda would hurry and go, but now she *was* gone, it was hard to know what to say to Gil. Made you want to cry to see a man so helpless, so unconcerned about living. She must try to get him home soon as the doctor said it would be safe for him to leave hospital. She had been a fool, she kept telling herself, to have quarrelled with him that night on the veranda.

"Isn't there anything you want to know, Gil?" she said.

"No," he said.

"The kiddies were asking about you," she said. "I thought it would be better if they came up on Saturday. You mightn't be so tired. Would you like them to bring some fruit?"

"Can if they like."

"I'll send some oranges and grapes."

Up the path Mr. Braxton honked the car horn and she stood, another visit ended. She bent and kissed his forehead, and he said good-bye. She walked slowly down the steps and to the car.

Driving home, Mr. Braxton asked what she thought of Gil's condition. She said she was rather worried. He looked a little weak, Mr. Braxton said, but that was sometimes better than if he was flushed-looking.

"Hope so," she said. She pondered. "I suppose it will all straighten out in the end."

"That's the way to look at it," Mr. Braxton said. He held tight to the car wheel as he turned the brewery corner into Livingstone Road. A very cautious driver, he never seemed so sure of himself as Fred. He stopped at the front gate, and she got out, thanking him for the ride.

She watched the tail-light of his car disappear, then she walked to the corner and looked up Massey Avenue. The air was autumn-mild, the night very quiet except for the music-and-laughter sounds of a party in a house across the road.

Fred drove up near the footpath, and she got in the front seat beside him. They said little for a while, and she didn't get out of the dumps until Fred had parked the Dodge on the beach and had his arm around her.

"How is he?" he asked.

"Doesn't look at all well, Fred," she said. "Such an awful colour."

"Reckon he's dangerous?"

"I don't know, Fred."

He didn't say any more for some time.

II

There was a bright yellow moon in the sky, it was light as day in the front of the car. The moonlight gave Fred's face a bluish look, and she could see the red veins in his cheeks like wire netting.

"You're not looking very well, dear," she said. "You must take care of yourself."

It had been a worrying few weeks for him, he said. First a man got well-nigh kicked out of his own home, then he smashed his leg, then things didn't go so well on the financial end of the stick. Christ, what a miserable bloody spin he was having.

It was a shame the way he was treated, she said, they'd be sorry for it some day.

He stroked her hair in an absent-minded sort of way.

"You know, dear," she said, "I've often wondered who told Gil about you and me. Must have been that Emily. Remember I saw her at a dance that time, and I bet she told Hilda I was there, and of course Gil would soon hear about it."

"Are you sorry you ever met me, Helen?"

"Don't be silly, Fred," she said. "What if Gil does know? I think he was suspicious before, but I don't think he was certain. Somebody *must* have said something."

"We have our enemies," Fred said.

"I certainly wish I could take my hook from everybody in Gladston," she said.

"Here, have a drink," he said. "Forget your worries." He poured two drinks.

III

She must break herself of the habit of drinking too much. It was getting so she had to keep a few bottles in the pantry cupboard, and one of these days the kids or somebody would find them and start asking awkward questions. One time she had been horrified at the thought of women drinking steadily, bnt now it seemed the natural thing to do.

"Suppose I should have popped in and seen how the kids were getting on," she said.

"They'll be all right," he said.

"They're all I have to live for besides you, Fred."

He filled her glass again. "How's Gilbert?"

"Oh, he's awfully keen on his school," she said. "Plays cricket now. Hope it doesn't interfere with his studies. Might neglect them if he gets too wrapped up in sport."

"Nothing like sport when you're young," Fred said. "Wish I was back in the days when I played rugger every Saturday afternoon. Those were the days."

"Must be terrible for an active man to have to be inactive," she said.

"I feel it pretty hard," he said.

Poor Fred, she thought.

Suddenly the idea came that perhaps she and Fred could go to the city, start another life together, forget all the worries of Gladston. But she couldn't do it; she was tied down.

If Gil had a turn for the worse, though, the first thing she would do would be to clear out with Fred. Maybe they could go to Mum until they got a start. She would write to Mum for advice. It would be wonderful to return to the city, meet all the friends she'd had in the old days, and she could walk down the street without everybody knowing who she was, and there would be opportunities for the kids, too.

But she couldn't write to Mum about this because hadn't Mum said how distressed she was to learn that her daughter was carrying on with another man while her husband was still alive?

Fred must have been thinking about the same things. He asked, "Why don't we leave Gladston?"

She was scared. "What about your business, Fred? What about the people you know in Gladston?"

He said he knew a good few people who had never been near Gladston, and his business was going to the pack anyway. "I'll make arrangements for us to go," he said.

"But what about the kids?" she asked.

"Take them with us," he said.

She thought a bit. Then she said, "I don't think it would work, Fred."

He looked at her. "No," he said, "I don't suppose it would."

IV

She was annoyed at herself and, to change the subject, told him how Ralph Coulter called the other day and wanted her to give him dancing lessons and said, cool as a cucumber, that he bet she'd been a hot dancer in her younger days, and he couldn't ask his mother to help him polish his steps, because she was too strait-laced.

"Just as though I was a woman of the streets, Fred. Golly, I was annoyed."

" I'd have given the brat a boot in the rump if I'd been there," Fred said.

She snuggled closer to him. She wished she had met him when they were younger; they could have grown old together. Even now they could be happy just with each other, preferably away from Gladston. But Gil and the kids made it useless to dream about herself and Fred.

" We're in the dumps tonight, aren't we?" she said.

" How about a dance?"

" No thanks, dear, I don't fancy it." She couldn't dance with Gil's face on her mind.

Fred backed the Dodge onto the road, and they drove for about half an hour. She dozed off on his shoulder, then awakened with a start to feel Fred shaking her gently. The car was parked outside his brother's hotel. The place was in darkness, but she could make out dimly the open door at the side that led to the stairs. She was shaky when she got out of the car, and had to lean against Fred. He almost had to carry her up the stairs.

Chapter Twenty-Seven

Comeback

I

THE AUTUMN was mild for Gladston; the veranda, sunny and swept by cool breezes, was really a bonzer possy. Within a month in hospital Gil felt better about things. His chest pains were not so bad, he didn't get the nausea rushes that made his head wham as though in a vice.

The Saturday morning George Simmons came to cut his hair he was in the mood for a good old yarn, but George, red-faced from his climb up Hospital Hill, didn't give him much show, and he cooled on the idea of the haircut when he saw the lid come off the box of hairdressing gear, the clippers worked a few times.

" Well, Gil, you're looking more pleased with yourself today. Didn't get a chance to call and see you before this. Been working nights a lot lately."

" Your missus was telling me you were pretty busy," Gil said.

"How you feeling anyway, old man? Reckon this place is doing you good?"

"I feel pretty good," Gil said.

"Somebody was telling me you were going to Waipuk," Simmons said.

"Don't reckon I'll be going," Gil said.

"Fair enough here," Simmons said. "You got a nice number in that blonde, huh? Wouldn't kick at that waiting on me."

"Nurse Evans is very efficient," Gil said.

"Bet she is. Had a good one the other night, Gil. Maori sheila."

Gil smiled. "Been thinking a lot about the old days," he said. "You wouldn't remember Kath Smith, George?"

"Was she a waitress at the Central?"

"No, you wouldn't remember her. Before you came to Gladston, I'd say."

"One's much the same as the next, anyway," Simmons said.

"Kath was different from the others," Gil said.

"You don't say. . . . Helen been coming up regularly, I suppose, Gil?"

"Usual times," Gil said.

"Big walk for her," Simmons said, snipping with the scissors.

"She usually gets a lift from Harry Braxton," Gil said.

"Thought I seen her the other day in a car but I couldn't place the joker driving," Simmons said. "Has Harry got a Dodge?"

"Wouldn't know," Gil said. What's the bastard driving at, he thought. He knew damned well what sort of car Harry had.

Simmons wiped the hair-dust away. "Feel better?"

"Thanks a lot, George."

Simmons collected his gear. "Myrtle said she'd be up on Tuesday with some cookies," he said.

He appreciated her kindness, Gil said. Hell, he thought. If anybody gave him a pain in the neck it was Myrtle Simmons, she did nothing but yap about other old biddies, and her cookies weren't a patch on anything Helen made. Last time she was up she got his goat properly by suggesting she read to him. He didn't think he'd reached that stage yet.

II

Restless, he looked in the locker for something to read. He took out the boxing book his son had left with him. He was glad Gilbert was taking an interest in sport, he didn't want any son of his growing up a ninny.

He glanced through the book at the paragraphs about odd ring happenings—Jim Driscoll's last fight, Fitzsimmons and Jeffries, Gene Tunney v. Tom Heeney, Les Darcy v. Eddie McGoorty—the ring records. He'd write something for the kid, he thought. So he wrote in the back of the book.

This is a very interesting book Gilbert, especially the names of fighters dating back to the year 1911, most of whom I saw in action when Gladston boys started to win New Zealand titles. At one period professional titles three in number were held by Gladston—Glen Jensen (featherweight), Red Burgess (welterweight), and Jim Douglas (heavyweight). Since then of course others have represented the district the most prominent being Hal Burgess, a mate of mine, who toured America. Glen Jensen was a pretty boxer with a nice style but carried a deadly punch if the opening occurred. Red Burgess was the rugged type of fighter with no defence and could absorb terrific punishment in getting at his man. Jim Douglas was all fighter and lucky to hold the championship. He could not take a punch and was easily beaten later (K.O.) by Bert Powell who in turn was beaten by Hal Burgess. Hal was handicapped by his shortness of reach and inclined to be lazy. I saw him lose two fights by taking things too easy. When wild he was a killer as one joker knew to his sorrow after passing a nasty remark prior to their fight in Christchurch. Two weeks unconscious in hospital and never able to fight again. Boxing nowadays is nothing to what it used to be. If you would like my opinion as to the best boxer I have seen, well without any hesitation I say Jimmy Clabby an American who toured New Zealand after the war and beat everyone he met. He was a perfect boxing machine and believe me a good boxer will beat a fighter any time, ask Dad.

There, that was something for his son to think about. He wouldn't guess his old man had known so many pugs. Yes, he had always taken an interest in boxing; it was a scientific sport and certainly different from wrestling. What he had said about boxing not being what it used to be was right, too. But you couldn't blame the boys for slipping, it all tied up with the way the world was going. Boxing was fighting, so was living. And if you got bashed around you had to have guts to make a comeback.

III

In an inside room a radio faintly played "Red Sails in the

Sunset" (ocarry my lovedone home safely tome). Baker, a dying man, was groaning a lot in the next bed.

Out across the flats he could see the bay shimmering in the sun, grey cliffs, a mass of white cloud, a pale blue sky. Birds were kicking up a fuss in the trees below the hospital. It was a great day, he felt very good.

He heard Nurse Evans' footsteps and sat up in bed, ready with a smile for her.

Chapter Twenty-Eight

Links in a Chain

I

HELEN COULDN'T stop staring at the face of the man mumbling *do you take this man. . . .* It was his eyes, one was glass, but she couldn't make out which one it was. She remembered her manners though when he asked her to sign the paper that showed she was witness to the marriage of Joseph Lloyd and Marjorie Young, and, screwing her face, she wrote her scrawly-round signature.

Marjorie looked at Helen and giggled, and Helen giggled a little, too. It was just like licensing a dog, she thought, it was not a marriage at all. They had got some papers from the office, filled them in, taken them back, and that was all there was to it. She couldn't help comparing her own wedding with Marjorie's. She'd never forget Gil and herself walking up the aisle of the little church in Auckland, the ride to their new home, the big party with all Gil's cobbers there and the enormous wedding cake. She had worn a short wedding dress, and after the marriage she wore it to parties and dances, so it was really quite handy getting a short dress.

Walking from the registry office with the newlyweds, she felt quite old. She looked thoughtfully at Joe. He was togged up in a pin-striped blue suit, white collar, and a red-and-blue diamond tie; Marjorie wore a lemon-coloured frock worked in with pink flowers and a broad-rimmed lemon-coloured hat with a pink ribbon. She fancied Joe was a bit stingy for all his good looks, his light brown skin, dark wavy hair, and beautifully white teeth. He paid fifteen bob a week for his and Marjorie's board but never so much as bought a pound of butter for the table.

Still, they were a young couple starting out on life together, and she supposed it was up to her to help them as much as she could. Nobody got very far on love alone.

II

Helen wondered whether Joe was worrying about the bill; he seemed nervous as he ate his afternoon tea. But it was an unkind thought, he was probably worrying because he was a married man now.

"Should really have had something stronger than tea to celebrate the occasion," she said.

Marjorie and Joe laughed.

"I could call on Fred; he'd be glad to treat you two to something seeing it's your wedding day."

Joe said not to bother, but Marjorie said, "Oh, why not?"

They didn't get married every week, Helen told them.

Over the teacups they yapped about the young couple's future. Marjorie said she and Joe would buy a little cottage and get a cow and a few chooks, and they would keep well away from town. They were going to have a wonderful life together, she said, smiling at Joe, and they were not going to quarrel and be foolish about things that didn't matter.

Helen said she supposed that in time there would be a lot of little Joes and Marjories running around.

Marjorie said "Of course," but Joe said they'd have to be careful for a while.

They laughed.

"Well, I'll pop down to Fred's warehouse and see about those drinks," Helen said.

She got rather a surprise when Joe paid for the afternoon tea, as though he'd been meaning to all along.

III

Down by the river she felt herself getting excited. It was wonderful how Fred affected her that way. Tenderly she thought of his face, his greying hair, his nose that was a little on the large side, and she thought how she got the fidgets when she didn't see him for a few days, and, momentarily scared, she thought how disappointing it would be if he were not at the warehouse.

But he was there all right. He was sitting at his desk going through a pile of ledgers and papers when she walked in. His tie was loosened, he looked as though he'd been without sleep for some time. His "Hello, Helen" sounded very dumpy.

"Busy?"

"Getting things straightened out for the young fellow," he said. "Want to make it easy as I can for him while I'm away."

It came as a shock. "Where you going, Fred?"

"Auckland, perhaps."

She felt lonely as anything; first she wanted to burst out howling, ask him to take her too, then all she felt was an emptiness inside, and it was as though she had known all along that he was going. "Well," she said, "if you have to go I suppose you have to."

"That's right," he said.

"Fred," she said, "I wanted a couple of bottles of something for Joe and Marjorie; they were married today."

"Go on?" he said, giving a bit of a laugh.

"It was just like licensing a dog," she said. "Not like a wedding at all."

He slammed a ledger shut, stood, and put his arms around her. He kissed her, saying, "It's the only way, love."

"I'll do whatever you say, dear," she said.

Then he told her of the anonymous letters he had been getting, and they had been written by the one person but other people must be talking, too, and he couldn't disgrace her, and the only thing was to leave Gladston. Besides, he said, he had been trying to break away for years. And her hubbie was getting better and would be coming home, and he didn't want to be on her mind when she would have plenty of worry as it was. Maybe they could write to each other now and again and some day they might be together forever.

She couldn't say what she wanted to say so she told him to be sure and call on Mum when he got to the city.

He said he would, he had always wanted to meet her mother. He suggested a farewell drink.

Before she knew it she was tiddly and crying like a mad thing.

Chapter Twenty-Nine

We're Only Human (R.K.O. Radio)

In the yarn Sergeant McGaffrey, a cop who plays to the the grandstand, captures notorious criminal Berger while sob sister Sally is a thrilled spectator. Instead of the expected plaudits and complimentary newspaper notices he gets censured and ridiculed in the prints. Berger escapes and McGaffrey publicly announces that he'll pinch him within a month. . . .

In the dusk of the Majestic Gilbert glanced at Barry Andrews. Barry seemed to be enjoying the picture, but, gosh, you couldn't concentrate on anything that was happening. Your mind was filled with other things, and it had been like this since you brushed against Carole Plowman in the lobby and said sorry and she smiled at you, looking at you for a few seconds while you shuffled along in the queue, and you'd been so stupid you hadn't thought she might like you to get a ticket for her seeing she'd come late. You tried to stop remembering Carole by thinking of something else, but you got thinking of Barry's birthday party this afternoon and that was just as bad. You hadn't been able to buy a present, and Mum could afford only a shilling so that's what Barry got from you. First you played basketball with Barry and his sisters and once when you caught hold of Mary Andrews you felt her breasts and she looked at you as though she knew what you had done, and you played hide-and-seek until five, then went inside for tea, and there were kids sitting round the dining-room table with Mr. Andrews, a big dark-looking man who owned a race-horse and supplied grain to farmers, sitting at the head, and he had to go just as the cake was being cut and that started everybody yapping and it was like a cage of monkeys, as Mrs. Andrews said. You had been annoyed because Mary Andrews had invited Moira Thornton to the party, and you hated Moira. She kept looking at you, and you knew she was waiting for a chance to say something about the way you'd flopped in the play *Robert E. Lee* by John Drinkwater that was one of those Miss Drake got the kids to act in for Friday's English class. You had been David Peel in Scene Two and Barry was Tom Buchanan and Laurie Bowden was Ray Warrenton, and you had got so nervous thinking about having to act in the play that you pinched the book and made out you didn't know where it had gone to, so none of you were able to learn your parts, but Miss Drake said you should have learned some of the play anyway and you'd have to make some attempt, so you had to stand before the class in any case and it wasn't so bad once you were standing there and you wished you hadn't hidden the book. Moira Thornton played the part of Elizabeth in Scene Three and Miss Drake complimented her on the way she acted, and you knew Moira was dying to talk about the play at the party, and you were glad when tea was over and everybody went in the front room and played games and Barry showed off his stamp collection. Mrs. Andrews wanted to know if you collected stamps too and was quite surprised when you said you didn't. Barry told her your hobby was making scrapbooks and made you feel proud when he mentioned the prize you won for the scrapbook last year. Yes, you certainly liked Barry, and you were pleased when the party ended and he said he would shout you to the pictures.

> Not only is his ambition the inspiration for this but having become romantically inclined towards Sally he is anxious to show her the kind of get-his-man officer he really is. While suspended he hears the police radio reporting a robbery. Determined to be the big shot he rushes in ahead of his erstwhile partner, tips off the presence of the cops, and in the ensuing mêlée a cop is shot and killed. The escapade only arouses the disgust of Sally, who would be sympathetic. . . .

Slumping in the seat, you saw yourself on the veranda at home with Marjorie's baby in a cot behind you, and you got up and kidded to the baby and heard Marjorie inside saying Gilbert liked babies didn't he, and then she poked her head out the front door to ask if the baby was all right and you said it was and she said she bet you would miss the little tyke when they took it away and you said you would. And Mum came out and Marjorie said you ought to ask for a new baby and Mum said no more kids for her thanks, she'd had her share and Marjorie would jolly soon get sick of kids and dirty nappies and everything once she was on her own up the coast. You would miss Marjorie, you thought. Funny how you got used to things being one way then suddenly they changed. But you didn't like Marjorie always asking whether you would miss *her*. It was like she was making fun of you when she asked that.

Later in another fracas with criminals McGaffrey is wounded and blinded. Though the accident brings Sally back to him the man living in darkness becomes mortally afraid. When he returns to duty he is yellow. . . .

Barry nudged you and asked if you liked the picture. It wasn't bad, you said. Barry held out a bag of chaws and you took one. Things certainly happened quickly in pictures. They could show you a person as a kid and soon after as a grown-up, different from in real life. You had to spend years and years being a kid, and you hated it, and you wished you could get a job, and when you were older you would be smart, not bashful like now. First of all though you'd have to go to High School like Carole and Joy, then you'd get a job and get married like Joe and Marjorie. Only *you* would marry a girl like Carole, who was different from most other girls. You wouldn't marry a stickybeak like Joy, for instance. Gosh, she made you wild reckoning you were sweet on Carole Plowman, and you said how did she know anyway, and she said she knew more than you thought, and you told her she had a high opinion of herself, and she said she did her share and was entitled to a little relaxation once in a while, and you said she ought to help with the messages, and she wanted to know if you'd been to Mr. Burgess lately for some bottles for Mum, and you told her she better watch what she was saying, and she said she knew Mum drank liquor, and you said Mum was old enough to take care of herself. Gosh, she was a stickybeak! Only you hoped Mum didn't drink too much, it would be terrible if she drank herself to death like they reckoned old Porkie St. John was doing. She must be knocking it off though because she hadn't sent you down to Mr. Burgess for more than a week now. You didn't like Mr. Burgess for teaching Mum to drink. You were glad Dad was supposed to be getting better and might return home, maybe he would be different when he was better, maybe he would be like other kids' fathers and maybe you would go to the beach together and Dad would help you with your school work and you'd be able to skite about him at school. And he would play with Bubs and Sydney and Frank and show them how to make things out of Plasticine. You were getting too old for Plasticine, they reckoned you were getting too old to play any games at all with the kids at home. Gee, it was awful being so gawky and not being able to play with smaller kids and yet not being old enough to be smart like Ralph Coulter.

All Sally's pleadings cannot restore his courage. But when

another crime is committed in which Berger is implicated, McGaffrey single-handed invades the criminals' hide-out to wipe out all including Berger. His success in rubbing out the mob coupled with the realisation he is no longer afraid brings him the applause he had always yearned for plus the love of Sally which will guide him in more discreet paths in the future . . . THE END.

The theatre lights went on, there was a lot of loud music. Following Barry through the crowd, you looked across the head-tops for sight of Carole, but you could not see her. Outside Barry suggested a milkshake, so you went into a milk bar and you sat in a booth sucking raspberry shakes through straws. You thought how wonderful it would be if Carole would come and sit with you and have a milkshake too. And you had been sitting there only two or three minutes when she did come in, and she was with a High School joker in a navy suit, and she stood at the bar with him eating sundaes. Barry kept talking about the picture, but you heard nothing more than a mumble.

Chapter Thirty

The Opportunist

I

HELEN BROODED as she did the ironing. The kids were in the dining-room listening to the man who told stories over the radio every Monday night at seven, and she was alone in the kitchen. Since Fred had gone, and Marjorie and Joe, too, this feeling of being alone had become worse, especially at night when she didn't know what to do with herself once the kids were in bed.

But Gil was coming home so she would soon have plenty to keep her busy. She didn't mind his leaving the hospital, but she bet it was his sisters' kicking up such a fuss that caused it; they might easily bring about his death with their interference. She was sick of the whole crowd, they never did anything for her or the kids. Still, if he was really better, perhaps she could get him to leave Gladston and go to the city, and they would live with

Mum until they got a house of their own. She would write to Mum and ask about a house. Mum would be pleased to learn Gil was coming out of hospital, and she would certainly be interested to learn that you and the kids had been examined probably to make sure there were no spots on your lungs.

Oh, but they'd need money to get away, and the Lord only knew they simply had no money.

Well, she would have to forget Fred if she was going to manage in Gladston with Gil. Fred might be considering her by not writing, but she wished he would write one small letter. This loneliness was awful. . . .

Bubs came howling into the kitchen, blubbered that Sydney had hit her, and lay on the sofa sniffing.

Helen said she had quite enough to do without worrying about howling kids. " Why don't you get Gilbert to tell you a story?"

" I was listening to the man's story, and Sydney hit me."

" Well, go and talk to Joy. As long as you leave *me* alone."

" Somebody mention my name?" asked Joy, appearing in a cool-looking print frock.

Helen stared hard at her daughter's face. " What's that on your lips, young lady?"

" Lipstick."

" Where on earth did you get that?"

" Marjorie gave it to me before she went. She said she wouldn't want it where she's going."

" Kids these days!" said Helen.

" Well, I'm off to the pictures," Joy said, putting her feet together and looking down at herself. She turned and walked lady-like up the passage.

" You see you get home early," Helen called after her. Young brat, using lipstick, she thought. Well, it showed how they were growing up around you. Soon they would no longer be children, they would be men and women.

She got on with the ironing. All her life she had been washing and ironing clothes. Most women got nice things to make up for the drudgery, went to parties and so forth—not her, though. She had seen a lovely dark blue dress in Kettle's the other day. It would suit her. But it would be a long, long time before she got a new dress—unless her ship came home and she won an art union.

II

Somebody knocked on the back porch and, wondering who the devil it could be, she turned the power switch off and propped the iron on its end.

Outside there was no moon, and the kitchen blind was down, so she didn't see who it was. The door swung shut behind her. She asked who was there. She didn't know it was Simmons until he said his name, only he said George and not Simmons.

"What do you want, Mr. Simmons?" she asked.

"Call me George," he said, grabbing her arm.

She drew back, the touch of his hand giving her the creeps. She wanted to yell out, but she was more indignant than frightened. She only wished she could get a chance to belt him across the face, put him where he belonged.

He stood on the top step holding her arm so's she couldn't move.

She told him to let go.

He said not to be like that, said they were friends, weren't they?

She suddenly lost her temper, said she was no friend of his and hated him. She tugged with all her strength, but he wouldn't let go.

"I know you, sweetheart; you're a sport. I'm a sport, too, Helen. How about it, eh?"

"Shut up, you cheeky swine. Taking advantage of a woman when there's nobody about."

"When her old man's in hospital? Don't give me that."

"I don't know what's come over you."

"You could go for any joker, couldn't you, Helen? You're only kidding me, you'll go soft. Look, we could have great times—"

"You better go before I call the police," she told him.

"Come off it. You wouldn't like your sister-in-law to park her ears to all I know about you. You and your bow-tie. Just you think a bit before you do anything you'll be sorry for."

"I'm not afraid of anything you can say," she said. "I've done nothing to be ashamed of."

"'Course you haven't," he said sarcastically. "But you know what these narrow-minded people are. Now, how about letting me in on the party, too? Nobody will ever know."

She was scared, could hear him breathing noisily.

He stepped onto the porch, pushing her before him. "Give us a kiss, love."

She pushed desperately, but he shoved his head forward, his face scraping against hers.

She was pressed back against the wall and, lunging sideways, slipped and fell. He fell on top of her. She wriggled like mad to get out from under him, felt her dress ripping, thought *O God save me from this filthy swine this fat bastard.*

Then he must have got too eager because she was free, and he fell on his side and she kicked him in the face and he cursed and she kicked him again.

She ran for her life inside, locked the kitchen door.

Sitting at the table, staring at the clothes she had ironed, she got the shakes, felt she wanted a good cry. Something seemed to choke her, and she put her head on the table and had a howl. How she hated that man! She had guessed what he thought about her, but she had never imagined it would come to this. He was a rotter, and God help him if Fred had not gone away. She wished Fred were here now, wished she could go to him for comfort in this hour of need. Now she knew who had sent Fred those notes; it was just the sort of thing you could expect of a man like Simmons. Well, she had shown him she was not as cheap as he thought. Just as well Gil *was* coming home; at least Simmons would not try any of his funny business with Gil about. Didn't matter what he said about Fred, either, because Fred had gone out of her life.

She sat at the table for a few minutes, then switched on the iron again and went on with her work.

Chapter Thirty-One

The Disturbing Influence

GIL WALKED down the hill from the hospital, scurrying his feet in the brown pine needles that lay thick on the ground among the trees. He felt satisfied with life. Everything was so peaceful here, like in a church, with only the birds making a noise. Every so often he saw the green of the bay through a break in the trees.

At the bottom of the hill he followed a creek for a spell, remembering how long ago he used to play with other kids on hill-sides like that going up from the creek, and they would slide down on cabbage-tree stems and over grass and around trees and stumps and bushes and to the bottom.

He spied a nice shady spot under a tree not far from the

creek and sat down. Thank goodness he could sneak away from that damned hospital for a while, he thought. It was a week since they'd let him out of bed and first he'd been pretty hesitant, had felt very tall and wobbly looking down on Nurse Evans; but pretty soon he was walking about normally, and he certainly got a kick out of it. No more headaches these days, either. A man was even planning to work up a vegetable garden when he got home. It would be exercise, and besides it would help spin out that pension when it came, and it shouldn't be long in coming now seeing the doc said he'd put in a word for him with the local pension crowd. And there were a few carpentering jobs he might do. Yes, he was looking forward to being back home. He'd be rather sorry to say good-bye to Nurse Evans, though he guessed her kindness was only part of her job. Little things about her were sort of decent, like when he was worried about the quacks wanting to examine Helen and the kids and thought something might be wrong and Nurse Evans assured him it was purely routine. And she told him she thought he could do light work when he got home even if the doctor said not to strain himself whatever he did.

It's moments like these you need a smoke, he thought. But smoking was out.

He heard twigs snapping on the hill and thought, Never get any peace wherever you are. He hoped whoever it was wouldn't notice him sitting there. But a few seconds later a voice said "Hello," and he looked up to see that crazy young redfed, Max Carson, who landed himself in trouble over at the works with his gabbing and got the boot, though this didn't stop him and he lectured on street corners and visited the hospital palming off his pamphlets and spouting about how the workers should organise and how capitalism was entering its last phase or something. He was a sandy-haired coon, very thin and very nervous, and he wore glasses and, as usual, carried a couple of books under his arm.

"Didn't expect to find anyone down here, Mr. Cunningham."

"Thought I'd be away from things, too," Gil said.

"You know, this is my favourite retreat when I want to catch up on my reading," Carson said. "Generally do some theory down here after doing the practical side up there."

Gil asked if there was any news.

Carson squatted on his hams. "Only news these days is Spain," he said. "Jesus, wish I could get over there somehow."

Gil asked, "What the hell you want to fight in somebody else's war for?" The young idiot was always harping on what was happening in Spain.

Carson started talking about Herr Hitler and Mussolini and fascism and how the working class all over the world was being menaced by Franco and those who backed him up.

The cow was mad, Gil thought. Only a madman would want to go to a war unless he had to. These redfeds were always thinking about killing someone; if they'd seen as much killing as he had they'd think different. Maybe they did have good intentions, but the best thing they could do if they were concerned about the workers was to do some of the work themselves, help make their own country a better place to live in. He could remember young Carson as a kid and he always was a bit of a disturbing influence, and his old man, "Atheist Ted" they called him, was probably to blame. Some things he said made sense, as when he talked of ordinary jokers slaving all their lives to fill somebody else's belly, and how the fat rich bastards did none of the fighting themselves after things ended in war. Oh, but you couldn't be bothered. Politicians were all the same; you couldn't waste time with them, 'specially if you had other matters to occupy your mind.

Carson asked, "You get round to reading any of those pamphlets I left, Mr. Cunningham?"

Gil said, "Didn't get a chance." He thought how he'd tried to read the pamphlets, but they were too dry altogether, and, anyway, he struck a brand new *True Detective* that contained some pretty good yarns.

Carson looked disappointed, sat hunched up pondering over something.

Gil felt an insect crawling along his leg and stood to brush it off.

"Just finished a good book," Carson said. "By a joker called Michael Gold—about the Jews in the slums of New York. *Jews Without Money.*"

"Can't say I've heard of it," Gil said.

"Listen to this," said Carson, opening one of his books and turning to the end. "'O workers' revolution, you brought hope to me, a lonely suicidal boy. You are the true Messiah. You will destroy the East Side when you come and build there a garden for the human spirit. O Revolution that forced me to think, to struggle, and to live. O great beginning!'"

Gil scratched his leg.

Carson looked up. "Great stuff, eh?"

Gil grunted. Jews were Jews, he reckoned, and most of them were moneybags and it was too bad some were poor and anyway they were in America and this was New Zealand and that sort of talk didn't belong in this country. Carson was like his old man—an atheist. You couldn't get far without God; he knew that much.

Carson said he was going, said he hoped Gil would have a whack at reading the pamphlets.

Gil said "Hooray," watched the other leap across the creek and walk over the paddocks.

Then, shrugging his shoulders, he turned back up the hill. Talking to Carson had vaguely irritated him, somehow it had spoiled his walk. To hell with the young fool, anyway, he thought. He didn't need to think about politics. He was going home to be a proper father to his kids; he'd take them to the beach, cut their hair, answer all their questions. He'd be very considerate to Helen, too, would help her as much as possible. He would work in the garden and do everything he could to keep the home going. And maybe he'd live to be an old man after all.

Chapter Thirty-Two

Good News

FROM MR. MOORE'S bakery Sydney Cunningham watched the postman riding up Massey Avenue. His fingers picked at the soft, doughy top of the half-loaf of bread he carried, and he chewed slowly as the postman came nearer and nearer. Looking back over his shoulder, he strolled to the corner. Half-way from the corner to home the postman passed him, waving a long envelope as he went by, saying there was good news for his father inside.

Sydney ran after Mr. Huxley. He hoped it really was good news so's he could be the one to take it to his father. He would run to Dad in the garden and Dad would pat him on the head and say he was his favourite son, then Dad would put his arm round his shoulders and they would walk into the kitchen together and tell Mum all about it. And Frank would be annoyed seeing Dad with his arm around him. Gee, he hoped it *was* good news, like Mr. Huxley reckoned.

BOOK TWO

Chapter One

Twelve Is Quite Old Enough

I

HELEN LEANED across the table and studied the cake, the aluminium icing syringe poised. "I told the old biddy to tell her son to keep his hands off my kids. I let her know if there was any hitting to be done around here I'd do it."

Mrs. Calcott, who was placing jelly lumps on the butterfly cakes, nodded. "Nobody else has a right to hit anybody's kids," she said, looking serious.

"I told her if my kids had done wrong they'd be punished, but I was the one to do the punishing," Helen said.

"It's awful when other people hit your kids, isn't it?" Mrs. Calcott said.

"Oh, it's not right," Helen said. "Heaven only knows the young devils do get into mischief, but I don't want that fellow Oldham laying a hand on them. He wouldn't do it if my husband was home." She squirted the blue icing with a flourish to complete the word BIRTHDAY.

"Some blokes will do anything if they get half a chance," Mrs. Calcott said.

"Especially if a woman's husband is in hospital," Helen said. "They take advantage of anything like that. I told you about the chap Simmons?"

Mrs. Calcott rested her elbows on the table, dug her fingers into her tangled grey hair, and said No, she hadn't heard about Simmons.

"He was the swine who attacked me one night out there on the veranda," Helen said, straightening up and becoming thoughtful. "I had a terrible job getting away from him. He jolly well didn't come around for weeks after that. He did turn up once when Gil was home that time and made out he was very contrite. I accepted his apology, but I told him I wanted nothing more to do with him. Haven't laid eyes on him since, though his old woman often calls for a chat. She's no angel herself. They've both been married half a dozen times. Awful, isn't it?"

"I wouldn't get married again," Mrs. Calcott said.

"No, if anything happened to Gil I simply couldn't marry another man," Helen said slowly. She looked at the writing on the cake: HAPPY BIRTHDAY TO GILBERT.

Mrs. Calcott said it looked nice. At least it was a cake, Helen said. Birthdays weren't the same for kids without a cake, even if it was only a bit of icing slapped on a sponge. Next thing would be to put twelve candles on it.

"Is Gilbert only twelve?"

"Mmm," Helen said. "I think it's quite old enough. Makes me feel I'm getting old when the kids have their birthdays. Won't be long before I'm a grannie, at this rate."

Mrs. Calcott laughed. She had a harsh voice, her laugh was croak-like. "He's a tall boy for his age."

"Takes after his father," Helen said. "Gil's just on six feet when he stands up, you know."

"My hubbie was a short man," Mrs. Calcott said. "That's why the twins are so small, I suppose. I wonder where those little brats are."

"They'll be all right," Helen said. "Probably in the paddock with Bubs."

"I better have a look," Mrs. Calcott said. She went out the back door.

Golly, she was a funny old thing, Helen thought. Always worrying about her kids. For all her outside roughness she was a soft-hearted old beggar. She must have had a hard life out there in the country with a husband who drank and belted her, no wonder she looked more like sixty than the forty or so she really was.

She felt very sorry for poor old Mrs. Calcott. All very well for Gil to turn up his nose about her being friendly with the Calcotts, but you got so's anybody who made your life the least bit happier had to be held on to, and the Calcotts certainly were a gay lot. She never knew anybody to throw parties like they did. Every pension day off went Mrs. Calcott on a shopping expedition, buying jellies, cakes, and beer instead of giving her kids the good food they needed. And expensive parties they were, too. Not just kids' parties like this one for Gilbert. She supposed she was a fool herself having a party, but there might not be many more parties for her kidlets, and it wouldn't hurt Trisk and Trisk to wait another month for the rent money.

She looked contentedly at the plates of cakes, dishes of jelly, fruit salads, and other things that made a kid's mouth water, and, licking some icing from her fingers, she told herself she hadn't done so badly considering. She wondered whether the brats were worth it. They certainly made her life a hell on earth sometimes, pinching apples from the neighbours' trees, getting up to every brand of mischief under the sun. Never mind, she and her kids were alone against everybody. If they didn't stick together they'd be a poor family. She was quite proud of the way she'd told off old Mrs. Oldham about young Oldham trying to hit the kids.

II

"What a face!" she told her eldest son, who came in with his nose in a knot about something. His cheek was cut, and his knees and arms were dirty, and he looked at Mrs. Calcott without saying a word.

"Why don't you tell them other kids to stop giving people lip, Mum?" he asked.

"What people?"

He spoke quickly, telling how the Danks kids had jumped on him when he was coming home and hit him on the nose. They twisted his arms and reckoned he'd told his brothers, Frank and Sydney, to give them cheek. Helen looked more closely at him. Those awful kids jumping on her son who wouldn't hurt a fly, she thought. She could understand it if they'd given Frank and Sydney a hiding, but Gilbert had so little to do with the young roughnecks. What a worry kids were.

Mrs. Calcott watched Gilbert sympathetically, he seeming to appreciate her sympathy though he usually acted as if she gave him the pip.

"I'll have a talk with those two," Helen said. "They'll have to go into a boarding school. They're getting too much for me."

"You always say you'll put them in a boarding school," Gilbert said. "Gee, I was just riding along when they jumped out on me."

"They'll provoke me too far," Helen said, "and I *will* put them in a school. Never mind, love, think about your party and you'll be all right."

"You going to tell them about it?"

"I'll tell them," she said. "But give me some peace now for heaven's sake. I want to get the things ready for the party. You going up to your father, love? He's expecting his tobacco today."

He said something about his brothers and why didn't *they* go up, and she told him it would only take a few minutes and surely it wasn't such a great sacrifice to make for his father lying on his back all day and every day. He said All right, he was going.

"You have to beg them to go anywhere," she told Mrs. Calcott.

"Mine are just the same." Mrs. Calcott grinned.

"Sydney and Frank make it hard for Gilbert," she said. "They're a cheeky pair of brats—typical boys, you know. I think I *would* put them in a boarding school if Gil wasn't against the idea of breaking up the home. It's hard to know what to do for the best."

"Well, I think you have a lovely family," Mrs. Calcott said. "My old man didn't care what happened to my kiddies. He didn't give a hoot about their schooling."

Helen thought how strange it was how everybody praised her family. She supposed she *was* lucky in a way. After all, her kids didn't do anything really bad, it was just that they were so mischievous. Mrs. Calcott was another one who'd had a hard time bringing up a family—three boys and three girls in her case. She guessed right from the first when she noticed her crying up at the hospital that she'd experienced the sorrier side of life. Mrs. Calcott being of a different nature from herself might make some difference, but still her old man was a proper fiend, and it was a good job he died although it didn't seem right to think that when you remembered that he was a returned soldier like Gil and perhaps the war had affected him.

She sighed and got on with icing the small cakes.

Gilbert came from his room and said he was going now. She said she thought he was halfway up there by this time and told him not to forget the letter on the dining-room mantelpiece for his father. She told Mrs. Calcott about the message from the Government that said the King and Queen were sending Gil a souvenir of the Coronation. Mrs. Calcott said that should be nice, and Helen said she thought it was very considerate of Their Majesties.

"Mr. Cunningham must have lots of patience," said Mrs. Calcott.

"Yes, he's a very patient man," Helen said. "Never complains. Poor Gil. There's nothing anybody can do for him. I just have to sit at home and put my trust in God and hope things'll turn out for the best."

Mrs. Calcott heard one of the kids screeching and rushed onto the veranda.

Helen stood by the table for a few minutes thinking of her

hubbie all alone up there in the hospital. It made her sad, but there was absolutely nothing she could do about it.

Chapter Two

Ordeal

I

RIDING HIS bike over the bridge from town, Gilbert glanced down at the stream that, thin and still between stretches of mud, reflected the white clouds floating in the blue autumn sky. He wanted to stop and watch two Maoris who had appeared from under the bridge and were trudging across the mud, dragging flax kits, leaving squelchy-looking footprints; but he'd have to hurry if he wanted to be back in good time for the party.

That familiar scary feeling twinged his inside, and he told himself he was getting nearer and nearer to the hospital and his father. Well, he wouldn't think about talking to Dad until he was in the hospital grounds. . . . He was twelve today, soon be in his teens, and he'd have a good time at the party with his brothers and sisters and the Calcott kids. Why hadn't he invited Barry Andrews? After all, Barry had invited him to his party, and it was queer how he'd been shy about inviting his best friend.

Pushing hard on the pedals, he reached the first bend in Hospital Hill. His cousin, Ralph Coulter, reckoned he could ride all the way up the hill, but Ralph said anything to make an impression. Mum always said you never got a lift up the hill because it was too much trouble for drivers to stop, then start again. Sometimes people got rides coming down the hill, though, and Mum was thrilled to the boots that time she got a lift from the Mayor of Gladston.

He looked out over the town. First thing you noticed was the brewery with the mud parallels of the river running along past it; this side of the river two lorries sped along the highway. Over back of the brewery was home, from here a faded red roof that you could pick out by the tall poplars at the bottom of the yard.

He bet his brothers were playing in the paddock already. Mum should have made them visit Dad, seeing they got him a hiding. Just to think of the hiding made him warm all over, so he thought of the party and how he was going to enjoy himself. It was probably a good job none of the kids from school were coming; he wasn't so nervous with the Calcotts the way he was with other kids. You could see their place in Peel Road from here pretty clearly—a dirty house with a broken-down fence out front. And they didn't live in the dirty part of Gladston, either; that part was way over near the sea.

He looked across the flats to the dark blue sea, white-pointed by the wave-tops.

II

He rode along the hospital driveway, avoiding the glances of a group of nurses who sat in deck chairs on the veranda of the Nurses' Home. He looked away as he approached a white-coated doctor walking towards him but wished right afterwards he'd given the doctor a chance to tell him it was not the official visiting day and he would have to turn around and go back down the hill.

Heck, why should he be so nervous about visiting his father? All he had to do was hop over the veranda railing, he thought, whistling low. Nothing dangerous about that.

He parked the bike, took the bag from the handlebars, moved quickly along below the ward veranda, and scrambled over the railing. His father lay with closed eyes. The other two beds on the veranda were empty, and that was good because you didn't have to talk in a whisper so's sick people wouldn't hear what you said and criticise your appearance.

Looking at his father's sunken-cheeked, sallow face on the white hospital pillow, the long thin arms on which brown hair straggled and the veins were prominent, he felt the trembling inside him stop; instead there was a mixed-up pride because this man was his father and he'd been a great carpenter and he'd gone to the war and done all the things only grown-ups could do. And he was sorry for having been glad when his father had to return to the hospital. Dad was strict, and once he'd chased him with a whip, but he was a good-looking joker, and you felt proud having him for a father.

He took the tobacco and two oranges from the bag, placed them on the locker beside the bed.

Dad smiled when he opened his eyes. "Hello, son," he said, reaching out to twist the chair before the locker.

Gilbert sat down on the edge of the chair. "You feeling all right, Dad?"

His father told him he wasn't feeling so bad, he was glad Gilbert had brought up the tobacco, he was dying for a smoke and the quack had told him to go easy on the baccy but a man had to get some enjoyment out of life. "How you getting on at school, son?"

"I'm doing all right, Dad. It's not too easy in Form I, but Mr. Bridgen said I was doing all right. He often reads my essays to the class. And I get high marks for drawing."

"You get your drawing ability from me. Remember those letters I used to write when you were younger and came to Gladston and I stayed up the coast?"

"Yes, you sketched funny people and houses at the end of them—I remember," Gilbert said, thinking how good it was to be chatting like this. He was silly to be scared of visiting Dad.

"I can see you'll be going in for a collar-and-tie job," Dad said.

"I don't know," Gilbert said. His father was criticising him. He didn't know that he did want a collar-and-tie job, he'd rather be a carpenter. "I might be a carpenter," he said, not too certainly.

Dad laughed. "Fancy Sydney will be the one to follow in his father's footsteps," he said.

Gilbert nodded. There was something about Sydney that made people like him. Different from himself; he had hardly any friends.

"Still working on those wrestling scrapbooks, Gilbert?"

"I started the 1937 one the other day."

"See where Sammy Stein got beaten in Wellington."

"Yes, by Hal Rumberg. He was lucky, though. If Stein hadn't hurt his arm in the last round he'd have won. That's the first time he's been beaten in New Zealand."

"Well, son, they seem to have some well-known wrestlers here this season, but give me boxing."

Gilbert tried to smile easily to signify "You like boxing and I like wrestling but we won't fight over it"; but his smiles always seemed to die stupidly.

He said he'd bring up his scrapbooks for him to look at, and his father said that was a good idea, adding, after he'd lain without speaking for a few minutes, that their mother had told him they were going regularly to Sunday School and he was pleased to hear that. Yes, Mr. Kent called for them every Sunday, Gilbert said, and Sunday School wasn't bad. But it was about the worst thing in his life, he thought, and he hated it.

He remembered the letter off the mantelpiece and handed it to his father who said he'd read it later. Squizzing through some magazines from the locker, he remembered the terrible dream about a man with a blue-and-white face standing over his bed, blood dripping from a knife he held, that he had one night after reading a *True Detective.* It was different from his usual dreams like the one where a rolling ball got bigger as it rolled then joined with several other balls that whirred on and on getting smaller and smaller until there were no balls though the whirring continued. And once there had been dreams of Marjorie Young and Carole Plowman; but this kind of dream now contained Izzy Calcott or some sheila at school.

III

"I'll have to go now, Dad," he said, standing up. "Got to get back to my birthday party."

"'Struth, that's right. Twelve today, eh? When you going to stop growing, son?"

Gilbert grinned. The same old question.

His father took a ten-bob note from the locker. "Something from your Dad," he said.

Gilbert thanked him very much. It was an enormous amount of money. It was the most money he'd ever had. When he had the paper run he got seven and six a week, but most of this had gone to his mother, and, gosh, when he and the other kids went to the flicks on Saturdays they'd be given threepence to go in and a penny to spend and that was all. Dad was a great joker, all right.

"Well, don't be late, son."

"I'll bring you a piece of my birthday cake."

"That's the idea."

Gilbert got over the veranda railing. He was rich. The money made him excited. He rode as fast as he could through the hospital grounds and let the bike coast swiftly down the hill. Visiting Dad hadn't been so bad after all, he told himself.

Chapter Three

His Majesty's Earnest Hope

GIL CUNNINGHAM lay back tiredly on the pillows, glad there was nobody to yap in the beds near his. What he wanted most out of life now was peace and rest. He'd been half asleep when Gilbert called, and it was as though the boy's visit hadn't been real, just another of those dreams you had about the kids and the people out of your past life.

Disinterestedly, he took the letter from the locker top. Probably from Hilda or some other relation. Been opened, too, he thought, and sealed up again.

He pictured his wife getting the letter from the postman, bringing it inside, looking curiously at it, turning it over, then deciding to open it. She wore a silk housefrock with torn armpits, her hair was fuzzy. She'd be puzzled about the letter because the address was typewritten and generally the only envelopes with typewritten addresses contained bills. That would worry Helen. He could see her frowning, could see her hand go up worriedly to her mouth.

He smiled and read the letter:

Dear Sir,

I am desired on behalf of His Majesty the King to convey to every ex-member of the Empire Forces undergoing institutional treatment in respect of disability arising from service in the Great War the assurance that all those who fought in the war are always in His Majesty's remembrance, and to express to you His Majesty's earnest hope that your sufferings may speedily be alleviated by the treatment which you are now receiving. The King also desires you to have a souvenir programme of Their Majesties' Coronation in the hope that it may be a reminder of a happy day in the history of the

British Commonwealth of Nations and one will be forwarded to you immediately on receipt of supplies from London.

Yours faithfully,

F. Jones,
Minister of Defence.

He considered the letter thoughtfully, sat up, and rolled himself a cigarette. Something interesting to show that young red-fed Carson who'd brought him unreadable pamphlets for weeks. Fought for your country and were then cast aside, eh?

That's what this bird reckoned. Well, here was a very nice gesture, very nice. You knew quite well the King and Queen were no more than figureheads—you needed no Max Carson to tell you that—but there was a thought to the action that sort of bucked you up.

Yes, they had a very young king and queen now, he thought. Seemed funny there being a king who shaved, the people had become used to old King George and his whiskers. They must have had a great time in England on Coronation Day. The papers reckoned they were still dancing in the streets days after the actual business was over. He wondered whether it had been a good thing their getting rid of the Prince of Wales. Yes, he decided, Edward the Eighth would have stirred up trouble with his carryings on; the king and queen played a big part in holding the Empire together, and such a high office was no place for irresponsible types.

He remembered young Carson had said how if Britain had spent a fraction of the money she spent on the Coronation towards helping the Loyalists or whatever they were in Spain world peace would be assured. Sometimes Carson got your goat properly. He was the one who brought up the point about the bus strike that was on during the Coronation. Said it was most significant. You couldn't follow the workings of these redfeds' minds.

He should have shown the letter to his son. The kid wasn't bad only he was so damned nervous he made you wonder, with not much interest, of course, whether you too had been that nervous when you were a kid and if you were no wonder you got biffed by older kids. Time had gone by all right, and his kids were growing into men and women. And just when they most needed their father's guiding hand he had to be in hospital. He hoped their mother saw they didn't disgrace his name, he had occasional doubts about her ability to bring them up the right way. He believed her grandmother practically lived on the mat and her mother was something of a hard-doer; that's why he got to thinking she was quite likely to go to pieces with too much discouragement. That Calcott biddy was no person for her to be friendly with. You should never be too friendly with people who weren't of at least your own class. God, she ought to be able to manage the kids now she had the pension.

He wondered if many other diggers would get Coronation souvenirs. Couldn't be too many diggers around just now seeing most of them had passed on. Happened to be still alive himself because he'd been so young when he left to do his bit and it was a matter of time before he passed on too but meanwhile here he was in hospital getting waited on and not forgotten, no, not even by Their Majesties, the King and Queen of England.

Nurse Johnson came walking through the ward, and he fired the cigarette over the veranda and placed the letter on the locker so's she'd notice it when she put his glass of milk there.

Chapter Four

Scent Can Choke You

I

THE KIDS climbed through the fence into the brewery paddock, promising their mothers they'd behave themselves and not get dirty.

Seeing it was his party and the others were his guests, he should suggest some game, Gilbert thought, but darned if he could think of anything. Clive might have a suggestion, but he didn't have many brains and gee he was a shrimp of a kid for sixteen.

Izzy helped by saying what about playing follow-the-leader, so they lined up behind her and she started running and she ran too fast for the small kids so Clive took the lead, followed by Izzy, Gilbert, Frank, Sydney, Rachel, Anne, and Bubs. Each held the waist of the one in front, and they made the snake shuffle along.

Gilbert took short steps so's he didn't kick Izzy on the heels and looked down at the green grass as they trampled over it.

Clive went a bit faster, making Izzy lunge forward, and, taking a firmer grip on her, Gilbert felt her body through her frock and he watched the backs of her soft-looking legs and told himself this game certainly made you excited and he wished Clive would leap suddenly ahead again so's he'd have an excuse for grabbing Izzy more tightly. And, sure enough, Clive went down a dip in the paddock before anyone else noticed it, and they tumbled on the ground, Gilbert rolling on Izzy and lying on top of her for some seconds.

"Why don't you dopes look where you're going?" Clive laughed.

Gilbert stood up and brushed his pants, and Izzy went crook at her brother because her white frock was grass-stained. She didn't look at Gilbert, and he felt she wasn't looking at him on purpose and that made him seem skitey.

Over by the brewery Bubs ran to where she said there'd been a duck's nest but it was not there and she kept explaining to the twins where it had been and what had probably happened to it. Sydney got up on the top stable railing and ran along, taking no notice of the older kids when they told him to get down before he fell and broke his neck. Then they got up, too, and walked cautiously along the railing, and Sydney called them scaredy-cats because they wouldn't run like he had. And Gilbert got wild at him and said he was stupid.

"Now, now, Gilbert, you don't want to lose your temper on your birthday," Izzy said.

Her saying that made him more annoyed. He hadn't lost his temper. He was proud of how he didn't lose his temper, different from Sydney and Frank, who were always scrapping. She had a cheek, and who did she think she was? He wished he hadn't invited the Calcotts to the party; he wished he'd invited Barry Andrews instead.

Bubs raced across the paddock to her mother, who had called from the fence, and her brothers and the twins ran after her. Gilbert strolled behind Clive and Izzy. It hadn't been important, he wished he didn't always get worried like this. What was the matter with him? Other kids didn't—oh, gosh, best not to think about it.

II

Coloured streamers hung from the kitchen ceiling, and in the middle of the table, laden with cakes and jellies and fruit and nuts and sweets and glasses of raspberry cordial, was the birthday cake of twelve candles. Mum had certainly taken more trouble over his party than she had over Joy's. But Joy wasn't worrying; she was acting like one of the grown-ups, placing the kids in position, calling them darlings the way Ma Calcott did.

Seated at the head of the table, he glanced at Ma Calcott beaming proudly in the passage doorway, now and then giving one of her loud laughs. He wished she'd stop grinning that silly grin of hers. He kept his head down and ate his jelly and custard slowly.

Not long after they sat down to eat Ralph and Donald Coulter turned up. Ralph wore his High School shorts and socks and a white tennis shirt that showed his sun-tanned neck and arms. His dark hair shone as he sat beside Izzy under the light. Gilbert thought how much he preferred Donald to Ralph. Donald, who wore a grey suit, was a nice quiet kid, pale-faced and not too strong looking, and no two brothers were more unlike each other, people said.

He noticed Ralph talking to Izzy. He felt jealous, though, gosh, he certainly didn't care who Izzy spoke to. None of his business. He didn't care.

What with hoping nobody said anything to him and trying not to look at Ralph speaking to Izzy, he didn't enjoy sitting at the table much. Everybody was eating a lot, and the small kids were chattering and racing one another to eat the most sultanas and walnuts.

Time to light the candles on the cake, Mum said, so the electric light was switched off and the room flickered with candle shadows. Faces were mysterious in the half-dark, and Ma Calcott, leaning over the table with the candle flame showing up her wrinkled face and gummy mouth, was like something out of a fairy-tale book.

He blew. Everyone joined in. The candle flames were snuffed out. The cake was cut, pieces handed around, and tea was over, thank goodness.

He kept looking at Ralph, knowing his cousin would soon make a wisecrack that he would not be able to think up an answer for.

"Now you children go into the dining-room and play," Mum said. "Gilbert, you can open your presents. Ralph and Donald might like to help you." She smiled at his cousins, the nervous smile she used for people like Aunty Hilda and the jokers who called for money, the smile that was different from the way she laughed at Ma Calcott and her big sons. Mum seemed scared of people like Aunty Hilda and the Trisk and Trisk man. Sort of like the way Ma Calcott was scared of you, as though she thought you were better than her; at least that's what you felt from the nervous way she talked to you. Or perhaps you were wrong; perhaps she saw you were a bashful kid—bashful was an awful word—and was merely trying to be sympathetic. If only he could become strong and casual like Ralph. Maybe he should join up with the Y.M.C.A. or something. Ralph went to that place, and he might ask him about it if he got the chance.

Remembering his promise to his father, he pushed past Joy, who was laughing at Clive about something, and said, "Don't forget a piece of the birthday cake for Dad, Mum. He said he'd like a piece of my cake, seeing he couldn't come to the party."

"Golly, no," she said. "We mustn't forget Dad."

As he followed the others into the dining-room he heard Ma Calcott commenting how thoughtful it was of him to remember his father, and he felt he'd done something great.

His presents were on the table, and, watched closely by Bubs and Rachel and Anne, he opened them up. There were a couple of hankies, a box of soap ("Joy must think you need a wash"), a tie, a copy of *My Favourite* and a wooden pencil case from Mum, and a book called *Epics of Empire* (Epic of Jutland; Blazing a Trail Across the Kalahari Desert; Malcolm Campbell —King of Speed; Five Englishmen Versus the Antarctic; How I Won the Victoria Cross) from Aunty Hilda and Uncle Bill and his cousins. The tie Ma Calcott had given him might come in handy if ever he got a suit, perhaps in another two or three years.

When it came to opening the presents, birthdays were all right, he reckoned. There would have been one more present if he'd invited Barry. Still, he was doing all right. Nothing had happened yet to make him appear foolish.

III

Rachel was a dark-haired, pretty kid, and Anne was fair-haired with weak eyes that made her squint. Urged on by their mother they sang "Little Sir Echo." Ma Calcott wanted Izzy to sing, but she made out she had a sore throat. Frank hid behind the door while Sydney recited Robert Louis Stevenson's "I Will Make You Brooches."

Gilbert kept out of Ma Calcott's sight. He thought how, at school, Bridgen laughed at the sing-song way he told a poem—up-down, up-down, finish, no emotion, a bad job completed as hastily as possible.

He was glad when Ralph suggested Postman's Knock and they played that for a while. Then they played hide-and-seek. He went to the linen cupboard next to the bathroom and crawled into the space between the bottom shelf and the floor. There was quite a bit of room, and he told himself he had a good hiding place. He was pulling the door shut when Izzy scrambled in beside him. He pressed hard against the end of the cupboard but still felt her body beside his. When the door shut and they were in darkness she started whispering. She wanted to know if he was still wild at her and reckoned he'd had the sulks in the paddock before tea. He hadn't, he said, his voice far away. He wished Frank would hurry and count to two hundred; he wanted to be out of the cupboard.

He could smell scent. He moved, and she asked if he was uncomfortable. He said he wasn't. He asked what she had on her hair, and she said some hair oil Teddy, her big brother, had got for his girl friend but the girl friend didn't like it so Teddy gave it to her and it was nice wasn't it. It was a good smell, he said, though really it was going up his nose and down into his throat and nearly choking him. In his throat there was something that made him wish he was somewhere else, anywhere so long as it was out of this cupboard.

"Coming!"

Frank walked past up the passage. They lay silent in the linen cupboard. He felt Izzy's arm rest against his body and her hand touched his shoulder and he was as taut as anything but he couldn't press back any further. Her face glanced against his ear. She said she was sorry, she was trying to turn around. She did it again, and he wasn't sure whether it was deliberate, but there was no excuse for her pushing against him when there should be plenty of room at her end of the cupboard.

He moved his hand and it touched her breasts and a flush spread over him. Izzy, Izzy. No use, he was scared. He'd dreamed, in the day as well as the night, of being somewhere like this with Carole Plowman, but it was different now that he was here with Izzy Calcott. It shouldn't be different. Izzy was a girl, though of course she wasn't as beautiful as Carole. But there would be the same mysterious things about Carole as there were about Izzy. All right dreaming about what you would do but, gosh, it was different now. He hoped Frank would hurry up and find them.

IV

Ralph said he'd found the *Champions* and *Triumphs* in the front room and Gilbert didn't mind lending them, did he?

He minded all right, Gilbert thought angrily, but with Mum watching what else could he say besides telling Ralph he could borrow a couple of the comics if he liked? Ralph had probably upset his whole filing system, and you couldn't have anything of your own, somebody always interfered with your private things. Ralph had a cheek, and it was queer how he'd buttoned up his shirt; most likely he had more *Champs* on him.

Even when he was saying good night from the front steps he couldn't stop thinking about his comics and about how Ralph, who got anything he wanted, would come to his place and pinch other people's things. Well-off kids could be selfish, though you couldn't complain about anything Donald did. Ralph was just a smart alec. Going to Y.M.C.A. might make him like that. Perhaps if you did exercise at Y.M. you forgot to be *bashful* and you developed a body that made other kids jealous. Well, his playing cricket hadn't made him less shy or improved his body, but Y.M. might be different.

In any case, he told himself, if he were rich he would not be selfish. No fear! When he went to his poorer cousins' parties he would not take a silly book. He would bring an envelope containing money, he would give nobody a chance to call him tight, he'd consider the people in the world less fortunate than himself. He was not sure, but somehow it seemed money could make all the difference in people's lives. Mum and other grown-ups were always talking about what they'd do when their ships came home, and they talked for hours about the lists of art union prize-winners.

He put his hand in his pocket and felt the ten-shilling note his father had given him, and he didn't feel so badly about Ralph having plenty to spend, though he was still annoyed about the *Champs*.

Chapter Five

Over the Sink

I

JOY MUTTERED to herself as she piled the plates in the pantry sink. Helen told her to stop moaning, the way she carried on about washing a few dishes you'd think she was hard done by.

Well, she better shut up, she wasn't too old to be smacked on the backside. Golly, *she'd* never had a party like the one her kids had had tonight. They didn't appreciate the sacrifices you made for them, took everything for granted.

Parties were a lot of bother, and she was glad her own birthday was next on the list because she never had a party, nobody noticed her birthday. Nobody except Gil and her mother. Seemed only a couple of months since she turned thirty-three and Gil gave her a pair of slippers; he always gave her slippers on her birthday. Yet it was really back before he went to hospital after his haemorrhage.

She selected a tea towel from the two or three lying in a corner where the kids had thrown them. "You're always moaning about something," she told her daughter. "You give me the pip."

"Is that so?"

"Yes, you cheeky brat, you think you're a real lady because you go to High School. It's a pity they don't teach you anything at that school besides typing and whatever you do."

"I'd rather be a typist than a shop-girl, anyway," Joy said. "I have to be educated, you know."

"Sometimes I wonder whether it's worth the expense. You're always pestering me for new books and money for sports clubs and concerts and things."

"All right, then, I'll leave High School, if that's what you want," Joy said. "Suits me, I don't care."

"Don't be cheeky," Helen told her. "I just want you to be reasonable. Didn't I clean up the mess after your party? It wouldn't hurt you to wash a few dishes on your own."

"The others ought to help," Joy said.

Helen lost her temper. "Shut up, for Christ's sake! If you don't shut up I'll break a plate on your head. I've had enough of your silly squabbling."

Joy swilled the water over the dishes in silence.

II

"I'm glad Mrs. Calcott brought her kiddies over," Helen said. "They don't have much of a life with a mother like her even if she does think the sunshine of them."

"They seemed to enjoy themselves," Joy said quietly.

Helen was sorry she'd lost her temper. Joy was exasperating at times, but she really wasn't a bad kid. Her education was expensive, but that didn't matter a scrap, she supposed, if it helped her to get a good job.

Joy worked her fingernail on the jelly-skin in the bottom of a glass dish.

" Be careful of that dish, love," Helen said. " I've had that for donkey's years."

" It's one of the dishes we had up the coast, eh?"

" Yes, and I hate things being broken that we've had for years. Heaven only knows we can't replace them."

" Be all right if we lived up the coast now, wouldn't it?"

" I don't think so," Helen said. " Too far in the backblocks for me."

" But we had some good times up there, didn't we?"

" Yes, they were happy days, but your father was well then. It'd be different now. No, when we move from here it won't be to the backblocks, it'll be to the city."

Joy looked thoughtfully at the dishes.

" What you thinking about, love?"

" I was thinking about the Calcotts and Dad not liking them," Joy said.

" It's not that he doesn't like them," Helen said. " I think he feels sorry for them. They seem coarse to him. But they're a good-hearted lot, and I bet they get more pleasure out of life than your rich aunties. I don't want their charity, but God has a way of paying back people who neglect their own brother."

" Dad's sisters are not as good as Grannie, are they?"

" Not a patch on her," Helen said. " But don't you call her Grannie when she comes to Gladston. She likes to be called Aunty. She's not keen on people thinking of her as a grandmother."

" She must be funny," Joy said.

" She's a dear old thing," said Helen, thinking tenderly of her mother, who did so much for her even although she was away in the city. Mum was a darling. Fancy sending that lovely big sewing machine when she heard of those terrible Singer people claiming her daughter's machine. Not many mothers would do a thing like that. Wonderful mother mine, it is a blessing to know I still have you and your love.

And Dad, too, she thought. She longed to see them both, and she only hoped they'd be able to come to Gladston for a holiday very soon. Dad with his big red face and white moustache, shaking all over when he laughed. Good job, too, that he did have a sense of humour because Mum could be rather trying in her own independent way.

" You hear the Calcotts talking about the party they're having, Mum?"

" What, another one?"

"Izzy reckons Jack is giving one for the girl next door to their place, and he said we were invited."

"We'll see when the time comes," Helen said.

"They're always having parties, eh?"

"Yes, they are."

"They must waste a lot of money."

"Mmm."

"But they have a good time."

"Yes."

"Well, that's the lot," Joy said, pulling the plug out.

"Thanks for washing up, love," Helen said.

"That's all right, Mum," Joy said. She walked into the kitchen, then turned as though suddenly remembering something. "Could I have two shillings for some books, Mum, please? I need them like anything."

"You don't want it now."

"Oh, in the morning will do," Joy said.

"I'll see what I've got in my purse," Helen said. She walked up the passage to her room. The young hussy. She knew she had been leading up to something. Kids couldn't do anything without wanting payment for it. What a hectic life they gave you.

III

She sat on her bed reading the letter she'd got that morning from Fred Burgess. Her heart ached when she read that he found life in the city unbearably lonely without her by his side, but it was good to hear that he had a likely job selling houses and sections that might bring him in, he said, quite a good income in the way of commissions. It would be glorious if he could save enough to buy a house of his own. Then, if anything happened to Gil, she could go with the kids to Fred and leave Gladston behind.

She'd read the letter many times, as she always did with Fred's letters. It was terrible when Gil was home and they dared not risk writing, contenting themselves with messages signed Peter and Fanny in the Personal Column. She had been silly ever to have thought she would forget Fred. She loved him, and he loved her.

Well, she really should be happy tonight. Apart from Gil being in hospital and more bills coming in, she was not doing so badly. The Calcotts were making life in Gladston somewhat brighter, and she was getting letters every other day from Fred, and there was a chance that her parents would soon be visiting Gladston.

And yet Gil could never be very far from her thoughts. The doctor had told her the truth, and she must face up to it. Little hope lay in sending him to a specialist or to Waipukurau or any other sanitorium. To think of him on his back and remembering him as he once was made her want to howl; the old days were truly gone, would never return.

Worry, worry, worry. She looked in the mirror, looked for more lines on her forehead, more grey hairs. She remembered the chap Mulligan who came to repair the radio the other day and how he tried to flirt with her and she thought, Well, perhaps she still had some attraction for men. She smiled at the memory of Mulligan, a thin wisecracking sort of fellow, a gay lad. Yes, he'd really tried to flirt with her. What a hope he had! For ever and ever and ever she would wait for Fred. Her Simmons experience had shown her what these shallow types were like. Fred was the only one for her. She just knew Mum would grow to understand him the way her daughter did, she'd soon forget her silly prejudice about his being a married man and see him in his real light. His family didn't want him, they had driven him from his home, so why should they be considered? It always brought new hope to hear from him, and some day she would go to him and she and her loved ones would be together.

She held his letter and felt very happy.

Joy poked her head around the bedroom door and asked, "Did you find the two bob, Mum?"

Annoyed, Helen said, "For goodness' sake leave me alone. That's all you kids think of—money, money, money!"

Chapter Six

No Place for Dreamers

I

Their faces glowing from playground snowfights, the pupils trooped back into class. Though the snow had been light and the flakes did not fall for long, everybody was excited about it, and it wasn't only being able to make snowballs that made it exciting, it was a brand-new experience and mysterious. The tins of water that had been left standing before school were ice-covered by playtime, and inside you the water was like fire. Phil Chalmers and his gang dropped ice down the backs of other kids and laughed madly when the kids shivered and tried frantically to get at it. With the mingling of many warm breaths, masses of mist rose in the cold corridors of the brick school building.

Gilbert bet his nose was red as a beetroot, the end of it was tingling, and despite his boots and thick grey and blue socks his feet were freezing, and he wished he'd worn the old woollen singlet that once belonged to his father and wasn't nice to wear because it prickled his skin. He was glad he had a seat at the back of the classroom beside the heater, only he wished Barry wouldn't keep asking to swap places so's he could be near the heater because it was a big thing for even your best friend to ask. And Bridgen might go crook if they swapped places. He was in Bridgen's bad books already because he'd gone to MacPherson's Bush yesterday with Mike Park instead of going to the school sports. The only reason they'd got a holiday, Bridgen said, was because of the sports, and the least he and Park could have done, seeing they couldn't see their way clear to participate in the school's sporting activities, was to have watched their schoolmates competing against the representatives of other district schools. And he wished he had gone to the sports anyway. Park was a selfish, self-opinionated kid, and the only reason he'd been asked to go for a ride was because Park's usual mates went to the sports.

From now on Bridgen would have no chance to call him a ninny. Starting today, he would take as much interest in sport as any kid in the school. In any case, he'd decided over a week ago to attend Y.M.C.A. classes with his cousin. Ralph was amused when he mentioned the idea but said he'd introduce him to the place, and Aunty Hilda was as pleased as Punch and told him he'd meet the nicest boys at Y.M.C.A. and it would fill him out, too. That was the main thing, of course. If his body was improved it might change his whole life. Those Charles Atlas advertisements, anyway, reckoned it changed your whole life to have a body everyone admired.

It had been strange waiting for today to arrive. He wanted to go to Y.M. and yet he didn't. Seemed something inside him kept making him worried about things even when he wanted to be happy and satisfied. Well, maybe he'd lose his nervousness when he had a strong body.

"I hate to intrude, Cunningham, but just as soon as you've finished day-dreaming you might spare me a minute of your time." Bridgen stood in an attitude of exaggerated patience, his hand on his forehead as though about to press down his swish-back hair in the way that was a habit with him.

Most of the kids turned their heads. Noticing Moira Thornton grinning, Gilbert felt like sticking out his tongue at her, as far as it would go. Edna Robinson hadn't even lifted her head when Bridgen spoke to him, which showed the difference between some tarts.

Barry put his finger on the school journal, whispered out the side of his mouth. "He wants you to start this."

Standing in the aisle with one hand on his desk, Gilbert began to read.

Bridgen interrupted. "Pardon me but I quite recently concluded reading that introduction. Sorry you weren't impressed, but I'll read it again and possibly I may show some improvement. And do you mind standing up straight—hand off that desk!—and listening? 'In his novel *Nicholas Nickleby,* Charles Dickens describes a terrible Yorkshire boarding house, Dotheboys Hall, his object being to attract the attention of the people of England to a kind of private school, many of which existed at that time—about a hundred years ago. Our story is about a kind young man, Nicholas Nickleby, who has come to be the assistant teacher at Dotheboys Hall, being introduced to the methods of the school by the owner, Mr. Wackford Squeers.' Now would you very much mind reading on from there?"

Gilbert read: "'There,' said Mr. Squeers, as they stepped in together; 'this is our shop, Nickleby! . . .' "

II

Gilbert made a note in the margin of the journal as Moira Thornton stopped her precise reading of a W. W. Jacobs extract to inquire about the meaning of *sagacious.* One of these days, perhaps after he'd gone to Y.M. for a bit, he would get up in class and talk like the joker Carson who lectured on street corners in town. Carson gave him copies of Communist papers, and he liked them for the pieces about wrestlers and boxers in their sporting sections. The other articles were too heavy to read, but some time you could look at them properly and make a speech on such subjects as rich and poor people and the war in Spain. Boy, it would give Bridgen a shock, and the Form II tarts would look at him with surprise and think what a clever boy he was and apparently he knew more than he let on.

Sometimes he wished he was not in Form II room. The Form I B kids under Major Howard reckoned the old boy's bark was worse than his bite, and it might not have been so bad if he had missed getting into Form I A seeing Bridgen was so strict and too much of a skite and always crawling to Baldy Shimmering. One thing, Baldy didn't seem to mind him although he had a bit of a set on Frank and Sydney and was always pinching their cheeks and telling them they were young roughnecks and should be like their brother. They certainly were cheeky kids, and they got him into trouble like getting him that hiding from the Danks, but he wished Baldy wouldn't keep coming to him about them as though he were to blame for what they did. Yes, and when he got built up at Y.M. he would challenge the Danks to a fight like the jokers did with their enemies in the Charles Atlas advertisements. He'd belt hell out of them, as Mum used to say to the kids when they annoyed her. . . .

He shivered, but he was scared to put his hands on the heater in case Bridgen saw him. His skin was red and purple, he must have poor blood circulation.

Thank goodness the week was just about over, only two more bad periods this week—Miss Drake's poetry class this afternoon and general discussion tomorrow morning. What a sensation he would cause at general discussion if he stood up and spoke loudly on Communism, whatever that was. He'd surprise the Form II tarts. But it didn't really matter; all tarts were silly the way they giggled about nothing and he only knew of one girl who seemed dignified and sensible and she was going to High School and was too old for him though he often thought of her sad-looking eyes and golden hair. Carole Plowman was beautiful, beautiful . . . lots more beautiful than Izzy Calcott, lots flasher. Izzy was a bit fat, and even though he sometimes wished she was his girl, just to show the other kids he too could get on well with girls, he was shy when she was around, and every time he remembered the party and the game of hide-and-seek he was embarrassed.

"I say, Cunningham?" Bridgen again.

"Yes, sir?"

"A polite inquiry. Are you with us in this lesson, tell me, or are you not? Eh? Would you like my permission to transfer down the corridor to Major Howard's room? Perhaps that's the trouble. You would prefer Major Howard, is that it? Does my brand of teaching bore you?"

"No, sir."

"You're quite interested?"

"Yes, sir."

Bridgen laid his journal on the table before the class. He turned, beckoned with his finger. "Come here, boy."

Boots squeaking, Gilbert walked down the aisle. Bridgen took hold of his wrist and asked him to unfold his palm. His hand was soft and warm, and Gilbert thought he must have better blood circulation than he had. The grip was removed, and Bridgen reached for the strap that lay beside a vase of flowers on his desk. He raised the strap and brought it swiftly down. Against his will, Gilbert withdrew his hand slightly, and the strap struck the tips of his fingers, dulling them. Frowning, Bridgen grabbed the wrist again and gave a couple of sharp whacks, saying, "Something to remind you that attention is one of the essential virtues, in this class at least."

Gilbert returned to his seat. Before he sat down he glanced through the window and saw an old woman walking past on the footpath below. She looked far away and as though she were walking in one of those London fogs you saw at the pictures. His hands had been cold before, but now prickling arrows jabbed the cold. He noticed Moira Thornton stare briefly at him, but he didn't care what she thought. He didn't feel ashamed, he felt as though Bridgen was not important and nobody else in the room was important. He wanted to be home, to see his mother, to lie on the bed in his room. Barry whispered that Bridgen was unfair and placed his hand on his knee under the desk. He smiled at his friend to show him that Bridgen wasn't such a terror as he thought he was.

Chapter Seven

The Radio Man

I

"It's got a lovely tone," Helen told Ernie Mulligan, the radio man. "It's just that there's a lot of noise every now and again."

Mulligan listened seriously. It was just after ten o'clock, and the kids were at school. The house was still. "Better have a look-see at the workings," he said. "May need a new valve."

"It might, too," Helen said. "It's given wonderful service, and I always say it's got the best tone of any radio I've heard, but I suppose we can all do with an overhaul at times."

" That's right, we can't go on and on indefinitely," Mulligan said, peering behind the radio.

" Only difference with us human beings is that we can't have new valves put in us," Helen laughed.

" True, true," Mulligan said. " Still, there are other ways of putting new life into oneself, eh?" He glanced up with a smile that seemed intended to mean a lot.

She smiled at him, hands behind her back. She felt at ease with him. Some people made her nervous and unable to talk naturally, but this joker had a way about him that put you at your ease. He was nothing much to look at. A thin man, on the short side, rather round-shouldered, but with quick movements and a twinkle in his eye. You could tell he was a good sport.

" I'm afraid some of us are not as lucky as others." It seemed a bold thing to say and sort of suggestive, and she was surprised at herself.

He stood up with a valve in his hands. " Now don't tell me an attractive woman like yourself doesn't have the most beautiful times."

She shouldn't encourage him, anybody would think she was flirting. " Oh, I suppose I have as good a time as any married woman with a tribe of kids."

" You go to dances, of course?" he said casually, studying the valve.

" No," she said.

" Well, the movies then?"

" Haven't seen a picture for donkey's years."

He raised his eyebrows. " No dances or movies?"

" No."

" Hmm."

" Why?"

" Well, naturally when you see an attractive young woman you just naturally jump to the conclusion that she has a wonderful time."

" I fancy you're a flatterer," she said. But she felt pleased all the same.

" Who? Me? Nothing-but-the-truth Mulligan, that's me."

Helen stood watching him fiddling with the radio, feeling a silly sort of excitement. He was a kidder, not to be taken seriously. She should go into the kitchen and leave him here. It had been so long since anyone had praised her appearance that she had believed her attractiveness had gone with her lost youth. Even Fred did not tell her she was beautiful; their love did not seem to need flattering words. Now Mulligan was suggesting things, and she wouldn't be normal if she didn't feel pleased.

"Afraid it will mean a couple of new valves," he said.
"Golly, the kids will be narked; they're following that 'Singapore Spy' serial, you know."
"I'll pop down to the shop and get the necessary," he said. "Won't take a couple of minutes."
"It wouldn't be a bother?"
"No bother," he said. He put the used valves in his pocket, and she followed him to the front door, smiling when she thought what a kidder he was.

II

She'd written to Fred about the Calcotts, and he'd replied saying he was glad she found some pleasure in Gladston, he only regretted he was unable to be there to give her all the comfort she needed. There was nothing snobbish about Fred, no criticising the Calcotts simply because they were on the rough side, and she had explained to him the sort of lives they led and how Gil didn't approve of her being friendly with them so it was clear that all that mattered to him was that she was finding enjoyment in their company. He wouldn't mind if she went to all the parties in the world, so long as she enjoyed herself. It was annoying that Mum should persist in offending him and although she was a good woman and the best mother going she should try not to be so spiteful and realise her daughter was battling along on her own and it was not as though Gil was up and about. She didn't like criticising her mother seeing it was only a week since the last parcel of clothes arrived and a couple of weeks since the enormous doll-house came on a post office truck for Bubs, but Fred meant quite as much to her as her mother, he did, he did.

—There's nothing wrong with talking to the man, I won't go further than that. He's not a patch on Fred. I don't have to tell myself I love Fred, and I wish this joker wouldn't make me feel I'm doing something wicked.

III

"Here I am again—like a bad smell," said Mulligan.

She showed him into the dining-room, feeling once more that he was an old friend, somebody she had known all her life.

"Driving up in the car, I got thinking about you not going to dances and movies," he said. "In a casual sort of way, mind you. Perhaps, I thought, you don't like that sort of thing."

"What do you think?"

"I think you like those things, all right, only you haven't been asked out lately, eh?"

"Now you're getting personal."

"I believe in getting down to fundamentals, but it's none of my business, of course. Sorry if I offended you."

"You didn't offend me," she told him.

He busied himself with the radio.

"Like a cup of tea?" she asked.

He said he wouldn't mind one, so she went out to the kitchen humming a tune. When she returned to the dining-room he was sitting on the chesterfield.

"That's the idea, make yourself at home," she said.

"I've been thinking about a dance I was invited to," he said. "Can't think who to take along for a partner. It's a country affair. Stop me if I annoy you, but would you like to keep me company?"

"Do you invite all your customers out to dances?"

"Only the beautiful ones. They seldom accept. But I keep on hoping. Very optimistic person."

"Oh, I couldn't go," Helen said. "For one thing I haven't an evening dress."

"That wouldn't be necessary, but perhaps we could drop the dance and make it the movies."

"I really don't know."

"Just thought you might take to a spot of entertainment. Promise to bring you home safe."

It wouldn't end with the pictures, she thought. Once it started it would go on to other things. Best not to let it get started.

"I don't think I could manage it," she said.

"You want to?"

"No—I mean, I appreciate you asking, but I don't see how I could manage it."

"Another time?"

"I don't know."

Slowly and thoughtfully, she drank her tea, he watching her. It was as though they were old friends who had reached a crisis in their friendship. Somewhere in the back of her mind were the thoughts of Fred and Gil and Mum, but what was important now did not seem dependent on these others. It was between Mulligan and herself, and she couldn't explain it right off, she needed time.

"I'll be passing tomorrow; mind if I pop in?"

"No, call for morning tea."

"Bye-bye in the meantime, then." He no longer seemed a smart alec, and that was very disturbing.

Round about noon, when she was preparing lunch for the kids, the idea of friendship with Mulligan did not seem wrong, and yet she was not sure. She could go on thinking it over the rest of the day, she thought, and through the night, and she would still not be sure.

Chapter Eight

The Lost Sheep

FOR ONCE poetry class had been all right. He had not been asked to recite, and he wouldn't have cared much if he had. The whacks from Bridgen had made him feel that anything they did to him at school was not worth worrying about. He had felt a little like this before, but somehow he felt it would be different from now on; he was no longer impressed by all they said and thought about him, they couldn't scare *him*. And so he would go on in his own way, and some day they would wish they had been kinder to him, and he would become strong and handsome, and he would win certificates or whatever you won at Y.M. classes, and they would want to be friendly with him, but on he would go on his own.

Carrying the white sand-shoes his mother had bought him and the rolled-up sleeveless singlet he would need to exercise in, he walked down the path beside the Coulter house.

Ralph had a racing bike upside down on the concrete yard. "Ah, the youngster with hopes of a Tarzan physique," he said. "Want to swing from tree to tree like Tarzan of the Apes, cousin?"

"Be all right," Gilbert grinned.

"Get the sheilas then, eh, boy?"

"Yes."

"But I forgot. You're the serious lad with no time for the opposite sex. Gilbert's not a boy like that. I forgot. Well, I suppose we lady-killers have our problems."

Aunty Hilda came out and told Ralph to hurry or they'd be late and it would be just as well to introduce Gilbert to Mr.

Hanley before the class started. Wearing a smart dark blue dress that Mum would have kept to wear down-town if she'd had it, she stood tall and haughty-looking on the top step. She asked how he was getting on at school, and he answered politely that he was doing all right and Mr. Shimmering considered his work very promising. As he spoke he thought how Aunty Hilda was supposed to regard him as her favourite nephew, but he did not feel that he loved her, she was not the sort of person you could love. She left them, asking to be excused as there was a bridge party in the drawing-room and the ladies would be wondering where she had vanished to.

He suddenly realised she had said nothing about the names he had called Ralph for pinching his comics. He had told Donald his brother was a thief and Donald had passed it on to Aunty Hilda and she had mentioned it to Dad and Dad wanted to know from Mum what the boy meant by making statements like that about his cousin. Mum had not been angry, though. She seemed tickled, as if what he had done was clever. Well, Ralph *was* a thief.

"Right, Gilbert my lad, we'll hit the trail."

They rode through town and across the bridge to the Y.M.C.A. Ralph, who commented on any girls they passed but otherwise said nothing, acted as though he thought his cousin was a dope who was too young to talk about anything intelligent.

Gradually Gilbert felt himself becoming jittery. He thought of the way he had felt after he got the whacks, but it did not help. He wondered what Y.M. would be like. He wished he didn't have to go through with it. Unlike poetry classes and general discussions, this was something he had caused himself. What would happen? It was going to be all right, it had to be all right.

He recognised some Second Formers among a group of kids standing outside the gymnasium, but they didn't see him or didn't want to. In a small office, the walls of which were decorated with photographs of young men standing in pyramid poses and leaping hurdles, Ralph introduced him to Mr. Hanley, a muscular, blond joker who looked very clean and wore a white jersey and white shorts. After taking his name, Mr. Hanley spoke heartily about the value of physical culture and how any normal boy would have the time of his life doing the many exercises planned to develop fully the potentialities of his body.

He followed Mr. Hanley into the gym and put on his sand-shoes and singlet. For about ten minutes he stood watching kids swinging gracefully from bars and turning somersaults on mats in the corners of the room. Then Mr. Hanley snapped a couple of orders, and the kids formed file. Gilbert stood uncertainly by the door until Mr. Hanley snapped "You, too!" at him, and he got behind the first kid he saw and was shoved away and told to go to the back, couldn't he use his eyes and see the tallest were at the back?

Round the room they marched, lifting their knees high ("Higher, higher, higher!"), and they ran ("Keep those feet up!") and walked on their toes, ran on their toes, walked, ran, until his new sand-shoes were cutting his heels and his feet were hot and sore. He was thankful when the halt order was given and they measured off at arm's length from those in front, watching while Mr. Hanley demonstrated smoothly and snappily various exercises which they then did. Gilbert was glad he was at the back of the class because he could make neither head nor tail of most of the exercises and had to follow the kid in front. Although his arms and legs ached already, the others seemed as fresh as when they had started.

One exercise followed another. His arms did not belong to him. They belonged to the bronze-skinned kid in the front row, or the one with a big nose and freckled body on the left of the class, or to Mr. Hanley, or Ralph, to anybody but himself. Mr. Hanley gave an order, and the others immediately went onto their stomachs, but he couldn't understand and stood wondering what to do.

"Hey, you!" Hanley pointed at him.

"Me?" he asked.

"Yes, you. What you standing there like a lost sheep in the wilderness for? Snap out of it! Get down. On your stomach, hurry!"

He dropped to the floor, shocked at the way Hanley had spoken to him. Gosh, you expected it from Bridgen because he was a schoolteacher and it was probably his job to shout at you, but this Hanley joker had no right to boss you around, you didn't *have* to come to his old Y.M.C.A.

Placing the palms of their hands on the floor, the kids raised and lowered their bodies, and he followed suit. It was hard to keep it up for as long as Hanley wanted you to, you wanted to rest, to lie panting on the floor. But he would go on counting—up, down, up, down, up, down, up, down—and you had to keep lowering your body and raising it, and when you thought the end had come he would be shouting orders at you once more. For a change they flipped over one another's bent backs . . . it lasted three-quarters of an hour, but it seemed more like hours.

When it was over he removed the sand-shoes from his cut

and blistered feet and hung them over the handlebar of the bike and, not waiting to put on his boots, he rode off, the memory of Hanley thudding in his head. A lost sheep, he had called him. A lost sheep in the wilderness. Orders, orders, just like school, worse even than school.

Presently he began to think about the things he would tell his mother and Aunty Hilda and Ralph to explain why he would never go to another Y.M. class.

Chapter Nine

A Crazy Thing To Do

I

On moonlight avenue, we met, we kissed . . . we parted . . . on moo-oonlight aaavenue. . . .

Happy days up the coast returned to her as she walked with her kids along Livingstone Road. There was a pale moon, but they walked on the roadway away from the dangerous hedge shadows. What memories were caused by songs like "Moonlight Avenue" and "My Blue Heaven" and "Ramona" and "I'm Dancing with Tears in My Eyes"! Everybody owned a gramophone, and the records were played over and over, and the songs those days could be listened to dozens of times, not like the silly songs they brought out nowadays.

She wondered if she would ever again experience the happiness she had experienced with friends like Flo Young; the sort of happiness that made day-to-day life bearable, not the sort you got from another person's company; that sort was to be treasured, of course, but it was personal, and even with it life could be dull and made up of work and worry.

"That's Mrs. Young's brother's house there, isn't it, Mum?" Joy said.

"What house? Who said it was?"

"I like that," Joy said. "You did, of course. Mr. Burgess, the coal man, lives there, and you said he was a brother of that Mr. Burgess who came to our place, remember? and you said he was a brother of Mr. Young, so naturally—"

"I forgot, that's right." Golly, you certainly had to be careful what you said to kids. It was a fib about Fred being Flo's brother, but saying he was had kept the kids quiet when he was calling. She hoped Joy wasn't thinking too much about it, she was at the knowing age.

"Doesn't Mrs. Calcott scratch her head a lot? She must have fleas."

No, she had forgotten already. But she would have to be careful what she said about Fred. She would just have to say nothing.

A steady machinery rumbling came from the dark shape of the brewery above them, and as they passed the yard gate there was the swishing of water and the muffled sound of men's voices.

II

From a block away they heard shouting and laughter from the Calcott house. Izzy and the twins ran up to them. A motor-bike came speeding noisily along Peel Road, and Izzy shouted, "Here's Teddy, Mrs. Cunningham! He's got a motor-bike now."

The machine's engine was cut off, and it drew up beside the rickety Calcott fence. Teddy Calcott, a boyish-looking fellow with crinkly brown hair and freckled face, jumped off feeling the seat of his pants. The Harley was a beaut, he said, but the seat was hard on a joker, and he'd probably get piles.

Teddy and his brother Jack were a bright pair, all right, Helen thought. They were well built, different from the younger ones in the family, but they took life very easily though they spanked cows and built fences when they were in the mood.

They stepped cautiously over the gaps in the veranda and entered the house, Mrs. Calcott laughing as she came up the uncarpeted passage to greet them and tugging at a thick woollen stocking that had slid down her leg. "Take your coat off and make yourself at home," she told Helen. "Hello, Bubs. Isn't she a darling?"

She showed Helen into her bedroom. Disordered bedclothes lay on the double bed under the window, and the light was dim, but you could see kids' dresses and bloomers scattered over the floor. Helen felt her stomach turn over when Mrs. Calcott prodded a half-full chamber-pot out of sight under the bed, and she wondered how people could live in such conditions. She laid her coat down and walked out into the passage.

In what Mrs. Calcott called the dining-room the floor was bare; there were a pile of records and a case of beer and several plates of cakes on the table. Clive Calcott was playing a cowboy tune on an old-fashioned gramophone, and he didn't look up when they glanced in the room but continued listening seriously.

Seated at the table in the kitchen were Jack and the next-door neighbour with her two daughters. They welcomed Helen as though she were a long-lost friend come home, and Mrs. Calcott introduced her to Mrs. Ellis, a big-limbed woman with a homely face and peroxidy-looking hair, and the girls, Agnes and Betty. "Wouldn't have missed the party for anything," Mrs. Ellis said. "By Christ, don't these Calcott boys like their parties?"

"What's life for but to enjoy?" asked Jack, his arm around Agnes.

"Don't worry, I'm all for parties, too," Mrs. Ellis said. "'Specially if I don't have to pay for the damned things."

Jack squeezed Agnes, said she was the guest of honour.

"A marriage on the way?" Helen asked.

"More like an engagement," Agnes giggled. She was rather pretty-looking and had dark hair and very red lips. Her sister looked sickly, probably because she used too much powder.

"You must come and see the jellies," Mrs. Calcott said.

Teddy laughed. "Great place she put them—in the bloody bath!" He stopped laughing when Betty said she thought that was quite a good place for them.

Mrs. Calcott poked one of the jellies, and her finger came out sticky and raspberry-red. "Doesn't seem to have set properly," she said.

What an awful mess, Helen thought. "I'd have made them for you," she said.

"The kids will clean them up tomorrow," Mrs. Calcott said.

Back in the kitchen Jack suggested a spot but his mother told him it was too early for that yet and Jack said there was a whole case to go through but they'd have a few hands of poker first if that's the way she felt. Helen was soon winning about two bob, but she was glad when they stopped because Mrs. Ellis and Mrs. Calcott, who reckoned they couldn't tell one card from another, kept leaning over her and watching her play.

Jack accompanied himself on a guitar and sang "Frankie and Johnny" right through, and he wasn't bad, either, Helen thought. Mrs. Calcott kept requesting "Clementine," but the boys told her there was time enough for that when they'd had a few spots.

III

Teddy poured beer into the cups, then added some wine.

Everybody except Mrs. Calcott, who never touched anything stronger than lemonade, had another drink.

The party so far had been a little dull, Helen told herself, but the drink inside her was warm, not that she liked it as much as the stout Fred used to buy her. She asked Teddy for some wine on its own, and he said she could have anything she wanted, he liked her, yes, sir, he liked Mrs. Cunningham.

"I see you don't need many drinks to liven you up," she told Agnes, feeling light-headed.

"Lordie, Ma'am, I'se always lively," Agnes said. "You ask Jack. Aren't I always lively, Jack? It's Betty that can't hold the liquor, isn't it? She's a real lily of a hophead."

"Hhh, you can talk," Betty said, pushing Teddy's arm away. "Don't catch me getting sick in the back yard anyway."

"Yes, you know, old Agnes got as sick as a dog in the back yard after the last party," Mrs. Ellis said. "What a sight for sore eyes. You were a sight that night, Aggie. Wasn't she, Jack?"

"Yes, she was a sight all right," Jack said. "I'm afraid you can't take it, sweetheart."

"I can so," Agnes said. "It was those bloody oysters you gave me. Would have held onto the drink if you hadn't given me oysters. Mr. Calcott, you know you shouldn't have given them to me."

"Didn't she beg them from me, Teddy?"

"No, you rotter; you forced them on her," said Teddy. "I seen you lying on her stuffing them into her mouth. Or am I thinking of another time?"

Agnes called Teddy a damned liar, and his mother told him to mind what he said.

"Have a drink, Mum," he said. "I was only sticking up for her."

"Thank you, I can stick up for myself," Agnes said.

"I'll say you can, sweetheart," Jack said.

Outside in the dark the kids were playing cowboys and Indians or some other noisy game. Helen heard Clive shout to Gilbert, then Frank gave a yell, and there was a scurrying right under the kitchen. "How about giving those kids a call, Mrs. Calcott?" she said.

"Let them have their fun," Jack said.

"I warned them not to get into mischief," Helen said.

"You have quite a family, Mrs. Cunningham," said Mrs. Ellis.

"Five of the brats," Helen said.

"My, your old age *will* be comfortable."

"So everybody tells me," Helen smiled. "They're not bad kids. They love their mother, that's the main thing."

"They're very nice children, and you ought to be proud of them, Mrs. Cunningham," said Mrs. Calcott.

"Here, have a drink," Teddy said.

IV

Jack got the gramophone and some records from the dining-room, and he and Agnes waltzed about the kitchen, and Betty wanted Teddy to get on his feet, too, but he reckoned he couldn't dance so she sat down and sourly watched her sister and Jack.

Helen thought of the many times she'd danced with Fred in country halls far away from Gladston's malicious gossip, and how he held her close to him just as Jack was holding Agnes. She longed to be in his arms now, to see his dear face would make her the happiest woman in the world. Surely it was not too much to ask of God—just send him to me, Lord.

But what about Ernie Mulligan? she asked herself. Every time he came to the house—regularly twice a week—she knew he was dying to hold her like Jack was holding Agnes, but so far nothing had happened. She liked him, and she hated herself for looking forward to his calls but, golly, she would sooner kill herself than go with another man while Fred was waiting for her. She *would* be silly not to realise that a man like Mulligan did not call merely for the sake of a cup of tea and a chat. He wanted more than that, and didn't she realise it? Oh, and how she longed to go to dances and have a man's arms around her! Seemed she had not noticed the longing until she had a few spots in her and saw Jack and Agnes being intimate.

She would have to straighten herself out. She was behaving as though there were some truth after all in what her mother had told her when she was a flapper in the long ago. She was working in the hotel at Rotorua and she knew she was going to marry Gil and Mum turned up and frothed at the mouth and demanded to know when she was going to stop flinging herself at anything in pants and who was this latest beau and it was plain that she would end up a bad woman and disgrace her parents' name and mark her words. As if she could help being popular. But Gil was her last fling, and he wasn't a bad fling. They went for long walks in the bush, bathed in hot-pools back of the cemetery, went to dances, had a wonderful time. It was hard, though, to keep loving even the best man in the world when there were kids and sickness and creditors. She had always told herself her love for Fred was unusual, and it almost made her howl when she thought things about Mulligan, who was not a patch on Fred. She blamed it on her lonely damned life. She would tell him to stop calling, remind him that he had a wife (cheap-looking blonde that she was), warn him people would start to talk and she could not bear a scandal. . . .

Jack and Agnes were cuddling on a stool against the wall. That boy was handsome enough to make any woman jealous of the girl he happened to be feeling up; wavy black hair, a nicely tanned face, a way of showing his teeth when he smiled. She saw Mrs. Ellis eyeing him, and knew she was not the only one feeling silly. Probably dried-up old Mrs. Calcott was the most normal person in the room at the moment.

"Nice boys, aren't they?" said Mrs. Ellis, keeping one eye on Jack.

"They think a lot of their mother, and I always say there's not much wrong with your children when they respect their parents," Helen said.

Mrs. Calcott grinned with pride.

"We're all family women, and I think women with families are the only ones who appreciate the trouble there is bringing up kids these days," Helen said. "Don't you think so, Mrs. Ellis?"

"Yes, love. And we all have to make do without our old men, too. Lost mine about four years ago. A good stick, but you know what men are, even the best?"

Helen nodded understandingly.

"There they go," Mrs. Ellis whispered.

The women watched Jack and Agnes disappear up the passage.

"Don't fall down one of the holes in the veranda!" Mrs. Ellis called. There was no reply.

They smiled at one another. Teddy lay with his head on the table, seeming asleep, and Betty sat morose and silent, her powder smeary so that in the pale light she was a bit like a ghost.

V

"No, Teddy, it doesn't matter, don't bother," Helen said. "You go back to Betty. I'll walk home with the kids."

"Be a sport, Helen, old girl, come on," Teddy said.

"No, I'd rather walk, Teddy."

"Make her hop on the seat, Mum," Teddy said.

"It'll be all right, Mrs. Cunningham, he won't take any risks," Mrs. Calcott said.

Helen laughed as she lifted her skirt and got astride the pillion seat. She told the kids to hurry on home. Gilbert warned her that Teddy was drunk and might run into something, but it was too late now, and besides, the way she felt she must have a thrill of some sort.

Hearing Bubs whimper, she started to get off the seat, but the motor-bike sped away from the fence with a great row, and she clung to Teddy's shirt. Like a mad thing the bike tore down Peel road, and she experienced a brief and wonderful excitement, and then it was over. The engine chug-chugged and stopped, and Teddy steered to the roadside. "Those bloody kids have been muddling with this," he said.

As she got off the bike she tore her dress. She felt sober. What a crazy thing to do! She might have been killed, and, for all her complaining and worries, she didn't really want to die. She thanked God for stopping the bike before anything terrible happened.

She looked anxiously up the road. Soon the running shapes of her five children appeared. Bubs was howling but stopped when her mother put her arms about her.

They said Hooray to Teddy, but he was too busy tinkering with his bike to notice them. They walked on home.

"Some party," said Joy.

Chapter Ten

Wishful Thinking

Eric MacNab, who'd been moved to the next bed a couple of weeks back, pushed his son aside so's he could see Gil. "You got that Coronation souvenir handy, Gil? Want to show it to the boy."

Gil looked up from the tray he was making. "Nurse took it away to show to some cronies, Mac. Must remind her about it."

"Des said he'd like to see it," Mac said. "Wanted to know why I didn't get one, too. I was telling him his old man left it a bit late. Should've timed it a bit better if I wanted a souvenir, eh, Gil?"

"Bad timing, all right," Gil smiled. He knew Mac didn't give a damn about the souvenir actually, only he was proud as a peacock of his son, talked for hours about him and his other kids and his wife, and probably the kid thought it funny his having a souvenir and his Dad not, and he'd want to see the thing just to show himself his father was not missing much.

"He can see it next visiting night, eh?"

"Sure, I'll get it back from Nurse Johnson."

Mac went on talking quietly and seriously to his son, the pair occasionally laughing over something.

Gil threaded the cane through the stems of the tray. He was becoming quite an expert at the work, he reckoned. It was something the Returned Soldiers' Association had thought of; they supplied the materials, and he and the other diggers passed the time away making baskets and various knick-knacks that were sold at a shop in town. It got boring, but you could take a rest from it and then try it on again. A change from reading and thinking.

Glancing at Mac and the boy, he wished momentarily that his own son was up yarning with him, but he didn't get on with Gilbert the way Mac got on with Des. Gilbert was like a stranger to him, they never seemed to hit it off. When the kid was younger you were fond of him for his quietness and for the knowledge there seemed to be in his large brown eyes, and you had hoped that he would grow into the sort of boy you could talk man-to-man with and take along on fishing trips and that sort of thing. Then, when the other kids came, you forgot the plans you'd made as he lay a tiny red bundle (he was a funny-looking baby) in his mother's arms until one day you realised he was a big boy and should be at the age to make a good companion to you, and it was a shock to find that he seemed frightened of you, and you tried to understand him but you couldn't, and you guessed it was the age he was at. He was not to blame for his gawkiness and shyness, but, God, he irritated you at times.

Well, perhaps Mac's kids would tire of visiting their father the way his own had tired of visiting him. They would have to be very loving kids to go against the example their mother set them. Mac talked endlessly about her, but you only had to look at her fur coat and over-made-up face to see she was a gal out for a good time, and she fidgeted all the while she was on the veranda, itching no doubt to hotfoot it down the hill to her bow-tie.

"Des just reminded me that the Springboks were coming," Mac said. "Too bad we can't see them, eh, Gil?"

"By Jove, yes," Gil said. "Reckon we might get Nurse Johnson to wheel us down to the Oval? Use a couple of wheelchairs. Might be an idea."

"We'll ask her," Mac said. "You may have hit on something there, boy."

"Won't do any harm to ask," Gil said.

"Des is great on his Rugby, you know, Gil," Mac said proudly.

"My boy's taking it on, too, I believe," Gil said. "Plays for the Central School side. You know Gilbert Cunningham, Des?"

"He can't be in the first fifteen," Des said.

"He's only starting," Gil said. "Don't think he'd be that good yet."

"I'm in the Tui School first fifteen," Des said.

"Good for you," Gil said.

"We beat the Central the other day," Des said.

"Very modest, isn't he, Gil?"

"Well, it's not every boy that's in the first fifteen," Gil said.

"Yes, I wasn't too bad myself in my day," Mac said.

'Struth, it would be great all right to be able to leave the hospital and join a mob of jokers going to a football match and stand on the sideline barracking his head off and after the game go to a pub and get well oiled, Gil thought. As in the old days when the footie was the only entertainment of the week. "I haven't seen a game of football in years," he said.

"Well, there's a chance we'll see one soon, and a big-time one, too," Mac said.

Nurse Johnson came out with a vase of flowers. "No visitors, Mr. Cunningham?"

"Be up on Saturday," Gil said. "Just talking about you, Nurse. Like to do us a favour?"

"I'd be thrilled to."

"How about taking us to the Springbok match?"

"Who's 'us'?"

"Mr. MacNab and myself."

"I'll think it over."

"You're not making any promises?"

"If you drink up all your medicine and eat your food properly, I promise to use my influence."

"That's decent of you. Hear that, Mac?"

"Feel a new man already," Mac said. "You're a real sport, Nurse."

"'Course doctor will have the last say." She gave them a big smile and bustled into the ward.

"Gosh, looks like you'll go, eh, Dad?"

Mac smiled, but he didn't answer his son. And Gil knew, as he threaded the cane, why there was nothing to say. Mac knew as well as he did that the only time either of them moved from hospital would be on the day the whitecoats drew the sheets over their heads and hurried them on spindle-legged trolleys to the silent, grey-walled room in the main block.

Chapter Eleven

The Big Game

I

IT LOOKED as though they'd be sold out of Springbok souvenirs by eight o'clock, and that would be jake, Gilbert thought, because it meant he'd be able to go to the Opera House with Sydney to see the Aussie comedian they'd been hearing over the Y.A. stations lately.

People in lizzies, lorries, buses, and gigs had come into Gladston all day, and wealthy station owners drove down from the coast in streamlined De Sotos and Zephyrs, and walking about after school you saw farmers standing in sidestreets and Maoris feeding on the river banks, the young Maoris singing cowboy songs and playing ukeleles, and there were crowds in the shops so that the shopkeepers reckoned it was just like Christmas. And now at night there was a proper carnival appearance about Stout Road, with gangs of youths walking up and down making eyes at the tarts, the Salvation Army band playing for all its worth, and kids blowing squeakers and toy bugles. Some of the football fans yapping in doorways reckoned this was the greatest South African team ever to tour New Zealand, while others stated that the local lads might surprise the visitors, who'd done a mighty lot of travelling since leaving home. And old men sucked thoughtfully on pipes as they recalled the magic of George Nepia and Bert Cooke. . . .

It was easy money, as the joker at the school gates at lunchtime had told them it was, and though at first it sounded awful to sell things on the footpath it wasn't bad once you were used to it and providing you kept out of the bright light. They had sold the booklets that they had been warned not to call programmes because the johns would grab them if they did, and now there were only a few souvenir buttons left.

Gilbert smiled at Barry. He would never have been able to sell the souvenirs without Barry standing by him even though Barry seemed shy about raising his voice and having people look at him. It was good to have a friend; Barry was the first joker he had been friendly with, and he liked him better than he liked anybody else in the school. He wished he was going to the concert with him instead of with Sydney.

A tall lean man in working clothes and with a cap pushed to the back of his head walked unsteadily from the alley beside the Royal Hotel. He was watching the footpath, but he looked up when Gilbert spoke to him.

"Want to buy a souvenir, Uncle Jim?"

"A souvenir of what, son? Good God, Gilbert my lad, what you selling now?"

"Souvenirs of the game tomorrow, Uncle Jim. A shilling each."

"Here, just a mo, here's half a crown; pin the thing on, will you?"

He pinned the button on his uncle's soiled coat, not minding the booze smell and pleased when he was patted lovingly on the head. Earlier in the evening Uncle Jim had bought a booklet from him, and it was certainly generous of him to buy a button, too, though he probably didn't know much about it. Uncle Jim was a couple of years older than Dad, but they were a lot like each other except that Uncle Jim was darker and had become very brown from working on building jobs in the country.

"Where you working now, Uncle?"

"Got in from the backblocks this afternoon, son. Thought I'd spend the week end in my summer cottage and see the game. Must've been confused, though. Find it wasn't me who had the summer cottage, it was the bloody boss. Well, maybe some day we'll all have cottages at the beach, eh, Gilbert?"

"When our ship comes home." Gilbert laughed, thinking that's what his mother would have said.

"Yes, boy, the day'll come when fellows like your old Uncle Jim will get their summer cottages," Uncle Jim said. "Have to stop pissing away the hard-earned cash though. Got to start saving. Go on the wagon."

Gilbert glanced at Barry and saw he had three more buttons than himself so he couldn't be such a good salesman. He should have let Barry sell a button to Uncle Jim, then they would have been just about even.

"And how's your Dad, Gilbert?"

"All right, thanks, Uncle. He was asking Mum about you. He said he hadn't seen you for months and months."

"Just got back to town. Have a whack at seeing him on Sunday. Well, must catch the bus, son, see you later. Hope you sell all your whatsanames. Whew, my head!" He mumbled as he walked on up Stout Road.

"Not a bad joker," Gilbert told Barry. He hoped Uncle Jim did visit Dad and mentioned in passing that he'd seen him selling souvenirs. Might interest Dad to hear his son was making his own pocket money and not cadging from his mother.

"Bet old Baldy wants to know how many kids showed initiative and sold these things," Barry said.

"Well, we're all right," Gilbert said. He stepped in front of an elderly woman and asked "Buy a souvenir, madam?" and she smiled and said she didn't know what she would do with one but she'd buy it all the same. He looked at Barry as if to say, That's how it's done.

II

Watching the laughing young fellows and their girls, he thought of girls, and he supposed that some day he too would have a girl of his own and even now a few of his classmates rode around town with girls and he supposed there was plenty of time for him to lose his fear of them.

Izzy Calcott seemed to like him, but he was as scared of her as he was of everybody except the family and Barry Andrews. . . . "Gilbert's a serious boy," "Gilbert's always got his nose in a book," "Gilbert's shy," "Isn't he tall?" "Hiya, Lanky!" "Daydreaming again?" "Cunningham, you have the unique talent for making the best poetry the most monotonous sounding dribble in the world." "Standing there like a lost sheep in the wilderness," yap yap yap yap yap. . . . He was sick of being a kid, he wanted to be a grown-up. Fifteen more months at Central; he counted the months that brought him nearer to High School. And from High he would go to University, but it was too far away for him to imagine what would happen after that.

Funny how Barry was quiet like himself yet wasn't as worried as he was about school. When Barry was spoken to he did not blush. He was pale-skinned, but he stayed just as pale when he said poetry or got bawled at by Bridgen. They said you had to control yourself and not think about what was happening and you'd be all right, but it didn't work out like that. You remembered the faces, and you felt lonely and you blushed like one thing. And after you had blushed and were once more sitting down or were out in the playground you felt skitey, and you wanted to laugh and joke with the other kids, but your nervousness returned as soon as you tried to do so. Why weren't you like the others? They didn't think you were a freak, and they didn't sling off at you, but they didn't talk to you in secret ways as they talked among themselves. Once he was voted the most popular boy in his class, but it was only because he had been top that term and because he belonged to none of the gangs there were among the kids in the class.

He had written down the names of the people he liked most. He liked his mother best, then he liked his father because every kid had to like his father, and he liked his brothers and sisters though Frank had a snotty temper and always caused rows, and he supposed he liked Izzy and the other Calcott kids, and Donald Coulter but not Ralph, and Uncle Bill and Uncle Jim but not Aunty Hilda and Aunty Rose, and Marjorie Young who married Joe Lloyd from their place, and Mr. Braxton who took Mum up to the hospital to see Dad and brought lollies for the kids, and his grandparents though he couldn't remember what they looked like . . . and Barry Andrews, of course.

But when it was all boiled down he supposed the only one in the world who really loved him was his mother, and even with her there had been times after she had given him a hiding when he had told himself he hated her, hated her.

III

They sold the remaining souvenir buttons and listened to the Salvation Army band playing "Onward Christian Soldiers." Then Barry said he had to get away home else his father would go off at him.

Gilbert walked along to the Opera House and met Sydney. With the money his uncle had given him he bought some Minties and a couple of bottles of soft drink. Seated in the Opera House stalls with his brother, he noticed Mrs. Simmons sitting in front, and, telling Sydney to shut up, he slumped in his seat and hoped she wouldn't turn around and yap, but she seemed to smell them out with her beaky nose and looked round and shrilly asked how their father was, and she looked closely at him so that he felt uncomfortable and asked about their mother and she'd been meaning to call on her for ages and she was only talking about her the other day. Yes, he bet she was, he thought. Mum reckoned she was one of the biggest gossips in Gladston. Well, she was getting nothing out of him. He wished she'd stop peering at him as though she thought he was hiding something from her. "I was saying to Mr. Simmons we must ask Helen Cunningham along to one of our five-hundred parties. Your mother would like that, Gilbert. You ask her. She wouldn't be getting out much with your poor father sick, and I think she'd like our little evenings." He promised to pass the message on, but he knew what his mother would say. He was glad when the curtain went up and the loudspeaker blared "God Save the King."

The Australian comedian stepped briskly onto the stage and cracked a couple of jokes before he was interrupted by a chap with a saxophone who wanted to play something but had first to struggle with the comedian, tap him on the head with the saxophone, and knock him out. Then, in a way that nearly brought tears to your eyes, he played "If You Were the Only Girl in the World."

A fat man with a voice like a woman's sang "Sylvia" and "Lilac Time," and everybody clapped for more, and Mrs. Simmons turned round and said it had been marvellous hadn't it and their mother would have enjoyed it, and they nodded. "Thank you, folks, thank you. Now let me introduce the guest of the evening, a lad I think will make his mark on the Dominion's singing world. He'll probably be another Richard Tauber or Richard Crooks, and he comes from your own town—I give you Stanley McDermott of Gladston." You were proud to think that Stan McDermott, who attended the Central School, should be good enough to be praised by overseas critics, but even while you clapped with the others you were envious of him for being able to stand up there in front of an audience and for being close to somebody famous like the Aussie comedian, and you wished there was something you could do that would make people take notice of you, and you felt like jumping up and shouting "Look at me! Look at me! I'm a clever kid, too!"

After interval the comedian gave a beaut "Dying Swan" dance that ended with his sinking lower and lower following an explosion from off stage until he jerked crazily a couple of times and died. The programme ended with community singing, and the hundreds of people sang as loudly as they could, and they all lost their worries as the comedian pranced on the stage before them, and Mrs. Simmons smiled at Gilbert and his brother and it didn't seem to matter that she was a nosy old woman so they smiled back. Everybody said there should be more of this sort of thing in Gladston and it was a change from the pictures.

A cold wind was blowing outside, and there was a large circle round the moon. They ran a couple of blocks to escape from Mrs. Simmons. Then they walked in silence watching the truckloads of Maoris speeding out of town and the big cars taking the well-off people to their summer cottages.

IV

The day of the Springbok game Gil Cunningham and Eric MacNab lay in bed up in the hospital. Their sons, Gilbert and Des, were going to tell them all about the game, but they couldn't help feeling sorry they couldn't have gone to see for themselves. They didn't miss much, though, because the local side got the father of a hiding.

Chapter Twelve

Husband and Wife

I

It was a cool spring night, and from where she sat Helen could see the many stars twinkling. Dimmed by blue cloth, the veranda light gave Gil's bedclothes a pale purple look, and his head was in a shadow. Hilda had been gone about ten minutes, and there didn't seem anything left to say. He had grinned when she told him one of Bubs' funny sayings but had said nothing. Sighing, she picked up the Coronation book from the locker top where Hilda had placed it.

II

King George's Jubilee Trust Dieu et Mon Droit, hhh must be French or Latin these Froggies and their funny-looking language, the Coronation of Their Majesties King George VI (five and one is six) and Queen Elizabeth a homely little body such a nice face not so dignified as old Queen Mary, quite an honour for Gil, and you had to be a returned soldier and of course an invalid too as they say it's a token of remembrance and it's something to show he's not been forgotten altogether though that sounds silly when you think he must have been forgotten by somebody, God or *somebody,* to be up here, but not by me as everybody knows, I'm doing my bit bringing up his children and keeping the home together because it's his wish that the kids shouldn't be put in a boarding school and I agree but they certainly make life a misery with their squawking and fighting and then I think well they're not bad kids and it's not their fault but will I be thanked? Not likely, kids grew up and left you and forgot all the sacifices you made for them.

They were a nice couple, and he was young and not too strong-looking and once your Gil was just as young-looking, unworried-looking, but that old Queen Mary did Georgie's worrying for him and kings were born with everything while men like Gil had to work all their lives and soon left their youth behind, he had fascinating wrinkles on his forehead when you first met him in Rotorua and a boyish smile and he was funny with his talk of being a big contractor and buying a home and you and he must have made a handsome couple because you were beautiful in those days, so the boys told you, and you went for exciting drives with him in a big Oldsmobile, it belonged to Bert whatshisname, and there was a crowd of young things like yourself all kissing and petting and going to dances, and he was a very generous boy and many times you told him not to waste his money on you and he would say Well darling I've gone through enough to get this little pile and darling I'm going to make the best use of it and spending it on you darling seems the best way in the world to me, and so there were boxes and boxes of chocolates and flowers and concerts and parties, and how you loved tall and gallant Gil Cunningham, and there was no Royal marriage but you bet you were as happy as the Queen for all that lady's jewels, fancy-pants, and whatnot.

Yes, Queen Elizabeth seemed a much better sort than Mrs. Simpson and just look at all the places in the Empire she was queen over, right round the page of the book—Union of South Africa, Commonwealth of Australia, Dominion of Canada, Dominion of New Zealand, Irish Free State, Kenya, Leeward Islands, Malta, Mauritius, Nigeria, Northern Rhodesia, Nyasaland, St. Helena, St. Lucia, St. Vincent, Seychelles, Sierra Leone, and golly lots more, well you wouldn't be a queen if they paid you to be one.

III

A man couldn't help the end-of-the-day weariness and it must be tiring for the wife, too, kids were a trial, the old lady used to say we boys, her Jim and Gil and Ray, were young animals but she was never really flustered and took you and your brothers and your three sisters in her stride, brought you all up and saw you start out in life. Well, everybody was broken up by Ray's death at twenty-three after eleven weeks of marriage and it killed the old lady, but did he have the worst of things after all? What had you got out of fifteen-odd years of marriage? You were tired, tired. Had to drop out just when the depression was ending and the future held all the Labour Government's promises. The country was showing the way to the world and things elsewhere might be going to the pack but it wouldn't be that way in New Zealand and no more fresh-faced New Zealand kids for Europe's battlefields, and that would be good for your kids because look what war had done to their old man, and it was cruel for the mothers when their children went to war, and you would never forget the tears the old lady had shed when you returned. Helen looks older but she seems to have brightened up, probably the Calcott crowd, can't see why she should enjoy those people, she never could mix with people like Hilda's friends, though, must be her bringing up. I'm tired. Glad the kids didn't come up, they worry a man. Carpenters, farmers, clerks? Would they leave Gladston, the Cunningham home town, leave the things the Cunningham pioneers had seen grow? You wished you could have seen them become men and women but just now you were too tired to care about it much. I want to sleep.

IV

How much longer would you be trooping up to this horrible place oh until he died like Mrs. Calcott's hubbie and Mrs. Ellis's too neither of that pair had the memories of young love apparently that you did and Mrs. Ellis still trying to cradle-snatch if she must get a man why not one nearer her own age than Jack Calcott disgusting poor old Mrs. Calcott had passed that stage long ago if she ever reached it probably she started when she was a kid and it meant nothing to her what her old man did and he kept on doing it and she didn't feel anything well you always knew what was happening and you were very careful and Ernie told you you were a bit cold but no you weren't cold you were only careful and you didn't mind driving with him but if he thinks I'm going to sleep with him he's got another think coming no harm in an occasional kiss but I'm no loose woman though sometimes I wonder at myself anyway he's gay company and I know I don't want him the way Mrs. Ellis wants Jack Calcott that old tart would take the boy away from her own daughter if she could and he shouldn't encourage her she nearly pees her pants every time he kids to her those Calcott boys have an animal way about them that comes from working with rough people and having no education by golly you'd make sure your kids got an education they'd have more chance than you had of enjoying a full life you hadn't had a real childhood because Mum was always on the move and Dad always away from home whereever that might be cooking in camps and you never saw him for months on end and Mum was a beggar sometimes those awful rigouts she made you wear that made you look old fashioned and had the kids poking fun at you and your sisters and your brother Danny so you kids kept together until suddenly you all seemed to break away from Mum at once and you went to the hotel and you supposed you got that independent spirit from Mum herself who was always starting out in some business or other but you were glad when you married Gil and didn't have to be independent though now you needed all the independent spirit you had and you longed for somebody really independent like Mum to sort of guide you well you mustn't give up hope but keep trusting in God and drawing your pension and washing clothes and scrubbing floors and cooking meals and dodging creditors those damned creditors came regularly every month the day after pension day and worried you all the dashed time about their bills Trisk and Trisk and Fields and Moores the whole bunch of them must think you got a fortune and they weren't the only ones either people like Hilda Coulter and Rose Cunningham and even Bella Simpson seemed to look upon twenty pounds odd as a terrific amount but golly the grocer's bill alone was nearly thirteen pounds a month and what about rent and clothes and those sheets you got from Wellington months ago and you weren't allowed to work to make more though goodness gracious some women got away with anything like that Mrs. Firth who had only herself and her hubbie but drew her own pension as well as his and he was working in a butcher's shop no matter that he had TB and it oughtn't to be allowed you certainly weren't going to buy from a shop where a joker with TB worked although if you didn't pay your present butcher you'd have to look around for another one had to keep the kids' tummies filled and why was it that a woman with a family and a husband in hospital was always persecuted more than women with a couple of kids and a husband in good health weren't the bigwigs forever singing out for bigger families saying it was your duty to have kids you were a fool to have kids only every time Gil returned from one of his jobs he would make up for lost time and probably it was better for him to get what he wanted from you instead of picking up something from those Maori tarts not that Gil would do anything like that he was always faithful to you a real family man and you'd have never thought about another man even Fred if he'd kept his health but he hadn't and you were like any woman you wanted sympathy so why shouldn't you get what fun you could out of life you got no thanks for being a martyr. . . .

V

In daytime and night-time ghosts from the past mocked you and they were muddled with those now alive so that your dreams were senseless things and you woke up to find yourself sweating, your pyjamas down and the bedclothes off. You had imagined that what had happened over there had passed from your mind but the memories must have been there all the time, and there was little pain in them, it was only that they got monotonous, and you would see over and over the body of the man without a head who had been talking to you a couple of minutes before the shell burst. And you thought about people like Kath Smith who had been part of your childhood and were now bringing up families of their own. You were not scared of either Heaven or Hell because these things were not real. You felt dull agony and lately strange contentment. Probably you were dying.

VI

When she saw that he was asleep she kissed his forehead and walked into the ward. By the bedsides the visitors were saying last-minute cheery things to the invalids, and those invalids who were now on their own were stowing the magazines and fruit and chocolate the visitors had brought into the lockers. The sister smiled so nicely when she told her Mr. Cunningham was asleep and said Yes, he liked his sleep. Anyway, Gil was in good hands, she thought gratefully as she hurried to get away from the hated hospital smell.

Chapter Thirteen

Twosomes

I

"BET YOU'RE glad to be away from the brats for an evening," Ernie said.

"It's a change," she said.

"Beats me how a woman like you keeps a hold on them. Or why."

"Well, my husband wouldn't hear of them going into boarding school."

"Best place for them. That's what those places are for."

"They *are* a worry."

"'Course they are. Think of the good times you could have without them. Why saddle yourself with kids when you could be enjoying yourself? Screwy."

"My own fault, I suppose."

"It is if you don't do anything about it."

"Poor kids, they didn't ask to be born."

"Nerts, you did your part bringing them into the world. Can't you see boarding schools were made for women who find their kids too much to cope with? Not only for the moneyed hens who can't stand the sight of little Michael's sticky dial."

"Oh, I suppose so, Ernie."

"It's right, honey. Put them in a home, and I promise you a good time. I've been around. Thinking of making for the States next year. What about that? How'd you like to drop in on Hollywood and say Hiya to Charles Boyer and Clark Gable?"

"Go on with you."

"Yes, we could hit the high spots. Just a twosome."

"What about your wife, Ernie?"

"To hell with that bitch!"

"Ernie!"

"Gives me a pain fair dinkum to think of her. You've got some queer notion in your head, honey, about wives and husbands having to stay faithful because it's the way God meant it to be. Well, He never said anything about it."

"So I've got that notion, have I? That's what you think."

"If you haven't, why don't you co-operate?"

"There might be plenty of reasons why I don't do what you want me to."

"Don't think I don't respect your motives. I do, honey, I do."

"Thank you."

"You feel pretty sweet on me, eh? I mean you like me a lot?"

"Yes, you're good fun."

"I think a lot of you, Helen. I like you as much as I've liked any woman, probably more."

"Is that a compliment?"

"Say, you got another bird on your mind? Is that the trouble?"

"Well, you're not the only one in my life, you know."

He sent the Chev wheeling sharply from the highway onto the dirt road that led to the Playtime Club. The headlights cut through the shadows cast by the roadside trees. "Honey, that's a big blow," he said. "Not particularly nice of you. I'm knocked back."

"I wonder if I'm a nice person, Ernie. I don't know myself. Lately I've been thinking about it."

"You're nice, all right. Only you put me off when I'm only trying to be helpful. Why tag along with me at all?"

"Tag along? Me? Who chased who, anyway?"

"Well, if I chased you, which I didn't, I was merely showing human interest, you liked it?"

"Yes, but I only went out with you because you wanted me to."

"Break it down, honey. You must have wanted me, or you'd have stopped back home nights with the kids."

"I don't care."

"Don't care what?"

"Don't care whether you bother or not."

He slowed the car. "Jeez, and I was only telling Al the other day I felt a new man lately and he said it must be the company I'm keeping and I said it must be. And now you say you don't care. You mean that? Even before we've started?"

"Like your idea of starting. Was that only practice what you did the other week? I don't go out with other men, you know, I remember things."

"Al said this was just another of my periodical enthusiasms and I told him no it wasn't, this was different from the others. Want to make a liar of me?"

"That wouldn't be necessary, you've done that on your own. And who's this Al you're always talking about? Is he your father or something?"

"You've heard of Al Summers. Business acquaintance of mine."

"He's a bookie."

"That's one of the rumours about him."

"I've heard about him. I don't think much of your acquaintances."

"Nothing wrong with Al."

"He's a crook, and everybody knows it."

"Well, he's not harming you, honey."

"I don't like mixing with crooks. I've always led a respectable life."

"Christ, from here this looks like a fight."

"I don't want to fight, but I don't like some of your insinuations. Do you regard me as a loose woman, Ernie?"

He stopped the Chev and put his arm around her. "You worry too much," he said. "Forget your worries, honey. I'm sorry if I offended you, and I don't know how I could have offended you, but I'm sorry, anyway. I apologise." He gave her a long kiss.

"You're nice, Ernie, but I don't think we better talk about the kids when we're out. It only makes for quarrels. I don't like quarrelling."

"So that's it. Well, I promise not to mention kids and boarding schools once more. Okay?"

She nodded. If he thought that was the only reason why she'd felt sudden revulsion towards him it was all right with her.

He started the car and drove on to the Playtime Club.

II

"You're a cunning one, you are," Flo Young told Helen.

Helen snuggled under the bedclothes, her body rubbing against her friend's. "Why, Flo?"

"Putting Bubs in bed to warm a place for you, my part's cold."

"I always do that. Of course when I get in I roll her over and she has to warm another place and, golly, doesn't she go crook sometimes!"

Flo laughed heartily, shaking the bed.

Good old Flo, Helen thought. It was two years since they'd seen each other, but Flo hadn't changed a bit, and it was quite like old times. "Had an idea you'd be down for Christmas, Flo, but I wasn't sure. You always promise to come down, then I suppose at the last minute you can't bear to part from Alex."

Flo laughed again. "Alex can look after himself, he doesn't complain."

"You're lucky having a man like him, Flo."

"He's comfortable," Flo said casually.

"Suppose it's the best sort of husband to have. One that's happy to be in the backblocks and doesn't mind his own company. No worry with Alex, is there?"

"He's very contented; I know he's always where I left him."

"I envy you in a way, Flo."

"Go away with you. You and Gil were happy together, and I know it."

"But look at us now, Flo. Isn't it terrible?"

"It's a great pity, all right. But you must keep looking on the bright side, whatever that is."

"I could, too, Flo, if I had somebody like you staying with me all the time. But you know how much I hate Gladston and the people in it."

"Never mind the people. You want to keep to the friends you've got and not worry about anybody else."

"I bet I'm brought up at their afternoon tea parties. I don't care, though."

They lay in silence for a few minutes. A car went past outside, then there was a midnight quiet once more.

"Heard from Fred yesterday," Helen said.

"How is he keeping?"

"He's doing very well, considering," Helen said. "Of course he says he misses me a lot."

"He would, too."

"You don't think it's wrong, Flo?"

"What, Helen?"

"About Fred and me?"

"Well, he's not in Gladston, is he?"

"No."

"Why worry then?"

"But if he was would you think it was wrong?"

"That's the sort of thing you decide for yourself."

"Sometimes I feel all muddled up. I want to see Fred, but then I think of Gil, and golly, Flo, I get dumpy as anything."

"Cheer up."

"Yes, it's awful. Always complaining these days. I'm glad you came, Flo. We'll go shopping tomorrow, eh?"

"Got a few things to buy. Marjorie wants some odds and ends, too."

"How are they enjoying married life, Flo? I may be wrong, of course, but I fancied Joe might be a little temperamental."

"No, he's all right. They're still a pair of lovebirds. Tickles me the way they argue, then flop in each other's arms. There's another kid coming."

"I say!"

"Marj says this'll be the last addition."

"That's what I said after I had Gilbert, and look at me now. Hope she does stop before she has too many, though. It's a lot of worry for a young girl."

"Marj is sensible, she won't let Joe be too greedy."

"Good on her."

"O-o-oh dear, I'm tired."

"You go to sleep, dear. I forgot you'd had a long day. Only I'm so pleased to see you, Flo, I could go on yapping all night."

Flo laughed and turned on her side. The bed creaked.

Helen lay with eyes open. She had missed her chance. But would Flo understand? Flo was broad-minded, and you felt she would be sympathetic, but how could you say what you wanted to say so that it didn't sound awful? Or was it so awful that there was no dressing it up?

"Flo, say if there was some—if somebody wanted to take me out now, would it be right if—"

"Mmm?"

"I was wondering if a man asked me to—"

"Mmm?"

No, it was not a fair question to ask Flo. It was another of the things you had to decide for yourself. Strange how you put off deciding things because you thought somebody else would come along who would see everything clearly and tell you just what to do, and yet now that Flo was here you were scared to say something wrong. So you didn't say anything.

She listened to her friend's heavy breathing. Well, there was plenty of time to tell her yet, anyway. She must get some sleep so's she'd be fresh for her round of the shops.

Chapter Fourteen

A 1937 Christmas

I

MRS. YOUNG came striding onto the veranda with an armful of parcels. Her face was red, and she looked hot. "By golly, you're a great one!" she said to Dad as she studied him briefly before placing her parcels on the floor by the bed. "Just look at him," she told Mum, who sat smiling on a chair. "Lying there like Lord Harry. Suppose you have all the poor nurses in the place waiting on you hand and foot."

Dad grinned at her, not minding what she said because that was how she always spoke and she could say the most insulting things to you but you could see she was only kidding, only sometimes you wondered if she really was kidding and whether she meant you to laugh at her but to take notice of what she said too.

"Should have taken my luggage home, I suppose," she said, "but I knew how disappointed our Lord Harry would be if I didn't come up and wish him a Merry Christmas and a Happy New Year."

"Well, you're looking very young and energetic," Dad told her. "Must be the country air."

"Don't feel too energetic, let me tell you. Walking up and down that Stout Road all day and, oh, my poor feet!"

"Suppose you're used to padding around in bare feet?"

"Never wear shoes up home. Can't stand this heat. Why is it always so hot in summer in Gladston?"

"Go on, Gladston's famous for her hot summers. Think of the tourists it brings. Our Chamber of Commerce would be hard up for propaganda if we didn't have hot summers," Dad said.

"Well, it's a bit too hot for me, thanks," Mrs. Young said. She waved a paper before her flushed face.

"Flo has to get all sorts of things for Marj, don't you, Flo?" said Mum.

"Usual grandmother story," Mrs. Young said. "You want to thank your lucky stars you didn't have more daughters to grow up and get married, Gil. They expect you to do everything for them from buying nappies to selecting pants for their old men."

"Girls *are* a trouble," Mum said. "The boys are not so bad in some ways, but I never know where Joy is. Suppose she's down the street with some boy this moment. Says she goes out with her girl friends, but I have my suspicions. Kids these days!"

They went on talking about girls and kids and babies and the weather. Mrs. Young sat with legs spread apart and, looking up from his *Puck,* Gilbert saw under her dress as far as the end of her stockings. She had tangled blue varicose veins.

What if she were Izzy and sitting like that? It would mean nothing. He would look at her, and that would be all, and it would be something more to think about at night, something to add to the thoughts of how Izzy's breasts would move beneath his touch and of a remembered hair oil smell and her lips on his and her body against his, and it would be no more than thinking because even when he wanted her to be his girl he was scared of the kids at school saying that she *was* his girl and mostly the dreams would switch from pictures of Izzy to pictures of some girl who wasn't real outside the dream. But for a moment he wanted Mrs. Young to be Izzy, and it was only the varicose veins that made his looking up the dress seem silly

Still the thought of Izzy didn't disturb him. He was pretty happy tonight. It was Christmas and school was over for the year and he'd passed into Form II and it wasn't as though he were up here with Dad on his own, there were Mum and Mrs. Young and Frank and Sydney and Bubs, too. And yet it wasn't like Christmas really, not like Christmas last year even when Dad had been home and had gone crook at you about Frank and Sydney stealing things from shops in town. It was a bit better now that Mrs. Young had blown in and the sadness that Mr. MacNab had helped to cause by his complaints against the hospital treatment, especially about the old joker who had been shifted onto the veranda and had died in front of their eyes, was going, and Mr. MacNab, who was waiting for his people to come up, was smiling at Mrs. Young, and she was talking in a way that included him, too. She was a good sort, all right, and you noticed the difference she made to Mum. Not so many rows, not so much complaining, and Mum could certainly complain at times, as though you could help being born and being a kid and making a bit of a row with the others in the house.

He swapped the *Puck* with Frank for a *Tiger Tim* and lay

on his stomach reading it, the grown-ups' talk going on monotonously in the background.

"Christmas is not what it used to be, Flo," Mum said. "Remember the parties we had up the coast? Everybody in the district rolling up at the hall across the river and dancing and singing."

"Things are quite dead up there now," Mrs. Young said. "Everybody's drifted away since the freezing works closed down."

"Think I had some of the happiest Christmases of my life up the coast," Mum said.

"Gil was a bit of a lad in those days," Mrs. Young said. "People said how quiet he was, but he could be gay when he had a few spots in him."

Gilbert sneaked a look at his father. He was grinning. "Don't appreciate a place till you leave it," he said.

"You wouldn't be taking it easy in bed if you had stayed there," Mrs. Young said. "But of course you can't stay in a place if there's no money to be made there."

"No, Flo, you must have regular wages where there's a family," Mum said.

"Yes, and there's more opportunity for the kids in a bigger place," Mrs. Young said.

"That's right," said Dad, who was not grinning now.

II

Gilbert thought of God and Jesus Christ who was born in a manger in Bethlehem and the Wise Men and the Virgin Mother and of Mr. Kent telling the wonderful story and himself not listening because it was sunny and he wanted to go down to the waterfront. He thought how once or twice lately he'd told himself there could not be a God up in the sky because, try as he would, he could not think where there was room for God and Paradise there; he had lain on his back in the paddock staring up at the sky and trying to see through the blue and the clouds but there was nothing but the movement of the clouds and the deepening and lightening of the blue, and there was never any sign of God or Paradise. He had told himself that if he didn't think so much he would not have those awful thoughts about there being no God, but all the same it showed he was growing up, and it was silly now to think once Mum and Dad had spelled out words so that he wouldn't understand what they were talking about.

The grown-ups were silent for a while, then Dad said, "Great how the youngsters go for comics," and they looked at you and the others.

Mr. MacNab said his son liked comics and Mrs. Young said you were a real bookworm and you looked up and grinned then went on reading without seeing what you were looking at.

And they got talking about what you and your brothers would probably be when you grew up and you heard Dad say that he didn't think you were sure what you wanted to be and you were angry because you were certain now that you were going to be a journalist and Dad knew that and was only trying to make out you were too young to know your own mind. Yes, your mind was made up, you were going to be a journalist and a bachelor.

"Here, boys, have some," said Mr. MacNab, holding out a stem of big, black grapes.

Sydney and Frank got up in a hurry, and Mum said to look at the young devils and told them they had more chance of getting fruit than Mr. MacNab and Dad, and Sydney and Frank looked disappointed, but Mr. MacNab wouldn't put the grapes down until they had taken some. Then the grown-ups listened to Mrs. Young telling a story about something that happened to her in a shop today, and you were glad because you had the jitters when they were looking at you.

III

"He's a sick man, all right, Helen," Mrs. Young said.

"Well, as a matter of fact, he looked better tonight than he has for some time," Mum said. "You cheered him up, Flo. He's been looking forward to you visiting him. So many wet blankets call on him, you know."

"I don't believe in talking about gloomy things to invalids," Mrs. Young said. "Joke with them, kid them along. What's the sense telling them they look sick? They know they're sick."

Somewhere in the hospital grounds a band was playing "Silent Night," and the younger kids ran to the top of the drive to see it. Gilbert followed his mother and Mrs. Young.

Down in Stout Road the crowds would be enjoying Christmas Eve, and there would be noise and happiness, he thought. But he did not want to be down there. He would like it if he knew he would enjoy himself, too, but he would not, he would stand around watching other people play and laugh, and he would be too shy to join in. It was not like last year, he didn't kid himself so much now; no more thinking he would become smart and casual just like that. Years would pass before he changed from a gawky kid, and he wanted to cry sometimes when he thought about it, but that would be no good, he had to make the best of what he was.

"We'll miss you, Flo, when you go back up the jolly old coast."

Yes, they *would* miss her. She had made the house brighter by her visit, and when she was gone Mum would be moody again and moan about her worries, and there would be rows. He would protest about doing a message and she would tell him he was getting lazier and lazier and once upon a time he had been a real help and he would point out that the other kids should do more and before long she would lose her temper and hit him in the face and try to pinch his cheeks to make him howl but he would not cry, he would go into his room and lie on his bed and not come out for tea, and later she would come in to him and say she was sorry and call him love, and at first he would be quiet and refuse to speak, then he would do her a favour by saying he felt all right, and she would look sadly at him and leave the room.

Sometimes he wished he were the only one in the family and had a different father and mother.

Chapter Fifteen

Teddy the Butcher

I

"How WAS your hubbie, Mrs. Cunningham?" asked Mrs. Calcott, scratching her head fiercely.

Helen seated herself on a stool behind the table in the Calcott kitchen. "As well as could be expected," she said, smiling a little sadly.

Jack Calcott looked up from the game of poker he was playing with Teddy and the Ellis girls. "Wait till I get my car, Mrs. Cunningham; run you up to the hospital any time of the day. I'd do anything for you, Mrs. Cunningham."

"You'll never be able to save enough to buy a car," Helen told him.

"Make no mistake about that," he said. "Another month and I'll have a cheque that'll make your eyes pop open. Going to buy a car or maybe a truck."

"Get a V8, Jack," said Agnes.

"Listen to Her Highness talking," he said. "She wants a Buick or a Pontiac right away. No starting with a small jalopy and trading it in later for a big one. Not her, she wants a limousine now."

"It was only a suggestion," Agnes said.

"I'll consider it," he said.

"Won't it be lovely?" his mother said, a smile all over her face.

"Makes such a difference when you have a car," said Helen, thinking of her rides with Fred and Ernie.

"You must take me down to see my sister," Mrs. Calcott said. "I wonder what she looks like. We haven't see one another since we were kids."

"I'll take you anywhere, as long as you pay for the petrol," Jack said.

Helen felt something rubbing against her leg and she reached under the table and a dog licked her hand and she gave it a kick and it yelped.

"Butch, get out from under there!" Mrs. Calcott shouted.

"Has he got fleas?" Helen asked.

"Lousy," Teddy said.

Under cover of the table, Helen gave another kick, and the dog—a dirty-coated foxie—whimpered across the kitchen and out the back door. Animals in the house gave her the creeps, she thought.

"Those kids are mad on cats and dogs," Mrs. Calcott said.

"If they don't get rid of that kitten they brought home, I'll chop its bloody head off," Teddy said.

"Oh come on you, open it, it's a jackpot," said Betty.

"It's got a scab over its eye, and I'll chop its head off and put it out of its misery," Teddy said.

"Hhh, what a he-man," Betty said. "Can you open it?"

"I'll chop its head off," he muttered, opening the jackpot for threepence.

Shuddering at the way he had spoken, Helen told herself she didn't know how anybody could have the nerve to kill an animal, the very thought gave her the woollies, and she was so scared of the sight of blood she couldn't kill even a chook, but it all depended how soft-hearted you were, she supposed. She glanced at the range where a stew was cooking and felt uneasy about the tea they were in for; Mrs. Calcott couldn't cook for nuts, and no wonder her old man belted her if the food he got was anything like what was put down in front of you and the kids.

Oh, well, it was good of the old dear to invite her to tea, and it was better than going home to a lonely house to muck about getting things ready. Since Flo had gone she was all on edge for somebody to talk to, and she would wander about the house looking in cupboards and taking up mats and there would be nobody but the kids running in and upsetting all your work, and she had quarrelled with Ernie and he had been really annoyed this time so she supposed she wouldn't see much more of him. She told herself she wasn't sorry to have a spell from Mulligan, but it seemed that despite herself she missed his banter and the suggestion of adventure that his talk of Al Summers seemed to give. Someone to talk to, to talk to, that's what she needed.

"You should have come over for Christmas, Mrs. Cunningham. The boys had a real wild party."

"I *was* coming, but a friend turned up and I couldn't get away," she said.

"I was rather tiddly," Agnes said. "We all were."

"You were stinking drunk, Agnes," Teddy said.

"I only had a few," Agnes said.

"A few too many, old girl," Jack said.

"It was a party, wasn't it? Isn't that where you have a spot? Wouldn't be a party without a drink, would it, Mrs. Cunningham?"

"I shouldn't think so."

"That's what I reckon. Come on, you jokers, play cards or I'll go home and read a book."

"That's a laugh," Teddy said. "*You* read a book?"

"Yes, ignorant," Agnes said. "Bet I've read more books than you have."

Mrs. Calcott swished a spoon in the stew while the card-players continued their game.

II

"Listen to the row those kids are making," Jack said. "What they doing in that room? They should be out in the sun while it's still there."

"Never you mind about the little ones," his mother told him. "The big kids will hit them if they go outside." She went to the back door and yelled to Teddy to hurry up in with the wood for the range.

Suddenly the door of the small room at the right of the kitchen flew open and Rachel ran out, a rotten apple following her and splonking against the wall above Jack.

"Bugger me Charlie!" he shouted, jumping up and making a grab for Rachel, who dodged him and ran outside. Bubs and Anne giggled as they followed her.

Helen thought what a little tike Bubs was becoming, and she wondered if Anne and Rachel were a bad influence on her baby.

Jack was quite nasty about the apple landing on the wall, not that it made any difference to the wall's appearance.

"They were only playing," Mrs. Calcott told him.

"Might have hit me," he said.

"And spoiled the part in your hair," Agnes said.

"No lip from you," Jack said.

"You needn't be offensive," Agnes said.

Jack went on looking surly until he got a full house and collected the pool.

Good heavens, what next? thought Helen when Mrs. Calcott invited her into the dining-room to see the new radio. It was certainly a beautiful set and about the most expensive on the market, and it looked out of place in the Calcott dining-room. Mrs. Calcott beamed as she turned the regulator up.

. . . spinning dreams of an old-fashioned garden
and a maid with her old-fashioned beau. . . .

Helen listened dreamily to the song; it was one of her favourites and suggested a world she had not really lived in but would have if she'd been given the chance.

Sometimes it seems that I can hear her in the twilight
At the organ softly singing Old Black Joe.
There's an old spinning-wheel in the parlour
Spinning dreams of the long, long ago. . . .

"It's a lovely radio," she said as she followed Mrs. Calcott back to the kitchen.

"We'd have a decent home if the old woman would keep it in order," Jack said. "Not much good buying things when they aren't respected."

Mrs. Calcott went red, and Helen felt sorry for her, but it was true what Jack said, though he shouldn't shame her in front of other people. Nothing showed what sort of a person you were like your home did, and she was glad she had nothing to be ashamed of in that respect, though there were times when she felt like setting a light to the whole box and dice with herself and the kids inside. She was scared to think how often she had been close to doing that, and she hoped that in the trying time ahead of her she would resist the temptation; for the sake of her kids she must control herself. She had been a good mother, just as she had been a good wife, and she would go on being one.

III

Rachel came screaming up the back steps. "He cut its head off, Teddy cut pussy's head off! Look at Teddy, Mum, he cut pussy's head off!"

Helen followed the others to the door. For a time the Ellis girls blocked her from seeing anything.

"You young hound," she heard Mrs. Calcott saying. "Teddy, what you want to do that for?"

Helen looked fearfully over the yard. Teddy stood grinning by the chopping block, his hand resting on the handle of an axe, the head of which was buried in the block. Head severed, the body of a small black kitten lay like a torn piece of rag.

Rachel and Bubs and Anne were looking at one another and then up at their mothers, not seeming to understand. Standing with their backs to the wash-house wall, Gilbert and Clive and Izzy seemed to be waiting for something to happen.

"Teddy the butcher!" Jack called.

"Sixpence a pound," Teddy said.

"You're a wicked boy," his mother told him. "You girls come inside, and Teddy, bury that somewhere and don't let the kids see where you dig the hole."

Helen noticed Agnes walk inside disgustedly, but her sister didn't seem affected. She felt sickened, and even if the kitten had been diseased there was no excuse for chopping its head off, it was brutal, and in front of the kids, too, it was enough to give them nightmares. She led Bubs into the kitchen and told her to play with the twins in the small room. Rachel was crying, and she heard Bubs and Anne consoling her.

Agnes had turned the radio on, and the noise blared through the house:

> The cross-eyed cowboy on the cross-eyed horse
> Goes round and round and round,
> Going here and there, but he don't get anywhere,
> Whoa! Giddy-ap! Whoa!

She wanted to be away from the place and she had less desire now than before for tea and it was as though the Calcotts were strangers. She longed to talk to somebody like Flo Young or Fred Burgess or even Ernie Mulligan, and she wished Flo hadn't gone home, and that Fred was in Gladston, and that she hadn't quarrelled with Ernie. Her unhappiness was returning, and she was frightened.

Chapter Sixteen

Murder in Lovers' Lane

I

GIL WOKE up suddenly, his body feeling like ice. Dully aware of the stillness of the moonlit summer night, he lay uncovered and shivering before pulling the bedclothes over himself. He'd never get back to sleep, he'd lie here until the morning nurse came with a thick cup of bodyless tea and awakened him, so she thought, to start another day.

He'd had a crook dream about the freezing works, and it started with him in his shirt sleeves hammering boxes together and a huge red-faced joker with a belly spilling over the top of his working trousers strolling up to him for a yarn and talking of the screw to be made in the chambers and of shorter hours and how it wasn't tough once you were used to it. And this joker led him to the locker room on the slaughtering floor, and he was given pieces of sacking for his feet, bacon-covering for his head, blue denims for his body, and he was led down to the chambers where he shovelled snow from the floor, chipped the ice from the pipes, bashed it, scooped it into bags, piled the bags up, lowered them to the storeroom, followed them there, heaved them onto slides, shoved them towards the rail trucks standing outside in the sunshine.

Also he was telling his wife he was tired, telling one of the kids to get his slippers and the others to cut out the noise, and he was sitting by the fire reading the paper while his wife ironed clothes at the table, and then he was lying in bed with one hand across his wife's body, and later he was moving this hand over her breasts and down to the, down to the thighs, and there was no stirring him, no stirring her, and he didn't know whether that had happened really or whether the failure belonged only to the dream, he'd remember any failing, surely, and he guessed it must be the dream. Well, he forgot the dream and remembered times up the coast when there *had* been a stirring as he lay beside her and worked in the dark to raise the long and irritating nightie and raised himself and with fitful breathing moved as he sank into the submissiveness of the beloved body.

—Occasionally he strolled from the chambers on a walk to get rid of the shakes, and he'd nose in at the killing and see the great blood pools reaching over the floor to the drains and see the throat-slashing of the dangling animals and say what a bugger of a job and dodge the lamb carcasses as they swung towards the freezers and finish his smoke and return to the snow.

How often did the nurse find him with his old john lying limply? Gave him the shakes to think how often. No wonder he had crook dreams.

II

Remember when you were a kid, Gil?

Too bloody right I do.

Remember the sheilas you had?

I remember just about everything. I remember kid's faces, remember their sayings even if I don't remember their names, remember the looks even of the ones now dead.

Did I tell you about the young bastard that gave me the scar on me face, Gil? I'm working on the Enfield, see, with the bloody pull-through, see, and and and and

Yes, Mac, and he said this and you said that and he took a poke at you with his and you got the and you've never lost it and you can't forget it or won't talk of anything but the damned I've heard it over and over and over and I'm sick of hearing it fair go.

Well, we'll talk about the kids, oh I told you Des got a couple of sixers the other day, scored fifty-seven and caught when he's going goodoh. Great boy, that.

Family pride's a fine thing, but reckon kids satisfy your liking for yourself, keep you going on forever and forever, name your kids after you and hint that they name theirs after you so that you go on and on. Why can't my boy understand? What have I done to him? I want to love him. Bashfulness, maybe, but even bashful kids get round to talking to their Dads.

Tired, Gil?

Yes, Mac.

Hellish tired, Gil.

Must be the heat. The heat gets you down.

That's a beaut, you're down, all right, that's a beaut, we're down, all right, boy.

Won't be long now.

You're certainly cheerful.

The breeze has died and it's hot and I get cranky these hot windless days.

—The words, swinging slowly from one to the other, received with no interest and anticipated before being uttered, formed casually into chatter that was reiterated and expanded but took on no meaning.

Nice night for a murder, he thought.

III

Down on Gladston flats a man and a woman are seated in a car in tree-shaded Lovers' Lane, so it would go in *True Detective*. All times of night cars are parked in this lane and a lot of things happen here that are not as unusual as some of the people concerned imagine.

The woman is a blonde with moist red-red lips and hair that has been tumbled up by the boy-friend's meaningful fingers that are now busy feeling her up, and she seems a good sort and is having some fun after a long day at the office where she typed four letters and spent about two hours telling a fellow-floosie what happened at a dance the night before. The only jarring note is that the man is married, but 'struth that doesn't bother the blonde because anyway she reckons married men more often than not make the best lovers and they're more considerate.

"Love me?"

"You're ravishing."

"Adore me?"

"Like this I do."

"O-o-o! Oo-oo!"

"Or like this."

"Darling, darling!"

"We're cramped."

"I'll slip this down."

"It's awkward here."

"Just a tick, darling."

"There."

"I love you, love you, love you."

BUT—a shadow breaks from the other shadows in Lovers' Lane and approaches the car and there are curses and a woman's scream and the sound of two shots and the blonde lies dying and the slayer is swallowed up by the shadows, and bravely the wounded man drives from the lane, blood dripping on thighs that so lately were emphasising his love for the girl with tumbled-up blonde hair.

—The *True Detective* reader felt sudden terror. No blonde was the woman, she was Helen, and the man was some joker he didn't know, and the slayer was himself!

No, he'd never have thought of doing a thing like that. Even when he had the haemorrhage he wouldn't have killed her. But that incident was closed and must be pushed from the mind. He wanted peace, and he must *try* to get some sleep.

The oversized hammer he now saw was to nail up boxes, was to nail up boards on Bill Coulter's offices at the freezing works, was to hammer him back into his place in this world.

IV

Sick and exhausted, he lay too tired to think further. He broke out in sweat and pushed the blankets down. His inside came up, and he tried to reach a towel but missed and puked on the veranda floor. His breathing came quickly and noisily.

Chapter Seventeen

To Hell with Worrying

I

"I DON'T think we better meet again, Ernie," said Helen. "I'm not good company for you any more. I got so much on my mind. Gil getting worse, creditors worrying me, growing kids to care for. I simply can't stand more worry. And it worries me nearly sick when I think about going out with you and what Gil's relations would say if they knew, how they'd tell him, and that'd probably be the end of him."

"Now you're sick of me?"

She moved slightly along the seat, away from him. She wanted sympathy, and he was getting his back up and was going to be selfish. Once again she felt an enormous dislike for him; those things about him that she had taken a fancy to were offensive now, and she criticised his thinness, his shortness, his round shoulders, and his insolent manner, and she asked herself why she had not considered them faults when he had first called about the radio.

They sat in silence, the garden beside the Playtime Club still, and the night air mild and perfumed with flower scents, and the far-away hall band playing a fox-trot.

She wished he hadn't ended her three long weeks of loneliness, a little longer and she'd have forgotten about him. But he had to turn up again and want her to go out, and she had imagined from the thankfulness she felt on seeing him that they would have a beautiful time together and so she had listened to him, but now she wished she hadn't, she wished he'd keep out of her life.

"You say your husband is getting worse?" He moved beside her, his voice sounding disinterested.

"I'm terribly worried, Ernie." She tried to speak normally to him, to loosen the tightness in her throat. "I've got the feeling there's not many more days on this earth for him. I don't know what'll happen if I lose him. How can I care for a family of growing boys and girls on my own?"

"Maybe he'll get better. Anyway, you've managed on your own for so long, you'll be all right. Don't worry, honey. Worrying won't fix things."

"The other day he had his foot out of the blanket, Ernie, and I felt it, and it was stone cold. I got an awful fright. It was freezing as though all life had gone out of it. They say you die from the feet up, you know."

"Probably the cold day."

"No, Ernie, it was a warm afternoon. Gave me a real scare. On the way home I thought of all the times I wished something would happen one way or the other so I'd know where I was, but I knew I didn't want him to die, and I thought of all the times we had together and I was dumpy and soon as I was in the house I howled."

Ernie lit a couple of cigarettes, passed one to her. "Honey, if you feel like crying now, lean on Uncle Ernie's shoulder and have one."

"I don't think you understand, Ernie. You're all out for a good time. Not everybody's as easy-going as you."

"Hell, I do understand. I could tell you I thought you had a lousy life, and I could complain about the depressing things that happen to me, too, how trouble would kill me if I let it get on top of me. But what's the use? We all have worries. The thing to do is to get as much enjoyment from life as life will give you. It's that simple. To hell with worrying."

She glanced at him curiously, the tightness in her throat relaxed, and she wondered if perhaps he did understand. "Other women seem to have more incentive to live than I have. I slave away, but what thanks do I get? Golly, I don't blame those women you read about in *Truth* who kill their kids in a fit of madness. I know what the poor devils have to put up with."

"If you want a good time why not have one with me when I can give it to you right away?"

"It's not good times I want really. I just want to live decently in comfort without being tormented all the time. But I'm grateful for the good times you've given me, Ernie. Think you saved my life the past few months."

"Nice to know."

"Only I'm so muddled up, can't think what to do. I keep thinking it might be as well if we didn't see each other any more."

"And you still feel that way?"

"I don't know."

"Well, how about forgetting it until you're sure?"

"We can't go on until something terrible happens to force us to separate."

"Good God, Helen, what sort of terrible thing possibly could happen? There's nothing to stop two people from being friendly. Feel like a drink?"

"I don't mind."

She followed him through the garden to the road where the Chev was parked. She studied his back and his eager way of walking and, remembering his advice about not worrying, she thought, Oh well he's not a bad little joker.

II

She lay tipsily against the back of the seat while Ernie slipped her white black-buttoned tunic over her head and pressed his face against her breasts.

She was comfortable in the deep seat except for her head, but he read her thoughts and quickly folded his coat into a pillow for her, stroking her forehead as she leaned back.

"Happy?"

"Mmm," she said fuzzily.

"You're drunk."

"Oh, I am not, Ernie!"

"Yes you are, honey. You're a lucky girl. Wish I could get utterly drunk, so drunk I didn't know what was happening."

"Ernie! You do know what you're doing to poor little Helen?"

"Sure, I'm doing this thoughtfully, knowing all that happens."

"Well, you're hurting."

"I love your voice, specially when it says things in its shy way. I don't love it so much when it complains, but, voice apart, I love you all the time."

"I was a very shy kid, Ernie. I didn't know anything until I was seventeen and started work in a restaurant. Then, golly, did I learn quick!"

"Bet you did."

"I had to learn. No idea the number of sheiks that—"

"I once had a piece out who reckoned she didn't believe in pants. Very handy, I might mention."

"You're shocking, Ernie!"

"Never meant anything to me herself. Hard to resist the no-pants factor, though. Possible to complete the evening in the car. That would be awkward with you, honey, for more than one reason. But mind if I see your legs? I've always admired your beautiful legs. You're not a small woman, and that suits me, too, but you have the most gorgeous pair of legs. See, with the shoe off, there is a perfect foot, and my fingers tell me there is perfect shape in this long soft limb and no housemaid's knee, either, and these soft soft clean thighs. But watch out for varicose veins with elastic as tight as this, honey."

"Suppose you think I'm another of your tarts. I told you I wasn't. That's why I wouldn't let you that time. I didn't want you thinking of me as a loose woman, Ernie. I'm not, I'm not."

"You need another brandy."

"I want to dance. That band's playing such lovely tunes. Can't we go inside and join all the people and I want to be where the band is, among the people in the coloured frocks. Aren't they nice coloured frocks, Ernie?"

"Here, drink this."

"Ooo, it's nasty."

"We'll call at the cottage, honey, and dance on our ownsome. Much better idea. No stale tobacco smell and body odours."

"All right, love."

"I'm forgiven?"

"You did nothing, love. It was silly old me. Always getting

wrong ideas. I didn't want to quarrel with you the other week, but something made me, and I wanted you afterwards. I'm silly."

"Relax, honey, and I'll hop around to the front seat, and we'll be dancing in a couple of ticks."

On the way to the cottage Helen lay drowsily studying her breasts as they rested full and contentedly, at times glowing in the light of approaching cars, and occasionally Ernie turned round to have a look too.

III

She gazed through the dim light of the bedroom to the curtainless window, the sound of the sea flowing rhythmically and sympathetically to her, and mind and body receiving it with complete happiness. Ernie's body was warm against hers, and she didn't have a care in the world.

Chapter Eighteen

The Smoker

I

THEY LIFTED their bikes over the fence into the plantation of pines up from the beach. The February sun blazed from a wide blue sky, and they were sweating. Inside his pants Gilbert's togs chafed his skin, and he was impatient for the water to swish about his body.

Izzy went off on her own, and the boys undressed in the trees by the side of the stretch of wasteland that was the Gladston rubbish dump. Followed by Gilbert, Frank, and Sydney, Clive ran through the trees and over the dunes and across the sharp sand full lick into the sea, lifting his legs high until the water became too deep and he took a header. Gilbert kept to the left of the long sewer pipe reaching out into the Bay because it was supposed to be unhealthy on the right side and the water was corker and cool, and it was beaut fun splashing around, until suddenly a large wave broke unexpectedly, and his mouth filled with salt water so that he wanted to vomit.

Izzy saw him rubbing his eyes and struggling to catch his breath and poked fun at him and wanted to know if he was drowning and he said he was all right, and he waded out behind her, studying the bright red costume that stuck closely to her body and the white rubber cap on her head and her curves, and thought how he wanted to touch her and yet didn't because he would not know what to do after touching her or what she would say. And to show her he was some swimmer he dived into another large wave, and once more his mouth filled with water, and feeling ill he walked back to the beach.

He lay on the sand watching the others. Out past his two brothers, who were walking along the sewer pipe, and across the sparkling green of the bay, there was a homeboat at anchor, and from behind the breakwater at the busier end of the beach a yacht appeared. Digging his fingers into the warm sand, he thought sleepily how noisy it would be down where the swings and slides and merry-go-rounds were, and there would be hundreds of kids licking ice creams and young men and women sitting close together on the sand and old people leaning against the promenade wall, and everything would be rowdy and disturbing. He hated crowds because it never seemed as though the people in crowds were separate from one another, each crowd had one pair of eyes, and the eyes were always on him, and he longed to be somewhere on his own, like in the quiet shady places in the library.

He saw Izzy's naked body quivering in a heat haze above the cliffs on the right of the bay and he got up and walked along the sewer pipe and told his brothers the mussels they were chipping off were diseased and they ought to hop in the water because swimming would stop them from getting infantile paralysis. Then he jumped from the pipe and, pushing his togs down to his knees, let the water swill between his legs. He watched Izzy and wished he could be a man so he could be like the fellows who took sheilas into the plantation at the dead of night and then went swimming in the nude with them.

II

Clive whistled to a couple of flashlookers who were riding horses along the dunes, but they took no notice and he said, "Nice pair of horses."

Gilbert lay on his belly, a towel over his head, gazing after the riders.

"Remember the horses we rode, Clive?" Izzy asked.

"Yeah, we had great times with old Johnson's nags until he got us a lamming, Gilbert. Told our old man about us pinching them, and we got a hell of a belting."

Gilbert said he'd never ridden a horse. There was one up the coast that everybody rode, but he never did. He was too small.

"My old man was a swine," Clive said thoughtfully.

Gilbert said nothing. He felt funny when kids spoke of their parents as "the old man" and "the old woman." You were taught that your father and mother were the most sacred people in the world and you must love them very much if you wished to please God, and you could not understand when other kids spoke of them casually as though they were ordinary people. You were beginning to feel ashamed that you should kiss your mother every morning when you left for school and you thought you would knock it off when school started again and yet to think that made you nervous as though it would be a terrible thing to do. Yet other kids couldn't kiss their mothers the way you and the others in the family did else they wouldn't talk as they did of them. And though you must love your father as much as you loved your mother you had not kissed him since you were a small kid and probably that was because men didn't kiss their sons but all the same none of it made sense. You felt there was something wrong about it all, but you didn't know whether you were to blame, or your mother and father, or God, or who.

He forgot about it. He was too contented and sleepy and hot to bother just now.

III

Up on the dunes they trod on the dry brown grass clumps off the hot sand. Back of the town abattoir they played King of the Castle until Clive pushed Izzy head over heels to the bottom of the dune and she hurt her ankle. Then they squizzed at some forlorn-looking sheep in the pens inside the abattoir wall and Frank and Sydney spoke of how cruel it was of the men to kill the dumb animals. Gilbert felt that his ears had roasted, and his nose tingled, and he told himself his back would make him squirm tonight, and he'd have a few more freckles.

They left the abattoir smell behind and followed a track into the plantation. Up here the trees were fairly tall, and there was little sunlight except in the firebreaks. You somehow wished you could become lost, but the plantation wasn't big enough for that to happen. They came upon a rusty half-tank standing like a hut in a clearing, and Izzy sat under it and felt her ankle. Gilbert and Clive sat looking at her. Frank found a couple of empty beer bottles near by and wandered off with Sydney to search for more.

"Good in a way about the epidemic," Gilbert said. "We get a longer holiday from school."

"I'd hate to catch infantile paralysis," Izzy said. "Have to go to hospital and not be able to play and go to parties. Gee, it'd be awful."

"We might have lessons over the radio, that's what they reckon," Gilbert said.

"Trust them to think up something like that," Izzy said.

"Doesn't worry me," Clive said. "Starting work next week. Getting a job in a bakehouse."

He envied Clive and he didn't, Gilbert thought. He wanted to go to work, too, but he wanted to have a good education first. He wasn't going to be one of those jokers with no money when he grew up, and the only way to get money was to learn things. "Think I'll go to High before I start work," he said.

"You're clever," Izzy told him.

"Not particularly," he said awkwardly.

"Yes, you are, Gilbert," she said.

"You and your mother coming to the peninsula with us in Jack's truck next month?" asked Clive.

"Mum says we are," Gilbert said. He had wanted Izzy to keep on telling him he was clever, and he was annoyed at Clive for interrupting.

"Have a fag?" Clive took a packet of cigarettes from the sports coat he was wearing above his bathing shorts.

Gilbert accepted a cigarette, noticing that Izzy placed hers between her lips like a grown-up. He was excited and at last it was going to happen and he wanted to and didn't want to, and he remembered speeches by Shimmering that made smoking seem desirable yet made it the cause of the most dread diseases imaginable, and he remembered a drawing in an old school journal of two young men, one healthy-looking with hands on hips and a football at his feet (The Non-Smoker) and the other thin-looking and round shouldered with hands in pockets and a cigarette drooping from his lips (The Smoker), and underneath the drawing the words *Play up, Play up, and Play the Game.* Chaps that smoked cigarettes were weak-willed, Baldy said, and no Central School boy should ever take up the filthy habit. And smoking stunted your growth, and the great athletes never smoked. And it seemed silly if you were always wanting a good body that you should make it hard for yourself by smoking, And what would your father say? Well, what did it matter what *he* said, anyway, and just one cigarette wouldn't harm you.

The other two appeared very casual, and Clive was blowing smoke rings. So this was why he was such a squirt of a kid. He hadn't thought Izzy smoked, though, and it just showed how much you knew about other kids. Well, even if all the kids in Gladston smoked cigarettes he wasn't getting into the habit.

He shifted uncomfortably and twisted secretly so that Izzy would not notice from his togs what had happened.

"Not bad," Clive said. "Myrtle Grove's about the best brand, all right."

"Good," Gilbert said quickly, wanting to splutter out the smoke that was tickling his throat.

He sneaked looks at Izzy. Somehow she did not seem podgy at all now and her brown hair fell thickly down her back and her breasts were large beneath the costume and he looked again and again at the start of them and he would not know what to do if she said he could feel them but they must be important because they were in your thoughts so often, and he noticed the rosiness that had tinted her pale skin, and the few hairs in her armpits when she stretched herself, and he did not look at her face because he knew if he did he would lose the feeling inside him and it was the most wonderful feeling and he did not want it to go.

Not far away a shaft of sunlight emphasised the still gloom of the plantation, and there were patches of yellow on the pine needles and thin grass in the clearing. Did Izzy Calcott explain the mysteriousness that was here, or was it the cigarette?

IV

They played for a while in the rubbish dump, and Frank and Sydney found a bag for their bottles and wanted to hurry up back to town to sell them. They got through the fence to the part of the plantation where they had undressed for the swim and almost stepped on a man and woman embracing. The pair did not notice them. Gilbert stayed watching a few minutes longer than the others. He had never felt more like a kid.

Chapter Nineteen

Night Journey

I

SHE STOOD in the front doorway and watched her kids sitting wrapped up in scarves and coats on the veranda waiting for the truck. The dusk was chilly, and rain did not seem far away. The ride to the peninsula would be long, but that didn't matter because she was sure this brief holiday was going to mean something important to her, and she could pretend that she was leaving for good this house that now seemed like a sulky, freshly-scrubbed child resentful about her and the kids leaving it empty for the week end. At last, she kidded herself, she was getting away from the house in Livingstone Road, Gladston.

She told herself the ride would do her good and the holiday would make a new woman of her and she'd nearly gone mad the past few weeks, and she hated to admit it, but it was mainly over Ernie Mulligan. She had not seen him since the night at the cottage, and though at first she had been glad she soon felt neglected and awfully dumpy, and she saw that he had finished with her and had tossed her aside as he had tossed aside so many other women, and though she wanted to believe it was best this way she still felt she would give anything to see him. With all her heart she hoped the holiday would clear her mind and make her believe in what was sensible. Fancy trusting a character like that! She had been weak. She had known from the start he was a self-opinionated fellow and shady in the bargain and would trample on his mother to get what he wanted. Might have been some excuse for her behaviour if there'd only been Gil, but when somebody like Fred believed in her—oh, to think she could degrade herself for the likes of that rotter!

She looked glumly into the dusk. Then she pulled the front door to, and it was as though the cheery click of the lock was the end of something.

II

"Yoo hoo! Come on, Mrs. Cunningham, we're going, we're going!" called Mrs. Calcott from the cabin of the truck where she sat beside Jack with Rachel on her knee.

Helen hurried out.

"What you got in that case, Mrs. Cunningham? You shouldn't have brought anything, we got plenty."

"Seeing it's my first holiday in years and I might never have another one I thought the damned creditors could wait for their money," Helen said. "Just a few things. My kids will eat their share, if I know them."

She climbed onto the back of the truck, wedged herself between some boxes, and Bubs sat on her lap. Gilbert, Joy, Izzy, Sydney, and Frank crowded together, and Anne went into the cab with her mother.

Izzy called, "Let her go, Jack!" and the truck moved off noisily. The mudguards scraped against the tyres as it chuttered into Massey Avenue, and it sounded as though it would fall to pieces any old time.

A knife-sharp wind whipped them, and she arranged a rug about Bubs. You couldn't be too careful with the infantile paralysis epidemic only just ended.

Sitting there with eyes closed, as the truck rattled out of town onto the southern highway, she felt she was flying from the known to the unknown and in between was confusion, and the thoughts that came so swiftly swept away even more swiftly, so that there was little time to grasp them, and nothing formed into shape. It was as though she were lost, and she looked at her kids for some sort of reassurance, and the first one she looked at was Gilbert and the feeling of loneliness did not go because he had the typical Cunningham look—the look that belonged to Gil and his brother, Jim, and his sisters, Hilda, Denise, Elaine, and Sarah—and this look always made her feel a stranger whose children belonged more to the Cunninghams than to her, and she searched eagerly for her own characteristics in the young faces and, finding them in Frank and Joy particularly, cheered up and told herself she and Gil and the kids were a distinct group of people and all others were strangers. No, she was not alone.

Halfway up the first hill Teddy and Clive came roaring on the motor-bike towards the groaning truck, the bike's long beam shining strangely on pale faces. Shouting at them to get a move on, Teddy raced past the truck, swerving as he did so and getting a curse from Jack. Soon they were high in the hills, crawling along narrow roads from which cliffs dropped sharply into darkness. Bubs had fallen asleep, and the older ones were scaring themselves by looking over the side of the truck and down at the unseen gullies. Occasionally Jack saved the battery by switching off the lights, and once they turned a sharp corner to find a large car almost on top of them and it seemed their last days had come but somehow the truck squeezed past on the outside of the road and went on climbing higher and higher while down in the gorges twinkled the lights from the camps of the workers building the railway through to Gladston. At last the truck stopped, and Jack called : "Ladies to the right, gents to the left!"

Helen strolled into the bush. Back at the truck somebody said to come and have a look at the lights of Gladston, and she was disturbed and thought that she was wrong, she was not leaving Gladston behind, and even after all these hours of travelling the lights of the town were still shining through the black night to remind her she must go back, must go back.

Bitterly she told herself she hated Ernie Mulligan and it was almost as though he was responsible for all her troubles and she could not forget him as she could not forget the town. Even in the loneliness of the silent hills they tormented her. Why couldn't they leave her alone?

III

On and on round hairpin bends, through creeks, past lonely roadside huts in the doorways of which sat roadmen smoking pipes with flickering candles behind them, down into gorges, on and on—until the creaking Ford drove into rain and Jack got out and fixed a tarpaulin cover on the back of the truck and the rain pressed down and the roads became muddy and suddenly the truck's engine stopped and there was a cold and miserable wait while Jack searched for the trouble. And, when once more they were on the move, the lights failed, and they were carried forward into the night like the blind, not knowing what was coming, afraid of the unknown.

Memories of Fred and Ernie and their comfortable cars tormented her. She thought of the many times she and Fred had sat watching the rain from the car, how she thought there was nothing better than sitting sheltered with your lover, how she waited while he went spearing eels. She thought how Ernie had never regarded her as Fred regarded her, as a good pal as well as a lover. Ernie had one idea only, and she would never forgive herself for letting him satisfy this idea.

A nagging started in her brain, and she kept reminding herself that she had made a break with Gladston and she was going to have a glorious holiday and when she did return to town she would have new courage to face her problems. It was a strange world; just now there seemed no reality outside the bumping truck and the invisible country spaces and the round yellow glow of the motor-bike's light following.

Long after midnight the truck slithered down into a paddock on the peninsula, and they could see nothing, hear nothing, only the long roaring crash of the sea. She stepped off the running board of the truck into ankle-deep mud. The flight had ended.

Chapter Twenty

On the Peninsula

I

BEFORE THE sun rose Joy walked from the women's tent to a shaky tin shed at the bottom of the paddock. She saw that they had camped in a small bay through which a creek ran to the sea, and, after perching on the can in the shed for a few minutes, she walked to the beach. The tide was out, and a narrow strip of water flowed between two stretches of sand to form two beaches, and she could not see the ocean over the dunes across the water strip, though she could hear the breakers. To her right, and grey-white against the dull sky, stood tall jagged cliffs on the top of which was a large head-shaped rock that reminded her of a picture of a rock impression of Abraham Lincoln's profile that she'd seen in a magazine at school. On her left the beach curved for several miles as far as a headland covered with black bush.

As she walked back to the tents, the sun came up, and she was glad it was going to be fine because it would be pretty hard to make the kids at school jealous of her if the holiday was a rainy one. Teddy Calcott came down the paddock, and his hair was tangled and his eyes had a sleep-look in them and his teeth were out so that he looked like his mother. She told herself he wasn't so good-looking after all, and that took away his last attraction in her opinion seeing he had no brains to speak of. She peeked into the tent at her mother, Mrs. Calcott and the girls, but the smell nearly knocked her down so she went to the creek to wash.

Her skin tingled from the icy water, and she rubbed hard with the towel. Then she noticed an old Maori man in sleeveless singlet and patched trousers and heavy boots watching her from the opposite side of the creek. He had close-cut grey hair, and his face was wrinkled, and he had a big belly. He held a flax kit.

"Haere-mai, ehoa!" she called to let him see she knew some Maori. She hoped it did mean Greetings.

He smiled back at her. He was selling eggs at a shilling a dozen, and she ran to tell her mother about it, and the Maori got rid of a couple of dozen and said he'd return later with some kumaras. He thanked her mother for her invitation to come over for a chat in the evening. Three pantless Maori kids met him when he walked up from the creek to an unpainted box-like house that stood among some poplars, and Joy called to them, but they went for their lives when they heard her voice.

Everybody was getting up now and telling one another how awful sleeping in a tent was and Joy noticed Ma Calcott digging into the boxes of food before she'd had a wash and this irritated her and she felt like turning up her nose. Somehow she knew there was a difference between her parents and the parents of certain of her classmates, and she disliked nobody as much as she disliked a girl who was snooty about her parents' position, but she never felt superior to any people apart from the Calcotts, and it made her wonder whether some of her classmates looked down on her the way she sometimes couldn't help looking down on Izzy Calcott and her family.

"You're different from your mother; she hasn't had a wash yet," she said to Izzy. Izzy said she was used to her mother, and she said this nervously, Joy thought, and probably she was a wee bit ashamed of her mother, and she couldn't be dumb, she must see the difference between her mother and Mum, for instance.

But she decided she wasn't going to quarrel with Izzy so she dropped the subject and, after breakfast, went down to the beach with the other kids. Teddy and Jack drove off in the truck to pick up a joker and go deer-stalking.

She and Izzy followed Clive and Gilbert up the beach and then through the blackberry bushes that grew thickly on the hill beside the cliffs. Izzy wore a white silk frock and you could see she wore a brassiere and you'd have to ask Mum to get you one, too, soon, you had to be careful at this awkward age. They started climbing and the earth disturbed by Izzy's feet kept falling on her and she seemed far too keen on trying to get right up behind Gilbert. Izzy seemed to have a fancy for Gilbert, but he was shy of girls, and anyway he was like her, he'd fancy something classier than the family belonging to Izzy. What about yourself, who did you fancy? Perhaps the Canadian drill instructor, or the dark, good-looking kid round by High who always had his collar turned up queeny-fashion? No, males made her sick. She didn't mind chatting with boys now and again, but you couldn't tell them your thoughts like you could with your girl friends.

They scrambled around the crags, and Clive wanted to get up on the head-shaped rock but thought he'd better not when they told him to go right ahead.

Looking at the rock, Joy felt sudden fear. She couldn't be sure but somehow this rock reminded her of somebody and she thought hard and then she knew; it was shaped like her father's head. It must be her imagination. No, it was Dad all right. Oh, gosh, she thought. She loved her father and she boasted about him but he was sick and she hated the smell of the hospital and that was why she didn't visit him very often. She wondered if this was one of those premonition things. It was queer, and the more she looked the more certain she became. Well, she would go up to see him every visiting day now. She would take this as a warning from God.

Silly, she thought. He won't die. Nobody dies. He'll go on living like he is now, and he won't die or not die because I go up to see him.

But she couldn't help thinking it was a premonition, and she was glad when the others started back to the beach and called to her. She was thoughtful as she picked a way through the blackberry.

II

After lunch they played cricket, and Gilbert, without bashing but bringing off some good strokes he considered, knocked the golf ball in all directions until finally a sixer landed in the middle of some blackberry and the game ended. The small kids made mud pies in the creek, and Izzy and Joy yapped with their mothers, so Clive and Gilbert went for a stroll along the road down which the truck had come the previous night.

When they could no longer be seen from the tents Clive, who had the pip over Teddy and Jack going deer-stalking without him and called them bastards every now and again, pulled out his cigarettes, and they sat smoking by the roadside.

"Those buggers forget I'm not a kid no more," Clive said. "Christ, I'm seventeen now and making me own living. I work more than them, but they still think I'm a bloody kid."

"What's it like in the bakehouse, Clive?"

"Be getting a rise soon. Boss said I was doing all right. I picked up things quickly, he said."

"I might go to work, too, instead of going to High."

"You're not as old as me, you'll have to keep on at school," Clive said. "Your mother wouldn't let you go to work."

"I'm just on thirteen, but I'm taller than you," Gilbert said. "They reckon I look older than my age."

"You're tall, all right, but you don't look as old as me," said Clive, breathing smoke through his nose.

Gilbert wanted to say that he did look as old as Clive, but he knew he didn't, and he wished he would grow old fast—he didn't want to grow any taller, my gosh—so he could go out to work.

"Know what I'd like now?" asked Clive.

"What?"

"A sheila."

Gilbert grinned and hid behind some cigarette smoke.

"I'd like a nice piece of black velvet," Clive said. "One of those quarter-castes, boy. They give you a good go for your money, they reckon."

Gilbert nodded and puffed quickly on his cigarette.

"I'd take her in the bushes," Clive said. "That's what I'd do. Bet that's what those other jokers have done. Bet they'll take some sheilas with them on the deer-stalking. That's why they didn't bring Aggie and her sister. They didn't want them spoiling their fun. That's why they didn't want me along. I can see through them."

Resentfully he began drawing a picture of a fellow on top of a girl in the dust. The stick he used for the drawing snapped in half with the force he put on it. Then he said, "Let's go look."

"You go, Clive," Gilbert said, scared. "I want to get something at the camp."

"Please yourself," said Clive, walking away.

Gilbert wanted to follow him, he did, he did, and if Clive asked him again he would go. But Clive walked up the road without speaking.

Back at the tents he found them having a cup of tea. Nobody commented when he didn't speak because he was supposed to be a very quiet boy in any case.

He walked along the beach with Izzy and Joy, still wishing he'd gone with Clive. He suddenly realised Joy was walking ahead and he was alone with Izzy and she was looking at him. She was wearing her red bathing costume and it was as though one of the many dreams he'd had since smoking his first cigarette had come true and he searched for words but what should have come—he didn't know what it should be except that it was something to do with the feeling he had when listening to Clive—would not, and he walked beside her, thinking she must notice the silence as much as he did. It was no use, he wasn't like Clive, girls didn't scare Clive.

He was relieved when Joy called, "Hey, you two look at this shell!" and he ran to her and pretended to be interested while she pointed out the strange markings on the shell. Izzy placed her warm hand on his shoulder when she leaned over to look too, and he told himself he disliked her.

III

Dying of curiosity, he watched Clive secretly. Clive, who ate his kumaras and fish hungrily and noisily, had a satisfied smirk, but he might be bluffing.

Eating your tea in the dusk near a campfire reminded you of the kids who were scouts, he thought. But he never wanted to be a scout, and he hated to think of being ordered around like the kids at Y.M.C.A. were ordered around. Bridgen was enough.

At last he said, "Everything go all right?"

"Not bad, son, not bad," Clive told him.

Gilbert was annoyed. He didn't like being called "son". Probably Clive hadn't done anything, he was only trying to make him jealous.

"Suppose you lay somewhere in the sun all afternoon?" he said casually.

"It's a possibility," Clive said.

"Where'd you go?"

"Up the road."

"See anybody?"

"Couple of Maoris."

"See any sheilas?"

"Grab us the salt, will you, Gilbert?"

Gilbert passed the salt. He pretended to lose interest in Clive and turned to listen to his mother and Ma Calcott saying how they hoped Teddy and Jack brought back some tender venison with them.

The old Maori from across the creek appeared with a young

Maori chap and an old woman and a girl. Mum told them to make themselves at home, and they sat down shyly outside the light from the fire. They said little until Ma Calcott brought out some beer, and that made them less shy, and there was a good deal of giggling.

Gilbert stared at the younger Maori woman. Her skin was olive, and he thought she was beautiful though her nose was inclined to be flat. She wore a blue-and-white-print frock and a red cardigan, and she was lying so that he could see the shape of her behind and the line of her thighs.

His mother was saying her Maori blood was the best part of her when he felt Clive poking him. He turned around, and Clive pointed to the Maori girl, but he pretended that he didn't know what Clive meant.

"Hot stuff," Clive said.

He didn't notice him.

"Name's Rangi," Clive said.

"Is it?"

"She told me it was, anyway."

Gilbert didn't speak. He knew Clive was a liar and was trying to make out he knew the girl but he couldn't, and anyway she hadn't looked at him and probably thought he was a kid and it was skiting on Clive's part. "Why don't you say hello?" he asked after a while.

"Don't want to embarrass her," Clive said.

"Oh, yeah," Gilbert said.

The Maoris sang a few songs, and they were good, and the way they sang "Red Sails in the Sunset," for instance, was better than it was sung over the radio. The young Maori sang a long story-song in his own tongue and it made his friends laugh and Mum laughed once or twice too and told them afterwards that she knew just enough Maori to understand the theme of the song and she was certainly tickled by it.

Ma Calcott got some more beer, and the grown-ups went on talking. The old Maori seemed a brainy old joker, and he listened attentively to all that was said and nodded a lot. He seemed like a *sage*. Mum said it must be great to live on the peninsula all the time, and he replied, "The peninsula she like the rest of the world. The people here want the good time, and they do not like fighting. We get enough to live on, and we fish and grow vegetables, and sometimes we lie in the sun. We want a bit of life, and it is the same away from here, in towns like Gladston, in cities like Auckland. But we do not think about it, we have it."

"Yes, you're luckier than the ones in the towns," Mum said. "Not so much rush and worry."

"People they always think there is something better around the corner and they talk about this and worry about it but when they get it they find it isn't so good and they worry for something more around the next corner," said the old Maori. "They don't see the best in their lives is with them all the time and they must stop worrying and enjoy what they have."

"He says it so wisely, doesn't he?" Mum said to the old Maori woman.

"People here call him crackpot, sometime," the woman said, laughing.

"I don't care what people call me," the man said. "They can call me miserable old stinkpot, or they can call me a good fellow, but I don't care. I've got my people, and so I am content."

"Sometime they call him prophet," the Maori woman said.

"Oh, I bet you can read cups then," Mum said to him. "We'll make a cup of tea, and you can read our cups."

But he refused, saying cup-reading was a superstition, and Mum looked around and noticed the kids were still up and told them to go to bed.

Gilbert went reluctantly to the tent. He noticed that Clive and Izzy and Joy hadn't moved, yet his mother expected him to go along with Frank and Sydney. She didn't appreciate that he was getting older. It was not fair. Most of all he was annoyed because Clive could look at the olive-skinned girl on his own and perhaps that kid had met the girl before tonight like he said.

The talk and singing and laughter seemed to go on for hours, and he fell asleep still resentful about the other three being considered old enough to listen to the grown-ups' talk while he wasn't. He dreamed of a naked Rangi and Izzy and awakened to find the camp silent and rain falling lightly on the tent. Frightened in case The Thing had happened and Mum or Ma Calcott would notice it when they made the beds in the morning, he felt nervously under the clothes and was relieved to find everything was jake.

He got up and went to the tent flap and looked out, and there was nothing but the drizzle and the noise of the sea. The embers in the fire glowed dimly, then appeared to die as he watched. He got back into bed.

IV

Only afterwards had she wondered whether the old Maori had said something that she should have tried to understand. Did he mean that the peninsula was the ideal place to live, or did he mean more than that? Well, she certainly did seem to see Gladston in a new light from here. She saw herself as a normal woman bringing up a family, and she should be as contented with her lot as any woman. It was simply that she worried too much and forgot that she did have friends in Gladston and had had quite a few good times in her life there. There was Bella Simpson, for one, and others with whom she could play cards and gossip. And yet—these women did not satisfy her. She knew there was a brighter life around the corner, and she didn't care what the Maori said, any life would be better than her present one. It sounded all right at first to live on the peninsula, but she'd had enough of small towns and the backblocks.

She studied the group of Maoris watching the Calcott boys fishing, and she thought they looked very consumptive, and the kids were skinny and old-looking for their age. Probably the Maori was a crackpot after all. What did he know of her particular troubles, anyway?

It had rained since early morning, and now a bleak wind came up, too, and the sky darkened, and the smoke from a bush fire across one of the bays hung low. Teddy and Jack couldn't get their dinghy past the shore breakers, so they decided to call it a day and start the trip home. The Ford had to be pushed before it would start, and everybody was testy and in no holiday mood.

There was more room on the back of the truck this time, but it was still uncomfortable, and the rain persisted and made them miserable. Then, on top of one of the hills, the truck's engine coughed and stopped. They were out of benzine and had to sit waiting in the sleety cold while Teddy rode off on his motor-bike to the nearest railway camp.

Jack came around to the back of the truck and lifted the tarpaulin. "Do you believe in the hereafter, Helen?" he asked cheerfully.

"I don't know, I suppose so," she said.

"That's a good job," he said. "That's very good because we'll be here after midnight, old girl."

Chapter Twenty-One

Street-Corner Radical

HE FELT important standing on the corner near the town clock talking to a grown-up, even though few people would be jealous of him seeing the grown-up was Max Carson, the young fellow who gave Dad pamphlets about Russia and working-class history and was supposed to be nuts. But you never could tell, some of the kids might notice and think Well, Cunningham must be brainy all right, and fancy being interested in politics at his age.

"Yes, your piece on the kids' page about the holiday was all right," Carson said.

"Thought I'd try and win half-a-crown," said Gilbert, feeling the clipping he'd carried in his pocket since the *Age* published his article.

"A nice feeling for words," Carson said. "Your Dad said you wanted to be a reporter. You like writing essays?"

"They reckon at school I'm pretty promising," said Gilbert.

"Journalism's all right as a profession, I suppose, but it's not so glamorous as it's cracked up to be in the pictures, you know."

Gosh, he knew that, he'd been warned about it plenty of times.

"Mightn't be so bad if what the reporter wrote was really printed," Carson said, "but they change the stories in the editor's room, and even if the stuff is not altered they make the reporter get into the habit of writing so that he knows his story will appear and not offend the boss."

You liked talking about papers and books, and anybody connected with newspapers seemed the luckiest person alive, and when you were sitting at the subscribers' table in the public library you would see men and women reading important-looking books and you would wish you could read them, too, and you would like to talk to the people, but you guessed they looked on you as just another kid who didn't know much.

You were fascinated by a good-looking, well-built fellow who was often in the library and knew the girls who checked the books, and you wondered what he was thinking when he read the magazines, and after a while he would glance at you as though feeling your eyes. On Saturdays you used to watch him playing cricket at the Oval, and he was pretty good and was a Gladston representative. And you supposed it was because he was interested in books that you were fascinated by him.

You pictured yourself as a well-known journalist and people would remember you from your schooldays in Gladston and the kids you went to school with would tell their friends about the swell essays Gilbert Cunningham wrote and your parents would be proud of you. You hoped Dad would stay alive until you became famous or did something anyway to make him proud of you. Mum reckoned he was getting worse, but you didn't think about that much.

"The thing to do, whether you become a journalist or not, is to keep believing in yourself," Carson said. "Set your mind on something and aim for it and never mind how you get there. Don't take too much notice of what unthinking people reckon. Would have cut my throat long ago if I took notice of the things I'm called. And don't you go getting tangled up with women."

Gilbert said he was going to be a bachelor.

"They can still get you into trouble."

Gilbert listened.

"More trouble than they're worth. But you won't be thinking about them yet a while."

That's all he knew, Gilbert thought.

"A man believes in something, and he has his work to do, well, auto-eroticism's better—preferable—" Carson shut up. He looked worried.

Gilbert watched the faces passing by along the street. You knew all the faces, though you mightn't know their owners' names. You knew the fat women and their husbands and the girls who were supposed to be fast and the ones whose people had money and the characters like the lame girl married to a bearded old man. You knew them all by their faces, the same old faces.

You didn't know what to think about Carson's advice. You told yourself you'd get on better with girls when you were older, and it was puzzling to hear Carson reckon sheilas were bad for you, but he was over twenty and ought to know. You'd change the subject.

Pointing to the book under Carson's arm, he asked, "That about Russia, Mr. Carson?"

" It's about the bourgeoisie—*The Fate of the Middle Classes.* Bit heavy for you, Gilbert."

" We don't read much about Russia at school. Mr. Bridgen says all Hitler's worried about is Russia, though. He says Hitler doesn't want to make war on England. You reckon Hitler's clever?"

" If it's clever to dress up evil ideas and delude the people as to who his backers are. Germany will make more armaments. She'll press for the return of her colonies. She wants Franco to win the Spanish War because that would be a knock for Communism, she thinks. And Communism—the true Marxist philosophy—is the greatest threat to Fascism."

Gilbert began to feel fidgety. He said he supposed he'd have to read more about those things.

" Plenty of time."

Gilbert said he liked history.

" They don't indicate sufficiently the lessons to be obtained from the past, just give you a lot about kings and dates and royalty gossip. Everybody should know what's happening in the modern world and New Zealand is not apart merely because of her Labour Government, and the fact that she's supposed to lead the world in social reform. Why, let me see—less than two per cent of the population of this country makes around about a fifth of the total private income. That means something."

Gilbert couldn't figure what it did mean, but he knew from the serious way Carson spoke that what he said must be true. He might be nuts, but he knew a lot, and it was good talking to him, only you were too young to be able to turn his talk over in your mind and let it sink in so you could make a speech in general discussion period as though you'd thought it all out for yourself.

" Gee, I better be going. Got some messages to do."

" Tell your Dad I'll pop up and see him on Sunday; he better get stuck into those pamphlets."

Riding along Stout Road, Gilbert wondered if girls were as bad for you as Carson reckoned.

Chapter Twenty-Two

Sleepyhead

"Is HE asleep?"

"Dropped off an hour ago, Nurse."

"Wonder if he'd like his milk now."

"Wake him up, go on. He can't be tired. Does nothing else but sleep these days. Can't get him talking on anything."

"I don't like to wake him. I think I'll let him finish his nap."

No, he was not asleep. He could hear the faraway voices, and he assumed Mac and the nurse were whispering, but possibly his hearing was crook and they were really bawling out at the top of their lungs. He could be sure of nothing beyond the desire to be left alone. He was not resentful, and he didn't mind milk, only he didn't feel like opening his eyes, and he damned well wasn't going to.

"He looks bad, Nurse."

"Yes, he has been in better spirits. But the days will soon be milder. How are *you* finding the weather, Mr. MacNab?"

"Bit better service in this show and I'd be happier."

"Go on with you. You're the sort that wants someone fussing around you all the time, aren't you? Your poor wife must have been run off her feet."

"It's the service here. It's chronic, fair go."

"Well, Mr. Cunningham never complains."

"Said he gave up complaining when he found it was hopeless to expect any improvement in the service. But I'm going to fight for my rights."

"I think we'll mould you into shape in the end, Mr. MacNab. We'll have you nicely trained."

"Think I'll put in a complaint to the doc. How about something to eat with my tea, and I'll postpone the complaint?"

"Oh, just look at that! On the floor!"

The startled voice made him curious, and he opened his eyes to find the nurse looking straight at him, and it was too late to shut them again, so he blinked them to make it seem he'd suddenly awakened.

"Sleepyhead," she told him.

He worked up a smile.

"You ought to be ashamed of yourself," she said.

"Haven't been asleep long, Nurse," he said.

She picked up something from the floor of the veranda. "It's not that," she said. "It's this lovely book you had sent to you. Lying on the floor. And stained, too." She showed him a tea stain on the Coronation souvenir.

"Must have fallen out when I was getting something from the locker," he said hollowly.

"And there's another book down here, too," she said. "Hmm, *Left-Wing Communism;* I bet that's interesting, Mr. Cunningham."

"Haven't read it," he said. "You can take it if you want to."

"No, I'll put it in the locker with the Coronation book. Goodness, what a terrible stain. It's a shame to spoil such a lovely book, especially after the King went to the trouble of sending it to you."

"Thought the wife took it home," he said.

She gave him a hell of a wonderful smile, adjusted the bedclothes, and went away to fetch his milk.

"How you feeling, Gil?"

"Not too good, Mac. You reckon they'd let me see the wife tonight?"

"Should think so, Gil."

"I want to talk to her."

"They ought to let her come up."

"I'll ask Nurse Johnson. I thought if Helen came up tonight I could talk things over, I want to straighten some—I wonder if that nurse would take a message—"

"She'll do it, Gil. Don't worry, boy."

"You feel cold, Mac?"

"No, I feel hot as—well, it *is* a little chilly come to think of it. Cover yourself up, Gil, you might catch a chill."

"Here she comes now. I'll ask her if she could take a message. A man ought to be able to see his wife when he feels like it."

Chapter Twenty-Three

Maytime

I

HER LIPS were annoyingly pale and did need lipstick, thought Joy as she studied herself in the mirror in her mother's room, but if she put any on Mum, who reckoned it was ridiculous for fifteen-year-olds to use make-up, would lose her temper and kick up an awful fuss. Cynthia Green was bound to be wearing some, and it was hateful thinking she would be one up on you. Posing haughtily, she turned sideways to get a better view of her breasts. Yes, Joyce Cunningham, she told herself, you're really growing up. What a pity *she* doesn't realise it!

She brushed her new fawn-coloured skirt, thinking it matched her brown twin-set perfectly, and she was thrilled at the chance of showing off the new clothes that her evening with Cynthia at the Majestic would give her. She glanced round the room, crossed to the door and shut it quietly, then hurried back to the mirror, and, taking a lipstick phial from her handbag, stared at her face thoughtfully before tentatively drawing the phial across her lips.

The door opened suddenly, and Gilbert said, "What you up to in here?"

Recovering from the shock, she hastily ran her tongue over her lips, slipped the phial back in the bag, and walked away from the mirror. "Mind your own business," she said.

"You can't go out tonight," he told her.

"And why not, Pop?" she asked.

"You know Dad's not too good, and they reckon anything might happen," he said. "Mum says the doctor is worried about him. You heard her say that. So you can't go out. She might want you."

"She said I could go. And that's that as far as I'm concerned, Mr. Busybody."

"She's worried, and she probably didn't hear what you asked her."

"Pooh! Let me past, I've got an appointment."

Repeating that she shouldn't be going to the pictures tonight, he followed her down the passage, and he was very annoying and seemed to get a swelled head like this far too often as though he knew more than she and had more feelings. Well, she loved her father as much as he did, and she certainly wouldn't be going out if she thought for a minute there was anything wrong about it. But she'd promised to meet Cynthia, and she certainly would be a fool to disappoint her.

She looked into the kitchen. The kids were looking at comics, and her mother was not reading the *True Story* on the table before her but staring into space.

"Good night, Mum."

Her mother continued to frown, then said, "Oh, hooray," as

"To the pictures. You said I could go, remember?"

Her mother continued to frown, then said, "Oh, hooray," as though she didn't care what you did.

She poked her tongue out at Gilbert to show him he wasn't such a smartie as he thought he was and walked out into the night, the memory of the quiet of the kitchen and her mother's frowning face and Gilbert's know-all expression remaining with her until she reached Massey Avenue corner. Then she began thinking of the romance there was in walking at night and soon pushed from her mind the thoughts of the irritations at home.

How beautiful it would be if she were walking along with some nice young man, and how surprised old Cynthia would be to see her with him! And one night perhaps the thing she was scared of happening, but in her heart wanted to happen, would happen, and a chap would jump from the darkness and attempt to assault her, to *rape* her, and she would struggle courageously but he would be too strong and would attack her, then suddenly repent and say he hadn't realised she was a nice girl, and would leave her, and then one day he would see her down-town and would raise his hat politely to her and tell her she had shown him what a terrible thing it was to be lonely and he had decided that he loved her, and she would say she loved him, too, and so they would be lovers, and—well, it would never happen but you couldn't help dreaming.

Gee, but she was irked (I am irked, she thought) about Gilbert trying to spoil her evening and Mum looking so sour and it made her feel she'd been wicked and anybody would think Dad was on his deathbed. Mum was exaggerating, her conscience was pricking her. She must think you were dumb sometimes. You could put two and two together. If she only realised how much you did know. Wow!

II

"You ready?" asked Cynthia. "Dressed to kill and nowhere to go."

"You really like my twin-set, Cynth?"

"It's ducky."

"Matches the skirt well, doesn't it?"

"Yes, it's ducky," Cynthia said. "Like mine?"

"You look super," said Joy, thinking Cynthia didn't have particularly good taste, and it was rather goofy wearing green clothes just because your name was Green, but yellow and green probably suited her as much as any other combination.

They walked from the toilet and stood outside the Majestic watching the people gather in the brightly-lit foyer.

"I adore Jeanette MacDonald and Nelson Eddy," said Cynthia, keeping an eye out for any boys who might happen along.

"They're lovely," said Joy, patting her hair and looking at her reflection in a milkbar window.

"Must be wonderful to be a film star."

"Think of all the beautiful clothes you could have."

"What about the boy friends?"

"You always think of that."

"Don't you?"

"I'm not always talking about boys, anyway."

"My big sister says it's best to talk about your feelings for boys and not hide them, else it'll do something to you. She says people have gone mad through keeping things hidden."

"No danger of that where you're concerned, Cynth."

"I'll say."

"Well, look who's coming," Joy said.

"Whee!" Cynthia said.

A couple of Form V Professional boys, wearing sports coats, greys, and open-necked white shirts, walked towards them. Joy suddenly became interested in the vividly coloured cutout of Jeanette MacDonald that stood in the foyer entrance.

"Good evening, girls. Alone?" His name was Rickard, and he was tall and sallow-skinned, and he had brown eyes and carefully combed fair hair.

"Hello," said Cynthia. "They say this picture's very good. Have you seen it?"

"Harry and I were about to enter when we noticed you two girls standing winsome and charming here. We thought you might possibly give us the pleasure of your company."

Joy looked doubtful. "I don't know," she said.

" Oh, I realise it's the woman's privilege to procrastinate," Rickard said.

" Some word," Joy said.

" Picked it up out of a book I was reading in math class the other day."

" We'll be late," Cynthia said. " Hurry up, you two." She walked into the foyer with Harry.

Joy and Rickard followed.

III

It was so thrillingly beautiful and so sad and so romantic and there were such lovely songs in it, like " Sweethearts," that it seemed quite appropriate when Joe Rickard slipped his arm around her. At interval she discussed the teachers at High with him and was pleased to find he liked the ones she liked and disliked those she disliked, and she decided he was a nice boy.

The way the sweet old lady told the story of her love for a handsome singer who was killed by a hatefully jealous man was simply too moving for words, and she was excited by every moment of it and would gladly see it again if she had the chance.

She told herself this was one of the happiest moments of her life. It was as though there were nothing but a kind of poignant loveliness about the world, and there was no pain, no ugliness; and she saw how, far from being cruel and bitter, death could be very beautiful. Pictures were good that way.

Outside after the show Cynthia said she felt like crying at times, and Harry told her she should have mentioned it and he'd have lent her his hanky. Cynthia said boys didn't feel things the way girls did, and Joy agreed.

They dawdled up Stout Road and stood talking at the beginning of Massey Avenue. When it was time to part the boys very seriously pecked at the girls' lips, and Joy imagined for a moment that she was in Nelson Eddy's arms. She walked up Massey Avenue humming " Sweethearts."

IV

She knew something was wrong as soon as she was on the veranda. The door was wide open, and the house was lit up. In the dining-room her brothers and Bubs were looking sorry for themselves. Gilbert didn't say anything when she walked in.

" What's up?" she asked.

" You're a great one," he said. " I told you not to go to the pictures. I told you Mum might want you. Uncle Bill's taken her to the hospital. Dad's dying."

She sat by her sister and tried to console her. She put her fist up to her mouth to stop herself from crying, and when she glanced at it she saw that it was smeared with lipstick, and she was unable to keep back the tears any longer.

Chapter Twenty-Four

A Link Is Severed

I

SHE KEPT telling herself she should never have gone home, she should have realised he was at death's door when she called up in the afternoon. No use assuring herself he had looked more contented, more healthy-looking that he had for weeks, no use blaming the nurse for leaving him for hours, she bet, and returning to find him dead. She, his wife, should have stayed with him.

Even after Bill Coulter had touched her sympathetically on the arm several times she wouldn't leave the bedside, and she knew Hilda and the nurse were standing behind Bill impatient for her to stop her weeping, but she couldn't, and she felt she *must* stay, there must be something she could do.

"It was so dreadfully sudden," Hilda was saying to the nurse. "Of course we've been expecting it for some time, but it did come as rather a surprise."

The cold haughtiness of that woman was horrible. Why didn't she go? Nothing seemed to upset her or her sisters.

She drew back the sheet from Gil's face. He was smiling and his cheeks had filled out so that he looked as he had when he was young, when they were first married. He had died peacefully, and that was something to be grateful for; his death had been far different from that suffered by her sister, Fay, a few years back, and she was glad that Gil anyway had not had a brain tumour. But what did it matter how he died? He was dead, dead.

"Think we better be moving, Helen," said Bill. "Nothing more for us to do."

Shutting her eyes, she let him lead her from the bed. She remembered Gil's clothes and asked if they should take them.

"They'll be all right, Mrs. Cunningham," the nurse said. "We'll take good care of them."

Helen glanced at her distrustfully. According to Mr. MacNab, Gil must have been dead a good while before it was noticed, and this was the person who had found him. She felt that somehow the nurse was to blame for something.

She wanted Gil's clothes, and who would dare stop her from taking them? She drew away from Bill, walked to the locker, and placed the contents on the floor—the change of underwear, the shaving gear the slippers, the magazines, the dressing-gown, the Coronation souvenir . . . But she could do no more.

So she stood up and walked away with Bill and Hilda.

II

"There was no pain," Hilda said. "He must have passed away in his sleep. I'm glad it was that way."

"But he's dead," said Helen.

"Yes, dear, and you must be brave," Hilda said. "If there's anything we can do to help, you must be sure to let us know. That's right, isn't it, William?"

"Of course," he said.

"Denise will be arriving tomorrow, and we'll call up and see you," Hilda said. "We'll help with the burial—"

"Don't talk about it," Helen said.

Hilda looked at her.

She was unconscious of anything but the thoughts that crowded her head, and her sister-in-law's voice had seemed unreal, and the things that had happened in recent months rushed from the droning car engine towards her, and Gil's smiling face was larger than anything else, but the others in her life passed in a procession behind his image, tormenting her, telling her she deserved all she got. She hated her tormentors, hated everybody in her life. Even Fred Burgess, looking soulfully and sympathetically at her. And in the city. And Ernie Mulligan, cheeking, wisecracking, sneering. And the Calcotts, laughing and bellowing coarsely. Creditors, gossips—oh, the hated faces.

Well, she was free—but it was not the freedom she had always hoped for even when it had seemed that he would never die. All at once the worries that would now be hers were overwhelming, and she felt trapped, and it was different from any feeling she had ever had before. And, another thing, while he was alive she had been part of Gladston, she supposed, because the Cunninghams were part of Gladston and everyone except the Cunningham womenfolk looked on her as a Cunningham. Now Gil was gone, and if she had been neglected while he was alive she could just imagine what it would be like with him dead. Apart from the attitude of his relations, she would lose some of the pension, though there would still be the family to rear. Her kids! What would happen to them? Some mothers would put them in a home right away, but she couldn't bear to do that. She'd have to hold onto them, give them every chance she could.

"I admire the way you stayed near him to the end, Helen," said Bill.

"I didn't see him when he must have needed me most," she said.

"Wasn't your fault, Helen. We rushed up soon as we got the 'phone message. It was bad luck."

"Ever since he sent for me last week I felt the end was near," she said. "He told me he felt like chatting with me, and that's what we did. We remembered the early days of our marriage, and he was like his old self. He must have known he was about to die. And I went up every day and sat by his side, and then the very time I'm away from him he dies. Every night I've lain awake worrying about him, hoping nothing'll happen. Haven't slept more than two hours any night for the past week."

"Nobody can criticise your behaviour in the slightest, Helen," said Bill. "You must keep strong and not let the strain break you up."

"He used to be cantankerous, the way most invalids are, but lately he was sort of resigned. I should have taken notice."

"You can take comfort from the fact that he died in no pain," said Hilda.

"I wonder if they gave him too many drugs. Do you think they might have done that, Bill?"

"Suppose he's been getting big doses lately, but I think they'd take every precaution," he said.

"Can't get over that nurse leaving him. Oh, but I don't suppose she's to blame."

"I don't think so," he said.

The car pulled up at the front gate of home, and she thanked them for the trouble they'd gone to. She walked inside, away from Hilda's voice repeating that she and Denise would be up to see her in the morning, away from that cold, unfeeling voice.

III

What was the sense in going to bed? She would lie awake for many night to come thinking of him, of life without him.

What *was* her life, anyway?

She could never start another one as she had once foolishly thought she might.

Here she was in Gladston, with few friends and the feeling that the world was against her. Well, she must keep the friends she did have. She must forget her sorrow.

If only she weren't the worrying kind. Why could she not be somebody contented and settled like Flo Young? She had been impatient up the coast and impatient in Gladston, and she would probably go right on being impatient to the end of her days.

She didn't want much from life. All she wanted was a chance for herself and her children, freedom from creditors, freedom to have the pleasant things that were surely everyone's right.

She believed in God, she harmed nobody, yet others who were selfish and spiteful got on while she remained in the same old rut. It wasn't fair.

If only there were somebody to whom she could turn for help as her children turned to her. Mum, perhaps. She was strong, that one, and let nobody run over her. But she was in the city. Everybody was in the city.

She hated to think of the day that would dawn in a few hours. Sympathisers, wreaths, the funeral, a thousand and one things to do. Mrs. Calcott would be over to look after the children. The poor darlings wouldn't understand, and Mrs. Calcott was just the one to keep them quiet. Ever since the holiday on the peninsula she had been telling herself she should not be so friendly with the Calcotts and she remembered such things about them as the time Teddy killed the kitten and the untidy state of their house, but now she knew that in future her best friends would be those who were poor, and it would take her all her time to keep from becoming as poor as the Calcotts, but she would do her best, that's all she could do.

—Oh, Gil, my darling Gil, why did you leave me?

She wept into the moonlight that shone through the window and spread over her bed.

Chapter Twenty-Five

Ceremony at the Family Home

I

ALONE IN his room, he read again the notice of his father's death that had appeared in the *Age*:

> After having been confined to bed for the past four and half years, a returned soldier, Mr. Gilbert Wyatt Cunningham, aged 41, died last evening in the Gladston Hospital. He bore his sufferings with remarkable fortitude to the end.
>
> The deceased, who was born in Gladston, was the son of the late Mr. and Mrs. James Cunningham, early settlers in this district. He was 19 years of age when he joined up with the Eleventh Reinforcements and saw service in Egypt and France before being invalided home after receiving severe injuries in one of the engagements.
>
> When he returned to Gladston, the late Mr. Cunningham made a good recovery and he was able to engage in the carpentry trade. He was later employed at the Gladston freezing works. Four and a half years ago the deceased was again troubled with his old injuries and was confined to bed.
>
> The sympathy of many friends will be extended to his widow and young family, Joyce, Gilbert, Francis, Sydney, and Helen. The deceased is also survived by Mesdames W. Coulter, G. Searing, S. Searing, H. Hale, and Mr. James Cunningham.
>
> A short service will be held at the residence of Mr. W. Coulter at 1.45 p.m. tomorrow prior to the funeral leaving for the Gladston Cemetery.

It was not until he read the piece in the paper that he began to realise what had happened; before that it had been too strange to understand at all. Reading about the many friends made him picture crowds of people talking sadly to one another and saying how they saw that Mr. Cunningham had passed away. Of course

Dad had lots of friends, Joy told him, but when Aunty Hilda had that notice put in the paper there was only one person she was really concerned about, and it wasn't Mum.

Though he read the notice over and over, he could not cry. Any normal kid would surely cry at a time like this, and he deliberately made himself think of his father in one of his good moods, smiling and not being sarcastic towards you, but the tears refused to come. He was puzzled about himself, and a bit scared, too. He had tried to make out to Joy that he was heart-broken, but he wasn't, he simply felt nothing, and perhaps he was suffering inside but didn't know it, but that was not true, either. He had slept soundly last night, and to think of his behaviour this morning made him ashamed.

Very early today Ma Calcott and Agnes Ellis had knocked on the door, and straightaway the old girl made one of her weak brews of tea, and for a long time she was in his mother's room, and they spoke low, speaking of death with Mum describing the peaceful way Dad died, now and then giving great sobs so that Ma Calcott would utter consoling words and shed a few tears herself. And Agnes had come into the kitchen to tidy up, and, seeing she hadn't known Dad, she wasn't particularly sad.

And suddenly he had wanted to be friendly with Agnes, and he mentioned to her that he didn't feel unhappy, and she said, "Oh, you must be, your father dying," and he said, "No, I don't think it's much good being unhappy now; it's happened and there's no sense getting miserable," and she said that was an odd attitude, and he said he knew but he just didn't feel unhappy.

And pretty soon she was telling him about the dance she went to the night before and how she'd felt like a lie-in this morning but her mother worried her to get up to go with Ma Calcott to the Cunninghams so here she was. She was a nice-looking sheila, he thought, and once he preferred blondes, but now he guessed he preferred brunettes. She wore a green smock over her petticoat and it was belted at the waist so that sometimes the neck would open up and he would see some of the secret part of her body, and he giggled excitedly with her as though they were not in a house of the dead. And Frank and Sydney had a scrap, and anxious Ma Calcott and Mum, who looked huge and round-shouldered in her blue kimono, came from the bedroom and asked them please to keep quiet. Ma Calcott did her best to look stern while Mum stood looking sadly at them with reddened eyes. "I suppose it's just as well," she said, "that they're too young to realise what's happened."

And as the day passed one person after another knocked on

the front door of the mournful house, and wreaths and flowers covered with coloured wax paper began to fill the small lobby. There were wreaths from Uncle Jim and Aunty Rose, from Mrs. Simpson and her husband, from Mrs. Simmons, who told him she'd call on his mother later in the week, from unknown friends of Dad, from old friends of the Cunninghams, and at first he had to concentrate on getting the right expression of sadness and humility to greet the callers with but after a bit the expression came automatically.

In the afternoon he opened the door to Uncle Bill, Aunty Hilda and Aunty Denise. Rich Aunty Denise was more high and mighty than her sister, and he wondered if the smart black costume she wore had been specially bought for his father's funeral. Aunty Hilda told him he must be a good little man now, but, after saying that he resembled his father, Aunty Denise ignored him. Ma Calcott scurried into the kitchen as the three of them walked down the passage. They shut the dining-room door behind them, but he could tell from what he heard by listening at the keyhole that they were discussing the funeral arrangements with Mum. They were there about an hour, and Mum showed them out.

So now he was waiting for Ma Calcott to get the tea ready and reading about his father's death and wondering why he could not cry. One thing about this, he often wanted an excuse for stopping away from school when anything awkward was going to happen and this was about the best excuse he was ever likely to have, only he couldn't help wishing his father had died on another day because today would have been all right at school. Well, he bet quite a bit of notice would be taken of him when he started back at school.

"What do *you* want?" he said irritably when Joy came in without knocking.

"Just filling in time," she said.

He was always suspicious when people came into his private room, as though they were planning to take it away from him. He was still thrilled about having a room to himself.

"Mum gives me the pip," his sister said.

"Don't you reckon she should feel upset about Dad? You want her to go on behaving like nothing has happened?"

"'Course not. But, gee, you know jolly well she's gone out with other chaps while Dad was in hospital."

"They were only friends," he said.

"Oh, she could please herself what she did. But why howl and blubber so much now? Makes me sick."

"You've got no feelings," he told her.

"Didn't I cry when you told me about him dying? I cried

myself to sleep. I bet you didn't, boy. Only I'm no hypocrite."

"Better watch what you're saying."

"Well, I'm *not* a hypocrite, so there."

"You want to learn the meaning of words before you go round saying them."

"Hypocrite?"

"Yes, who's a hypocrite?"

"Well, who was giggling with Agnes Ellis this morning, eh?"

"Why don't you get out of here? Can't get any privacy even in your own room."

"Aw, pooh," she said. "For a so-called brainy one you're some drip." She walked out.

As if anything she said was news, he thought. He knew about his mother and her men friends, and he would lie awake after she had gone out one of those nights and wonder what she was doing, just as he wondered what she did when she went into the bathroom and locked the door behind her and he listened but all he could hear was the tap running and he thought maybe she was peeing in the bath but that was silly seeing the lavatory was only at the back door. He could think the same things as Joy if he wanted to, but he told himself his mother was an adult and he was a kid and she knew more about things than he did. She was old enough to look after herself.

Oh, gosh, he'd have to go to the funeral. He didn't want to go, but all of them, even Agnes, said he must go. He and Joyce and Frank. He would wear his school uniform, and Frank would wear the navy suit-coat that had once been his, and they'd have to go to the Coulter house where there would be crowds and crowds of people. He was certainly getting out of nothing by missing school.

II

They crossed the lawn to Uncle Bill's car. Mum wore her old costume and round-shaped close-fitting black hat that left a half-circle of hair poking out over her forehead. She carried a handkerchief in one hand as though she was about to burst out howling any moment. She got in the front seat of the car beside Uncle Bill, and he got in the back with his sister and brother.

As they drove down Massey Avenue, the blue smoke from the cigarette Uncle Bill was smoking drifted to them. The car moved smoothly along, and it was quiet and kind of stuffy inside. He looked at the brown leaves on the trees in the avenue; it was a sunny autumn day, and a breeze blew dust puffs from unmetalled sidestreets. Nobody spoke.

On the footpath outside the Coulter house a dozen or so people stood chatting. He could imagine them whispering about the widow and the children. Uncle Bill led the way to the front door. Mum held her head down.

The house was a large, tidy, and brooding place at any time, but now it seemed more brooding than ever. Where there was death there must be quiet, and it seemed that even the houses respected the order.

They were met in the hall by three old ladies, all alike with grey hair and wearing long black coats, and these ladies, who were distant relations of the Cunninghams, kissed Mum in turn and clicked their tongues over him and the other two. " So sorry for you, my dear . . . God's call . . . an end to brave suffering . . . heavenly peace."

Neatly arranged in the sitting-room so that the visitors could inspect the cards were many wreaths and flowers. He looked for the remembered bellows on the hearth, and they were there sure enough, and so were the purple satin cushions on the deep blue lounge suite. Aunty Hilda guided his mother around the wreaths, she working up appreciative smiles and asking in a low voice who such and such a person was, and it was strange how many of the wreaths were from people she hadn't known existed. Aunty Hilda was quite thrilled about the little white flower crosses she had bought for each of the kids. " I knew you wouldn't have time to think of it, Helen, so I went ahead and got them myself. They *are* pretty, aren't they?" And Mum said it was good of her to think of it.

The walked down the hall to the dining-room, and there on the table was Dad's coffin.

—He gulped. Would he cry?

Taking him by the arm, his aunt led him to the bay window and stood him there with Frank and Joy. When he sat on the window seat she whispered that he'd better remain standing as there were several grown-ups to be seated. His mother was placed on a large settee on the opposite side of the room.

One by one the people came in and were directed into position by Aunty Hilda. He heard the three old ladies discussing the remarkable likeness he bore to his late father. And they discussed the measurements of the coffin and agreed that the poor boy had been very tall, very tall, and it was without a doubt the longest coffin they'd seen, but then again some dead chap called Alfred had needed a very long coffin, too, though, if their memories served them right, this one was every bit as long. And one of them told Aunty Hilda what she estimated as the length of the coffin, and Aunty Hilda said she was quite right in her guess, and the old lady nodded her head with satisfaction.

Silly old things, he thought. Why couldn't *they* have died? God was supposed to take only those who are ready to go or whom He considered had lived their allotted span, so why should He take Dad instead of them? Maybe He thought they were too dippy for Heaven yet awhile.

Mr. Braxton and Uncle Jim entered, Uncle Jim looking awkward in his blue serge suit. There'd be no more chaws from Mr. Braxton now that there was no need for him to take Mum to the hospital.

—No, he wouldn't cry. Not in front of all these people.

Ralph Coulter moved among the people in a dark double-breasted suit and acted as though it were his father who had died.

He looked out the window at the yellow vines on the trellis, and he thought how the leaves dropped to the ground right along the side of the house and were swept away with a bamboo rake held by Aunty Hilda. Leaves falling beside the old house Mr. James Cunningham had built in the early days of Gladston. Probably they fell when Dad was a boy playing and they fell while he grew up and they fell now he was dead and they would go on falling, falling while Ralph Coulter grew up.

"Hey, you," his sister whispered.

The preacher had entered, and heads were bowed in prayer. The voice that came from the stocky, bald-headed man droned out long phrases, and if you shut your eyes you could imagine this was a dream, and if you opened them all you saw was a strange, darkened room with many strange people in it and a strange object on the table.

Listen . . . Gil Cunningham had been a respected and well-loved man. Among returned soldiers the story of his unfailing fortitude and cheerful outlook had been told as an exceptional one, even in the experience of men who had passed through war hospitals and civilian institutions over a long period. And now this brave man, one of those heroic boys of yesterday, was about to meet his Creator, and he left behind a sense of loss in the hearts of those who had been acquainted with him, and admiration for his noble spirit, and. . . .

He looked up, but Aunty Hilda frowned at him, so down went his head again.

III

He told his mother to look at all the cars. They reached almost to the end of the block. There was a big crowd of onlookers, including the usual women holding babies and gazing over gates. She smiled at him and she had been crying and he remembered how sharp-spoken Aunty Denise had been to her, telling her she was not doing herself any good carrying on the way she was, and he thought how dignified and self-controlled his aunties had been and it was as though they were standing through a band concert or something.

The pallbearers—Uncle Bill, Uncle Jim, Mr. Braxton, and three men his father had worked with at the freezing works—came slowly along the path and to the hearse, tongues stilled while eyes watched the coffin.

He breathed out as he sat back in Uncle Bill's car. Joy and Frank leaned back, too, trying to keep out of sight. He wondered if that was the last time he would enter the Coulter house. He hadn't been there very often, and when he had it was generally something to do with Dad, and he didn't go much on what they said about his being Aunty Hilda's favourite nephew because it didn't seem to have done him any good even if it was true and anyway he didn't care. Like Mum said, relations weren't much use unless they helped you in ways that counted.

He got thinking about his mother's talk of going to the city, and he supposed they would have the chance of going now. But he didn't think they would go. It was something Mum always talked about, and it would never happen. No, he would be able to go to High with the other jokers, all right. Mum would not leave Gladston.

Very slowly the procession moved off. After the moments in the Coulter dining-room it was good in the car and he didn't mind how slow they went because he knew that at the end of the journey there was the burial of his father and he wasn't looking forward to it.

"It was true," Joy said suddenly.

"What?"

"You know that rock on the cliff down at the peninsula? Shaped like a man's head? I thought it looked like Dad, and I bet it was a premonition. That's what it was."

He kept quiet because there was no explaining the silly things girls said and this was no time to start an argument.

He watched to see whether the people on the sides of the

highway showed proper respect for the dead by removing their hats. —He still did not feel like crying.

The hearse stopped at the cemetery gate, and the cars were emptied. There were bulky white clouds in the sky, but the sun had found a clear blue patch.

The mourners followed the pallbearers along dirt paths that looked as though they had just been worked upon with a grader. He watched the dust settle on the well-polished shoes of his uncles and he looked down at his own boots and the dust was gathering on them, too.

They were in the oldest part of the cemetery. The only graves being dug here were in family plots, and Dad was to be the last in the Cunningham plot. He knew his mother had wanted Dad buried in the returned soldiers' section, but she had given way to Aunty Hilda. The plot was on the cemetery's edge in the shade of tall gums and pines, and there was plenty of room for all the mourners, including the two lines of returned soldiers.

He had thought the coffin might be sort of dumped in a hole, and he was glad it wasn't going to be like that. You couldn't even see the earth mounds for the wreaths and flowers.

Beside the coffin the preacher droned another prayer, and he heard his mother give a choking sound and he touched her arm. He noticed Aunty Hilda watching. Then Joy began to cry also.

Earth was sprinkled on the coffin as it was lowered, and a couple of men threw red poppies into the grave. A bugler played the Last Post.

And his father had gone.

He would never see his father again.

—The tears came at last, and he moved nearer his mother.